Kids First—Primero Los Niños

Chicago School Reform in the 1980s

Kids First—Primero Los Niños

Chicago School Reform in the 1980s

Charles L. Kyle
and
Edward R. Kantowicz

Illinois Issues
Sangamon State University
Springfield, Illinois

Dedicated to the memory of Freddy Mercado

Library of Congress Cataloging-in-Publication Data

Kyle, Charles Lambert, 1943-
      Kids First—Primero Los Niños: Chicago School Reform in the 1980s / by Charles L. Kyle and Edward R. Kantowicz.
         p.   cm.
      Includes index.
      ISBN 0-9620873-8-6
      1. Education—Illinois—Chicago—History—20th century.
      2. Education and state—Illinois—Chicago—History—20th century.
      3. Community and school—Illinois—Chicago—History—20th century.
      4. Public schools—Illinois—Chicago—History—20th century.
      I. Kantowicz, Edward R. II. Title.
LA269.C4K95 1992
370'.9773'11--dc20   92-29667
                                          CIP

Portions of chapters 1 and 5 previously appeared in the *Latino Studies Journal*. Reprinted with permission.

Chicagoans United to Reform Education (C.U.R.E.) used the cover logo in the Chicago school reform campaign. The logo, which was designed by Janice Boehm, is used with the permission of C.U.R.E. Cover design by Larz Gaydos.

Supported in part by a gift from Prince Charitable Trusts.

Illinois Issues
Sangamon State University
Springfield, Illinois 62794-9243

Contents

Chronology

November 13, 1979   Moody's Investors Service downgrades the Chicago Board of Education's bond rating, initiating a financial crisis.

November 28, 1979   Schools Superintendent Joseph Hannon resigns and Angeline Caruso is named interim superintendent.

December 21, 1979   Chicago teachers experience first payless payday since the Great Depression.

January 6, 1980   Governor James R. Thompson negotiates bailout plan for Chicago public schools.

January 12, 1980   Legislature passes school bailout plan and establishes Chicago School Finance Authority as fiscal watchdog.

January 15, 1980   Governor Thompson and Mayor Jane Byrne appoint members of Chicago School Finance Authority.

January 28, 1980   Chicago teachers strike to protest the slow implementation of the bailout and the continuing payless paydays.

February 11, 1980   Teachers' strike ends.

April 16, 1980   Mayor Byrne appoints new board of education, Chicago's first with a majority composed of minority group members.

September 24, 1980   Desegregation consent decree between Chicago Board of Education and federal court.

March, 1981	Ruth Love appointed first black schools superintendent.
April 12, 1983	Harold Washington elected Chicago's first black mayor.
April 26, 1983	National Commission on Excellence in Education releases report titled "A Nation at Risk."
March 26, 1984	The Latino community marches on Clemente High School to highlight dropout problem.
April, 1984	Aspira dropout study released.
July 1, 1984	Legislature passes SJR 82 authorizing Hispanic Dropout Task Force.
July 23, 1984	Board of education votes not to renew Ruth Love's contract as superintendent.
November 20, 1984	Murder of high school basketball star Ben Wilson touches off antigang furor.
December 3, 1984	Chicago teachers begin 10-day strike.
January 9, 1985	Illinois Commission on the Improvement of Elementary and Secondary Education issues report.
February 6-8, 1985	Hispanic Dropout Task Force holds public hearings.
February 6, 1985	Designs for Change issues dropout report.
March 15, 1985	Hispanic Dropout Task Force issues report.
March 25, 1985	Manford Byrd, Jr., appointed schools superintendent.

April, 1985   Chicago Panel on Public School Policy and Fi-
                       nance issues dropout report.

May 30, 1985   City council passes Mayor Washington's anti-
                       gang proposal, setting up the Chicago Inter-
                       vention Network.

June 24-30, 1985   Legislature passes various dropout prevention
                       bills recommended by the Hispanic Dropout
                       Task Force.

June 27-July 1, 1985   Legislature passes safe schools zone bills.

July 2, 1985   Legislature passes omnibus school reform bill
                       (PA 84-126).

September, 1985   Chicago teachers stage brief strike before win-
                       ning a two-year contract.

March 4-5, 1986   Chicago Board of Education holds half-hearted
                       budget hearings, open to the public, at local
                       schools as mandated by school reform act.

April, 1986   "Council Wars" deadlock is broken by special
                       elections giving Mayor Washington control of
                       city council.

June 23, 1986   Chicagoans United to Reform Education
                       (C.U.R.E.) meet for the first time.

August, 1986   Mayor Washington convenes first business-
                       education summit meetings.

October, 1986   First school report cards, mandated by the
                       omnibus school reform act, are published.

November, 1986   Miguel del Valle elected first Latino state
                       senator.

April 25, 1987   C.U.R.E. holds public conference and releases its school reform plan.

September 8, 1987   Longest teachers' strike in Chicago history begins.

September 11, 1987   First parent demonstration against the teachers' strike takes place.

October 2, 1987   Largest parent demonstration of the strike occurs.

October 5, 1987   Teachers' strike ends.

October 8, 1987   Peoples' Coalition for Educational Reform forms human chain across the Loop, calling for thoroughgoing school reform.

October 11, 1987   Mayor Washington convenes an expanded summit conference at the University of Illinois at Chicago to kick off a drive for school reform.

October, 1987   C.U.R.E. expands its roster of community organizations and hires the Haymarket Group as political consultants for school reform.

November 6, 1987   Secretary of Education William Bennett blasts Chicago public schools as "the worst in the nation."

November 25, 1987   Mayor Washington dies of a heart attack.

December 2, 1987   Eugene Sawyer chosen acting mayor by the city council.

January 22, 1988   Parent/community council submits their school reform plan to the mayor's summit.

February 3, 1988	C.U.R.E. completes their "Kids First" school reform bill.
February, 1988	A "rump summit" begins holding parallel sessions to the mayor's summit.
March 15, 1988	Voters on the northwest side overwhelmingly approve a referendum proposal for school-based management of the public schools.
March 21, 1988	Mayor's summit approves preliminary school reform plan.
March 30-31, 1988	Education committees of the Illinois House and Senate hold joint hearings on the summit proposals.
April 7, 1988	Senator Arthur Berman introduces education shell bills, SB 1839 and SB 1840, in the legislature.
April 8, 1988	C.U.R.E. introduces its bill in the legislature as SB 2144 and IIB 3707.
May 11, 1988	Secretary Bennett delivers second blast at Chicago public schools.
May 16, 1988	UNO announces its support for the C.U.R.E. bill.
May 19, 1988	Mayor's summit issues final report.
May 20, 1988	Republican Senator Robert Kustra's SB 2261, which would break up the Chicago school district into 20 new districts, passes in the senate.

June 2, 1988   Senator Arthur Berman's SB 1839, the first attempt at a consensus school reform bill, passes in the senate.

June 6, 1988   The Alliance for Better Chicago Schools (ABCs) holds its kickoff rally.

June 15, 1988   HB 4101, another attempt at a consensus bill, passes in the house.

June 20-29, 1988   School reformers and legislators confer in House Speaker Michael Madigan's office to agree on final version of the school reform bill.

June 30, 1988   SB 1839, the consensus reform bill, fails to pass the senate by one vote.

July 2, 1988   SB 1839 passes both houses with a delayed implementation date.

September 26, 1988   Governor Thompson issues amendatory veto of SB 1839.

December 1, 1988   SB 1840, a revised school reform bill, passes both houses of the legislature as PA 85-1418.

February, 1989   Business executives incorporate Leadership for Quality Education (LQE) as a vehicle for continued support of school reform.

April 4, 1989   Richard M. Daley elected mayor.

May 1, 1989   Chicago School Reform Act officially takes effect.

May 25, 1989   Mayor Daley appoints interim school board and deputy mayor for education.

June 30, 1989   Legislature passes income tax surcharge, half of which is designated for education.

October 11-12, 1989   First local school council elections are held.

January, 1990   Ted Kimbrough takes office as schools superintendent.

April 15, 1990   First new principals chosen under school reform act.

October 3, 1990   New board of education takes office.

November 30, 1990   Illinois Supreme Court declares school reform act unconstitutional.

January 8, 1991   Legislature passes HB 3302, validating past actions of local school councils and permitting Mayor Daley to reappoint existing LSC members, while legislature decides how to meet constitutional objections.

April 2, 1991   Mayor Daley reelected.

June 18-19, 1991   Senator Berman convenes summit conference of school reform groups to agree on a consensus bill that will meet the supreme court's constitutional objections.

June 27, 1991   HD 885, a statewide school accountability measure, passes.

July 18, 1991   SB 10, revising the voting procedure for local school councils to meet the constitutional objections, passes.

Authors

Charles L. Kyle grew up in Oak Park, Illinois. He is a sociologist, who earned the Ph.D. from Northwestern University, and is currently assistant to the president, Triton College, River Grove, Illinois. He is author of *The Magnitude of and Reasons for Chicago's Hispanic Dropout Problem: A Case Study of Two Public High Schools* (The Renato Rosaldo Lecture Series Monograph, Mexican-American Studies and Research Center, University of Arizona, 1990) and *Indivisible—Good Schools Equal a Healthy Economy* (Loyola University, 1939, available from Educational Resource Information Clearinghouse). He has been active for over 20 years in Latino issues including immigration reform, community empowerment, and school reform.

Edward R. Kantowicz grew up in Chicago, Illinois, earned the Ph.D. from the University of Chicago, and was professor of history at Carleton University, Ottawa, Canada. He is currently a free-lance writer and historical consultant in Chicago. He is author of *Polish-American Politics in Chicago* (University of Chicago Press, 1975) and *Corporation Sole: Cardinal Mundelein and Chicago Catholicism* (University of Notre Dame Press, 1983), for which he received the Publication Award from the Cushwa Center for the Study of American Catholicism.

Introduction

The Politics of School Reform in Chicago

In the decade of the 1980s, national concern mounted over the failings of American education. Parents and educators, business and political leaders feared that the public schools were not preparing young people for the economic challenges of the twenty-first century. Student scores on standardized tests had fallen, high schools had lowered their requirements for graduation, and rising numbers of adult Americans were functionally illiterate. American students spent less time in school than European or Japanese students, and many more of them dropped out before finishing high school. Increasingly loud voices called out for school reform, lest the nation's youth be wasted and the country's economy fall behind Japan, West Germany, and other countries.

A presidential commission sounded the loudest alarm, warning that the nation stood at risk from a "rising tide of mediocrity." Yet the Reagan and Bush administrations were unwilling to commit substantial resources to education, so state governments took the initiative and local school districts across the country became laboratories of school reform.

Few would have predicted, as the decade began, that the city of Chicago would launch one of the most audacious experiments in school reform. The nation's third-largest city was noted more for its segregated neighborhoods, fierce ethnic quarrels, and hardball politics than its educational leadership. Chicagoans often quoted, seemingly with pride, the famous dictum of ward boss Paddy Bauler, "Chicago ain't ready for reform."

Yet the shortcomings of Chicago's public schools became so severe they cracked the shell of hardened cynicism Chicagoans wear when viewing their favorite spectator sport: local politics. The decade opened with a sharp financial crisis that nearly pushed the public schools into default, then the federal Justice Department, after years of litigation, imposed a costly desegregation plan on the city's schools. Researchers discovered at mid-decade that the dropout rate in public high schools stood at nearly 50 percent, not the 9 percent officially admitted by school administrators. When the city's first African-American[1] schools superintendent, Ruth Love, failed to deal candidly with these astounding statistics, the board of education terminated her contract in a messy, public bloodletting. A literal bloodletting, the murder of Ben Wilson, a popular high school athlete, highlighted the growing gang violence in the city's schools.

The national outcry for school reform echoed in the Illinois legislature, which passed a hefty package of school legislation in 1985, yet few of these reform bills seemed to make much difference. One of them did, however, heighten public concern. A 1985 Illinois law required every school district and every individual school in the state to publish a report card on its achievements in the fall of each year. As the decade wore on, these report cards revealed a shocking story of institutional failure in the Chicago public schools. Only two of Chicago's 64 high schools recorded standardized test scores higher than the state average. Reading and math scores fell below average in 3rd, 6th, 8th, and 10th grades. Failure rates were higher, daily attendance and graduation rates lower. Adding insult to injury, U.S. Secretary of Education William Bennett visited the city in November 1987 and proclaimed Chicago's schools the "worst in the nation."

---

1   The term *African-American* has been used widely since about 1988 when Jesse Jackson helped popularize it during his second run for the presidency. Since this book is a historical work, largely concerned with events before and during 1988, we have chosen to use the term *black* in most instances. Our sources, both written and oral, tended to use this word, which replaced the term *Negro* in the late 1960s. However, we have used *African-American* in the introduction and final chapter, both of which are written in the present, and in a few other instances where the context seemed to demand it.

Chicagoans are used to bad publicity, particularly from easterners, but local events conspired to drive home the seriousness of the education crisis. Shortly before Secretary Bennett delivered his blast, the Chicago teachers walked out of class for the ninth time in 18 years, staying out on strike for 19 days. Community organizations, closely allied with Mayor Harold Washington, the city's first African-American mayor, finally brokered a solution that gave in to most of the teachers' demands. With the unionized teachers and the school board bureaucracy seemingly insensitive to the damage caused by the strike, Chicagoans were ready to listen when Secretary Bennett remarked caustically, "The first step in solving the problem is reducing the system's bureaucracy. Explode the blob."

Mayor Washington convened a summit conference of businessmen, educators, parents, and community leaders in the wake of the 1987 teachers' strike. Washington died soon after, but the parent/community council, the most radical segment of the education summit, hammered out a school reform plan that they dedicated to the late mayor. The council concluded that the best solution was to give parents more control over the local schools.

This outcome was neither foreordained nor accidental. During the two years before the Bennett blast, the teachers' strike, and the mayor's summit, a remarkable multiethnic, multiracial coalition had been gathering to push for radical reform of the Chicago school system. Michael Bakalis, a unique scholar-politician who had previously served as state superintendent of public instruction, convened a racially mixed group of educators and community activists who called themselves Chicagoans United to Reform Education (C.U.R.E.). They proposed the election of local school councils with real power in the hands of parents, teachers, and community representatives. When Mayor Washington convened the education summit, C.U.R.E.'s plan was the best available and the summit negotiators adopted its main features.

In the legislative session of 1988, the Illinois General Assembly passed a school reform act creating local school councils at every school in the city. These local school councils (LSCs) were not merely advisory. The reform act granted them authority to hire and fire the school's principal, to manage the discretionary budget for the school, and to devise a long-range school improvement plan.

The multiracial coalition put together by C.U.R.E. expanded in the spring of 1988 as local businessmen, increasingly frustrated in their attempts to hire a skilled work force from public school graduates, joined with parents' groups, community organizations, and education advocacy agencies to lobby the legislature. Community organizations chartered school buses to transport parents from the barrios and ghettoes, and the CEOs of the city's largest business firms flew to the capital in their corporate jets. Illinois legislators were used to noisy demonstrations, but they had never seen such persistent, day-to-day lobbying by such diverse groups. Members of the reform coalition, now renamed the Alliance for Better Chicago Schools (ABCs), sported yellow lapel buttons that read "Don't Come Home Without It."

The final details of the school reform act were hammered out in long bargaining sessions between the reform coalition and the Democratic party leadership of the legislature. Speaker of the House Michael Madigan made his office available for the sessions, leaving a trusted lieutenant in charge with instructions to find a consensus plan. What resulted was the radical reorganization of school governance. When the Illinois Supreme Court objected to the voting procedure for LSC elections and struck down the school reform act as unconstitutional, the ABCs coalition came together again and worked with the legislature to amend the act in July 1991.

Twenty years previously, in the turbulent 1960s, similar experiments were tried under the rallying cries of "community control" and "power to the people." Over the years, the notion of a local school council lost some of its ideological baggage and educators renamed it school-based management. Whatever the name, it remained a radical idea: to give the parents of schoolchildren a genuine sense of ownership in the local public school and sufficient power to affect what happens at school.

It certainly seemed amazing that Chicago politicians and educators would cede some control to parents and community representatives. Just as amazing was the key role played by Chicago's most neglected, and least powerful, ethnic community, the Latinos,[2] in setting the stage for school reform. Latin-Americans from Puerto Rico, Mexico, Cuba, and Central and South America formed about 16 percent of Chicago's population in the 1980s and about 25 percent of the school enrollment, but they comprised only 5 percent of the registered voters. At the beginning of the decade, Latinos were virtually shut out from local government, with no aldermen, ward committeemen, or state representatives.

Yet the Latino community spearheaded the early calls for school reform. Aspira, an educational self-help group, commissioned research that blew the lid off the dropout problem. Community organizers staged protests highlighting both the dropout and the gang problems in inner-city schools. Community leaders testified eloquently before the legislative task forces studying the schools and lobbied effectively in Springfield. One of their number, Miguel del Valle, decided he could do more good for the schools inside the capitol than out on the streets, so he won election as the first Latino state senator in Illinois. When the school reform act passed and elections were held for the first local school councils, Latino voters turned out in larger numbers than elsewhere in the city. Chicago's Latin-Americans finally found their voice in the politics of school reform.

Latinos were not alone in calling for reform. Two school advocacy agencies, Designs for Change and the Chicago Panel on Public School Policy and Finance, published dropout studies that confirmed the Aspira research and showed the problem to be citywide. African-American community organizations played

---

2   The word *Latino* is the umbrella term for all groups originating in Latin America. The alternate term, *Hispanic*, is also commonly used. We have chosen to use *Latino* throughout the book, though *Hispanic* appears frequently when quoting others or in the names of organizations. See chapter four for a fuller discussion of the political significance of these terms.

a crucial role in mobilizing parents of public school children at the time of the teachers' strike. White ethnic homeowners, many of whom sent their children to parochial schools, also realized that reformed public schools would be vital assets to their communities. Ultimately, Latinos formed just one element in a grand coalition pushing for radical reform.

The most important feature of the school reform movement in Chicago, therefore, was its multiethnic, multiracial character. In a city of fierce ethnic resentments and racial tensions, Chicagoans united to change the system. At key moments of doubt and divisiveness, they agreed to compromise their differences and put Kids First—*Primero Los Niños*.

Chicago launched its radical experiment in school governance and accountability largely out of desperation. Latino schools experienced a dropout rate approaching 70 percent, and the citywide average stood around 42 percent. Many of those who did finish high school were barely literate, and local businessmen found it increasingly difficult to find suitable employees from the ranks of public school graduates. Ordinarily conservative opinion makers advocated extraordinary solutions. A columnist for *Crain's Chicago Business* proposed half-seriously that the state throw the public schools into receivership and appoint the Catholic cardinal of Chicago as receiver. The *Chicago Tribune* argued in dead earnest that only a voucher system, allowing parents free choice of private schools at public expense, would solve the problem. Finally, the legislature conceded parent and community control of the schools.

Only a broad coalition of educators, businessmen, politicians, and community organizations coupled with a crisis atmosphere could have produced this result. It is too soon to tell whether this remarkable coalition has saved the public schools. Yet, the story of its successful multiracial movement is worth telling for its own sake, as it throws a whole new light on Chicago's turbulent political history.

When we embarked on this study, Michael Bakalis, who convened Chicagoans United to Reform Education, predicted that "every group you talk to will claim they were the prime movers behind school reform." He was right. Yet, this only serves to demonstrate how remarkable the reform coalition was. Every participant felt important, vital, indispensable.

Because each coalition member's experience was unique, different authors could choose various starting points for a history of school reform in Chicago and highlight different individuals or organizations. We have chosen to begin with the Latino community, the group we know best and the one whose role is least likely to be appreciated. Other authors will, no doubt, make different decisions. No matter what the starting point or the shades of emphasis, we have tried not to slight any of the main actors or distort the key events. Ultimately, a coalition of diverse groups and individuals who all agreed to put Kids First—*Primero Los Niños*, made the difference.

1

Una Semilla Viva: The Seed of School Reform

At 7 P.M. on March 26, 1984, Freddy Mercado stood shivering in a cold rain outside the door of St. Mark's Church. Freddy, a Puerto Rican teenager, had dropped out of school the year before but had recently returned to the classroom. "Tonight," Freddy thought to himself, "is the most important night of my life." He was wearing the white arm band of a parade marshal; over five hundred people had gathered at St. Mark's that cold, rainy night to pray and to march.

Freddy couldn't believe it. The community was entrusting its care to him that evening. In fact, all the parade marshals were young people chosen from the Aspira clubs because the community was marching for them. Pallbearers would carry a mahogany casket from the Catholic church at 1048 N. Campbell to Roberto Clemente High School, a few blocks away at Division and Western. The casket symbolized the barrio's lost youth who had dropped out of school and died in gang warfare. Flickering candles carried by the rest of the marchers symbolized the hope of the community for their remaining youth. The march on Clemente began a long campaign by Chicago's Latino parents to claim ownership of their local public schools and force them to do a better job of educating their children, a campaign that ultimately proved successful when it merged with the efforts of black and white parents.[1]

From inside the church, Freddy heard Hector Carasquillo and the choirs from Our Lady of Grace and St. Francis Xavier churches singing a song that Hector had written especially for this night. As Freddy listened to the words, he began to cry. "No es importa si tu hermano es drug adicto. No es importa si tu hermano es matador. No es importa si tu hermano es gangista. Lo que es importa es que una semilla viva!" (No matter if your brother is a drug addict. No matter if your brother is a killer. No matter if your brother is a gang banger. What matters is that there is a seed still living!)

"Una Semilla Viva" seemed to be written for Freddy. He had been a hard-core gang banger, indeed a shooter, and he would have been on the streets this very night if Roberto Rivera from Aspira had not challenged him to change his life. Freddy had resisted at first, and even took a few swings at Roberto, but he finally left the Latin Kings and returned to school. This decision cost Freddy a lot. The Kings cornered and beat him on more than one occasion; he had permanent scar tissue over his eyes where his eyebrows should have been. But he remembered how often Roberto would say, "You'll make it, Freddy, but you have to study harder and do things to help the community." Now, this night, Freddy was a proud young man because he had been chosen to usher the community from the church down Division Street to the stage of Roberto Clemente High School. Yet he was nervous too, since Clemente stood on the turf of his former gang's archrivals, the Disciples.

When the Network for Youth Services (NYS), a coalition of 30 neighborhood organizations, decided to stage a candle-light march, everyone knew even before discussing the location that the march would go down the center of Division Street and end up at Roberto Clemente. For Puerto Ricans in Chicago, Division Street is special. It harbors the heart, and the pain, of the barrio. The street cuts through Humboldt Park, the dividing line between two mighty street gang nations: the People and the Folks. As these gangs vie for turf and drug sales, Division Street often echoes with the sound of gunfire. Puerto Rican people nurture a love-hate relationship with Division Street. Its sounds and smells recall their homeland on the Island, but its burned-out storefronts and vacant lots also bring to mind the nights of fury in June 1966 when some of the barrio's residents rioted against economic exploitation and police brutality.[2]

Similarly, Roberto Clemente High School epitomizes both the community's pride and its shame. The modernistic, seven-story school replaced the old Tuley High in 1974. Alderman Thomas Keane, then the ward boss for the area and Mayor Richard J. Daley's city council leader, appropriated funds for the school as a result of community pressure and demonstrations. The board of education named the high school after the Hall-of-Fame baseball star who died in a plane crash while taking food and clothing to the victims of an earthquake in Nicaragua. Yet Clemente High had not lived up to its promise. The huge factory-like building warehoused its students more than it educated them, and the Anglo principal, teachers, and counsellors seemed more eager to "push out" problem students than help them. In the 1980-81 school year, Clemente earned the dubious distinction of the highest dropout total in the city. Out of 3,990 students who enrolled at some time during that year, 693 dropped out.[3]

Latino people on the north side share the feelings of writer Nelson Algren toward the beauty and toughness of Chicago. As Algren wrote about Division Street at an earlier date, "Like loving a woman with a broken nose, you may well find lovelier lovelies. But never a lovely so real."[4]

At 8 P.M. on the night of March 26, Reverend Jorge Morales from San Lucas United Church of Christ, Father Edward Maloney from St. Mark's, and Bishop Placido Rodriguez, auxiliary bishop of the Catholic Archdiocese of Chicago, began the ecumenical prayer service. The hundreds present prayed with the clergy for the souls of the young people killed on the streets. They prayed for Freddy and the other young people still alive that they might study harder and become doctors and lawyers. In his homily, Bishop Rodriguez soothed the fears of those who hesitated to march: "It is not a privilege to have your children attend good schools," he exclaimed, "it is a right."

The participation of the Catholic church in a movement to reform the public schools proved historic, for the church had traditionally followed a hands-off policy toward public education. Many suspected that Catholic clergy and educators viewed the inferior quality of public schools as a blessing, since it ensured an eager clientele for their own parochial schools. The presence of a Catholic prelate, such as Bishop Rodriguez, legitimized the march in the eyes of Catholic parishioners and dramatized the seriousness of the dropout crisis.

The young parade marshals from the Aspira clubs had prepared carefully for the march at an all-day workshop titled "Reject Rejection." Puerto Rican educators had founded Aspira in New York City in the late 1960s to help Latino students reach higher and achieve more in school. Maria Cerda, whom Mayor Daley had chosen as the first Latino member of the board of education, became the first chairman of Aspira's Illinois branch in 1969. Aspira had two main purposes: to foster Latino leadership in the high schools through a network of Aspira clubs, and then to send these student leaders on to college. In Chicago public high schools Aspira students met weekly with a teacher moderator, who helped prepare them to take college entrance tests and fill out financial aid forms. The clubs frequently escorted their students on field trips to local colleges and universities and welcomed outstanding Latino doctors, lawyers, and other professional role models into the high schools.

As early as 1971 Aspira Inc. of Illinois had commissioned a study of the Puerto Rican dropout problem. Dr. Isidro Lucas, who taught languages at St. Xavier's College and then at the University of Illinois at Chicago, secured a federal study grant and discovered that the dropout rate for Puerto Rican students stood at 71.2 percent. No one believed him. The Chicago Board of Education wrote a six-page critique of Lucas's report, then buried it.[5]

For Latino youths, the Chicago public schools were not friendly places. One of the marchers, Cesario Martinez, told why he joined the procession that night. Cesario was the oldest of six children whose parents came to Chicago from Puerto Rico in the early 1960s. Shortly after they arrived, his father died of cancer. Because Cesario couldn't speak English and the school he attended had no ESL (English as a Second Language) or bilingual program, the teacher assigned him to an EMH (Educable Mentally Handicapped) class where he spent all his time drawing with crayons.

After aggressive lobbying of the board of education by Maria Cerda, its Latino member, and the threat of a class action lawsuit, Cesario and many other students were taken from the EMH classes and placed in ordinary classrooms. So, in the seventh grade, Cesario Martinez joined his classmates, but by that time he was so far behind that he couldn't grasp what was being taught. He could neither read nor write. His mother's welfare checks purchased barely enough food for her children, so Cesario quit school in seventh grade and went to work delivering groceries. Now, years later, working in a dead-end job at a car wash, he decided to take part in the march for the sake of his own young daughter's future.

Cesar Chavez, the legendary farm worker organizer, had planted the seeds for the candlelight march on a trip through Chicago six months previously. The workers from Aspira and the Network for Youth Services felt frustrated that recent efforts to publicize the dropout problem were hitting a stone wall. "Don't blame anybody else," Chavez counselled, "take the responsibility and rededicate yourselves. Mobilize the people but make allies, not enemies. Transform the people's private pain into a public issue." A group of about 15 organizers took Chavez's words to heart and gathered for a retreat at Northern Illinois University in DeKalb. During two days of prayer and intense conversation, the idea of a candlelight march was born.

Roberto Rivera, who had given up a good job as an administrator at Northern Illinois University to work with Aspira, was laid off when grant money for his position ran out. So he coordinated the march for nearly six months without pay while living on unemployment compensation. Miguel del Valle knew firsthand the humiliation suffered by Puerto Ricans in the public schools. Like Cesario Martinez, he had been held back a year for lack of English, but luckily a sympathetic teacher had recognized his native intelligence and double-promoted him the following year. Del Valle went on to organize the Union for Puerto Rican Students at Northeastern Illinois University and earn a master's degree in guidance and counselling. Now, as director of Association House, a social settlement near Clemente High, he committed himself to the march, for many of the students who dropped out came to his youth employment program seeking aid.

Del Valle and Rivera were beginning a long journey that would take them into the political arena. In 1986 del Valle won election as the first Latino state senator in Illinois. Rivera went to Springfield with him as his chief of staff, and together they helped maneuver school reform through the upper house.

After offering prayers and singing songs in the church, the congregation lit their candles and formed a procession behind the casket. No one objected to the choice of a coffin as a symbol. Some even thought the pallbearers should be parents of young people killed in the streets, but the organizers overruled them, fearing the experience would prove too much for the parents to bear. Those who gathered that night had already attended too many wakes, most of them at the storefront parlor of Caribe Funeral Home on Armitage Avenue. For the people marching in procession, this was no publicity stunt; it was a collective cathartic experience. Previously, a parent whose child had dropped out of school or joined a gang thought he or she had failed as a parent; he or she individualized the pain. Now they saw that they were not alone and they turned their personal pain into a public protest.

The bobbing coffin brought back memories to all who marched behind it. Some remembered the mother who got into a fight at the funeral home when gang bangers insisted she bury her son wearing their gang colors. Others could see the women fanning another grieving mother and rubbing her forehead with alcohol so she wouldn't pass out. They heard the haunting sound of choirs singing "*Resucito*" (He has risen) to the accompaniment of guitars and congas. And inside every head reverberated a mother's scream when they closed the casket on her teenage son. "After you close that coffin and hear that mother cry, it's a sound you never want to hear again," a Catholic priest remarked. The coffin that led the procession down Division Street made sense to everyone.

Carolyn Newberry, a social worker from Erie Neighborhood House, and Tomas Sanabria, from the Network for Youth Services, had been responsible for getting a march permit. They called city hall, they tramped down to the hall in person, and they even enlisted the help of their alderman, but to no avail. Evidently, the police didn't want a permit issued, fearing a gang bang or another riot. Too much had happened on Division Street in the past.

As the time for the march approached, the organizers decided to go ahead without a permit. No one could object to a prayer service in church and they could call the march itself a religious procession. If Bishop Rodriguez led the procession, Commander Walsh, the Irish Catholic cop in charge of the district, wouldn't dare interfere. This strategy worked to perfection. Commander Walsh pulled up to St. Mark's in a squadrol with its blue lights flashing. When he observed Bishop Rodriguez lining up with the crowd, he got out of his car and asked the bishop, "What can I do to be of help, Your Excellency?"

The marchers left the church and proceeded north into the darkness of Campbell Street, then headed east on Division. Gabriel Lopez carried a crucifix at the head of the procession. Lopez worked for Aspira; he was later to join the staff of Michael Madigan, Speaker of the Illinois House of Representatives, and help shepherd the school reform bill through the lower house.

The organizers of the march took the first turn as pallbearers: Miguel del Valle, Roberto Rivera, Aida Sanchez, Jose Herrera, Enrique Colon, Carmelo Rodriguez, Pedro Delgado. They made sure that representatives from the 30 member organizations of NYS each took a turn with the casket. Joe "Whatever it Takes" Rosen, a retired public school district superintendent, had arranged for the use of Clemente High School auditorium. Jaime Rivera rented the casket from a theatrical company, insisting on an expensive mahogany model. Even Freddy Mercado and some of the other youthful marshals took a turn hauling the grim burden. As the coffin grew heavier, they laughed and joked that the principal from Clemente High must have crawled inside.

Representatives of Latino organizations throughout the city joined the local Puerto Rican activists from the northwest side. Carlos Heredia came from the Mexican area called Little Village with a group from Por Un Barrio Mejor (For a Better Neighborhood). Hank Martinez brought a group from the Mexican-American Civic Committee on the southeast side where the steel mills used to be. Mary Gonzales, the founder of UNO (United Neighborhood Organization), led a group from the Mexican barrio of Pilsen, and Danny Solis led UNO delegations from other neighborhoods.

The three Latino members of the Chicago Board of Education—George Muñoz and Raul Villalobos, both Mexican-Americans, and Myrna Salazar, a Puerto Rican—marched behind the casket. Mrs. Clara Rosiles, a Puerto Rican district superintendent of schools and sister-in-law of Bishop Rodriguez, marched with her husband.[6]

Both Protestant and Catholic religious societies, such as the Cursillistas (members of small Christian communities) and Los Carismaticos (fundamentalist Bible-centered Catholics and Protestants), supported the march. When asked to express their feelings that evening, many of the devout replied: "We are the church, it is not the church buildings. So our faith must lead us where God wishes us to go and witness to our belief. We have faith in the power of God, but while our faith is strong, we don't have much hope the schools will ever change."

As if to illustrate the reasons for this pessimism, the Chicago Board of Education released three different dropout rates to the news media the day of the march. At noon, the board stuck to their official line that the dropout rate for the city was only 9 percent. By the five o'clock news, they admitted the rate might be nearer to 20 percent. On the 10 o'clock news, a spokesperson for the board quoted a dropout rate of 45 percent.

Michael Bakalis, a professor of education at Northwestern University and a former Illinois superintendent of public instruction, was primarily responsible for the media coverage that beamed a spotlight on the board's equivocations. Two days before the march, the organizers told Bakalis they couldn't catch the attention of the major newspapers and television stations. A month previously they had held a preliminary meeting with neighborhood parents at the Trina Davila Center across from Humboldt Park. They only expected 75 parents and educators; over five hundred showed up. There weren't enough chairs; there wasn't enough food. The overflow crowd should have been a newscaster's dream, but only two neighborhood newspapers and Channel 26, the Spanish-language station, sent reporters. None of the major media were showing any more interest in the upcoming march.

Bakalis called up two friends who run a Chicago public relations firm, Jasculca/Terman and Associates. Rick Jasculca and Jim Terman made a lot of phone calls over the next two days and arranged for both major papers, every local TV station, and several news radio stations to cover the event. Without this publicity, the march would have failed. A seed can't grow without light.

Bakalis walked with the throng on the night of March 26 and addressed the crowd seated in the Clemente High School auditorium. He urged a total reorganization of the public school system, and warned everyone present that the movement for school reform would be a long, tiring struggle. The Chicago school system was a monolith composed of thousands of unresponsive bureaucrats, he told the crowd, and trying to change it will be like hitting a rock with a hammer: "It will seem hopeless, but if you keep at it, one day the rock will crack into thousands of pieces."

As Bakalis spoke, members of the National Commission on Secondary Education for Hispanics were conducting hearings close by.[7] The commission visited Chicago from March 24 to March 27 as one of many stops on a nationwide tour. Their presence at Division and Western was no accident.

David Vidal, the executive director of the commission, had attended the parents' conference at Trina Davila Center the previous month and had determined to keep the commission members away from such high pressure rallies. When march organizers asked him to bring the commission to Clemente on the night of March 26, he flatly refused and began seeking a neutral site for that night's hearings. He deliberately avoided activists, such as Roberto Rivera, but because the whole Latino leadership of the north side was behind the march, Vidal fell into a trap.

David Vidal asked Celeste Peña, the administrative liaison for community affairs at St. Mary of Nazareth Hospital, for the use of a conference room. Peña obliged by booking the commission hearings into the doctors' dining room the night of March 26. Vidal was not a Chicagoan so he didn't realize that St. Mary of Nazareth Hospital, whose published address is on Division Street, and Roberto Clemente High School, whose address is on Western Avenue, stand adjacent to one another. The picture window of the doctors' dining room overlooks the path of the candlelight procession. Just to make sure, Roberto Rivera circled the pallbearers under the window twice so the visiting commissioners couldn't miss them.

This trick led to the biggest breakthrough of the evening. A reporter for the *New York Times*, E. R. Shipp, was covering the commission proceedings, but when she saw the march she left the hearings to follow the bigger story. As a result, America's "newspaper of record" printed a picture of the candlelight procession and published the story of Chicago's Latinos protesting the catastrophic dropout rate in the city's high schools.[8]

Even Vidal was impressed. He told a Chicago reporter, "It shatters the myth that they [Latinos] do not have an interest in self-betterment."[9]

By the time the march broke up at 10 P.M. on March 26, 1984, a living seed had been planted in a Puerto Rican barrio that would eventually flower into school reform legislation giving parents control over all neighborhood public schools in Chicago. The city's most neglected minority community planted the seed of school reform.

Freddy Mercado, however, didn't live to see the flowering. In the two years following the march, Freddy got his life together. He graduated from high school, found a job, and started attending a community college, but he drifted away from Roberto Rivera and the other adults who had helped him break with the gangs. Then in early 1986, in the midst of a tightly contested aldermanic campaign that would eventually elect four Latino aldermen, Roberto Rivera ran into Freddy on a street corner near Humboldt Park on the near northwest side. He invited him to sit in on a campaign meeting, but Freddy couldn't sit still and kept getting up and walking around outside. The last time he left the storefront meeting, he was gunned down by a street gang.

Notes

1. One of the authors (Kyle) was an organizer of the march on Clemente, and this chapter was written largely from his recollections and those of his fellow organizers: Roberto Rivera, interview by authors, 20 September 1990; Gabriel Lopez, interview by authors, 4 January 1991; and Miguel del Valle, interview by authors, 29 January 1991. Newspaper accounts were published in *Chicago Sun-Times*, 27 March 1984, 23; 28 March 1984, 18; *New York Times*, 28 March 1984, 16. Gabriel Lopez wrote a fuller account for the neighborhood newspaper, *Logan Square Free Press*, 5 April 1984, 8. Tim Bannon provides a lengthy behind-the-scenes look at the organizers of the march in *Chicago Reader*, 27 July 1984, 3, 37.

2. Felix Padilla, *Puerto Rican Chicago* (Notre Dame, Ind.: University of Notre Dame Press, 1987), 83-98, 144-55.

3. *Chicago Tribune*, 25 November 1981, 9.

4. Nelson Algren, *Chicago: City on the Make* (Chicago: McGraw Hill Book Co., 1951), 23.

5. Isidro Lucas, "Puerto Rican Dropouts in Chicago: Numbers and Motivation" (Chicago: Council on Urban Education, 1971); Isidro Lucas, interview by authors, 26 September 1990.

6. The list could go on indefinitely as the roster of marchers was a virtual Who's Who of Latino leadership: State Representative Juan Soliz; Maria Sandoval, who founded Mothers Against Gangs after her son Arthur was murdered on a school playground; Jose Zayas, founder of an alternative school for dropouts; J. Zully Alvarado, first executive director of NYS; Walaska Delgado, a senior at Kelvyn Park High School who served as president of the Aspira clubs; Jaime Rivera, who inaugurated a state-of-the-art, food services vocational program at Clemente High; Tomas Sanabria, who worked six months without pay at NYS as a memorial to his brother who was killed by a street gang; youth workers Guillermo and Gregorio Gomez.

7. The commission was one of many founded in response to the publication of "A Nation at Risk," a federal government study of America's schools (see chapter 3). The commission's study, titled "Make Something Happen: Hispanics and Urban High School Reform," was issued in December 1984.

8. *New York Times*, 28 March 1984, 16.

9. *Chicago Sun-Times*, 28 March 1984, 18.

2

Bankrupt Schools in the Nation's Most Segregated City

The Chicago public schools were no strangers to controversy, nor, for that matter, to street demonstrations. Throughout their history, the schools had faced enormous problems of inadequate finance and political interference.[1]

In the 1920s, Mayor William Hale "Big Bill" Thompson made himself a laughingstock by attacking teachers and textbooks for unpatriotic "British propaganda" and conducting a buffoonish show trial of the schools superintendent, William McAndrew. The Great Depression of the 1930s led to the dismissal of 1,400 teachers and payless paydays for those who hung on to their jobs. Significantly, the school board did not reduce the number of janitors on the payroll, for these were appointed by the ward committeemen of the Kelly-Nash Democratic machine. Some janitors received higher salaries than school principals.[2]

After the schools weathered the financial storms of the depression, they were systematically looted by Kelly's patronage appointees on the board of education. Finally, in 1945, the National Education Association issued a scathing report on Chicago schools and the North Central Association threatened to withdraw accreditation. Mayor Kelly decided not to seek reelection in 1947, his hand-picked school board president resigned, and the state legislature passed a law creating a new, more powerful position of general superintendent of schools. Herold C. Hunt, formerly superintendent in Kansas City, assumed this post in 1947 and proceeded to clean house and establish professional standards.

The long history of scandal, however, left a legacy. After 1947 the mayor appointed members of the school board from a slate of candidates nominated by a nonpartisan advisory commission. The board, in turn, always went outside the city in hiring a superintendent to minimize political influence. Furthermore, the superintendent was granted enormous leeway to carry out his will without significant interference from the school board. After 1947 Chicago employed a "strong superintendent, weak board" system of schools administration.[3]

Though Herold Hunt stabilized the system by injecting honest and professional procedures, Chicago schools still experienced nearly constant turmoil. In the decades of the 1960s and 1970s, the schools confronted demands from black parents and community leaders for integration of the classrooms. The teachers' union acquired collective bargaining rights in 1966, and their escalating salary demands and frequent strikes increased financial pressures on the system. Finally, in 1979, the Chicago Board of Education suffered a sharp financial crisis that left the schools all but bankrupt.

From Willis Wagons to Magnet Schools

Chicago's tightly knit ethnic neighborhoods made it the nation's most segregated city, and such housing patterns produced de facto segregation in the neighborhood schools. By 1963 nonwhite pupils comprised 54 percent of the elementary school students, and 90 percent of these black youngsters attended schools that were 90 to 100 percent black.[4]

Superintendent Benjamin Willis, who succeeded Herold Hunt in 1953, ignored the growing segregation in his schools and became a lightning rod for the civil rights movement. Willis had thrown himself like a whirlwind into the task of building new schools for Chicago's burgeoning youth population, which rose by 180,000 between 1953 and 1966, and he initially enjoyed great esteem and prestige. One historian has concluded "that not one rumor of scandal ever rose" during

Willis's building boom. This is a remarkable achievement in Chicago.[5]

Ben Willis, however, was an imperious man, curt with subordinates, contemptuous of the school board that appointed him, and inaccessible to parents and other outsiders. The post-1947 tradition of the all-powerful superintendent reinforced his natural tendencies. Even Mayor Daley left him alone. Furthermore, Willis believed firmly in the "four walls" theory of schooling (i.e., teachers should teach and nothing outside the four walls of the classroom should affect them). Segregation and poverty in the neighborhoods outside the school walls were utterly irrelevant to the educational task. When black ghetto schools filled to overflowing in the early 1960s while many white schools sat half empty, he refused to bus black children into white neighborhoods. Instead he dropped portable classrooms (swiftly dubbed Willis Wagons) into the playgrounds of the overcrowded schools. In his view, schools should not engage in social engineering. De facto segregation was not his fault and it was none of his business.[6]

The U.S. Supreme Court had outlawed the legally established separate-but-equal schools of the southern states with the landmark *Brown v. Board of Education* case of 1954, but southern politicians dragged their feet against enforcing this decision and northern school districts assumed it did not apply to them. Then in 1961, the Court ruled that the school system of New Rochelle, New York had drawn its district boundaries in such a way as to enhance de facto segregation. This opened the way for similar legal challenges to school segregation elsewhere in the North.[7]

Aided by the NAACP, a group of Chicago black parents filed suit in 1961 alleging deliberate segregation of the public schools. Superintendent Willis refused to divulge the number of vacant classrooms in all-white neighborhoods and resisted all demands to transport black students to such empty classrooms. The board of education settled one lawsuit, the *Webb* case, out of court in 1963 by agreeing to fund an expert study of the problem. Willis's arrogance, however, ran counter to the board's conciliatory motions and made him the focus of mounting protests and demonstrations.[8]

A loosely knit alliance of black and white groups called the Coordinating Committee of Community Organizations (CCCO) documented conditions in the schools and brought them to the attention of the press and the federal Civil Rights Commission. When the board of education instituted a permissive transfer program in the fall of 1963, Willis refused to implement it and engineered an artificial crisis by resigning on October 4. One historian has commented, "It was as if the superintendent had engaged in a one-man strike in an essential industry...."[9] The board refused to accept his resignation and rescinded its transfer policy instead. CCCO hit the streets, declaring a one-day boycott of classes to demand Willis's removal. Approximately half the students stayed away from school on October 22, 1963.

The Advisory Panel on Integration, appointed in settlement of the *Webb* case and headed by University of Chicago sociologist Philip Hauser, reported its findings on March 31, 1964. De facto segregation produced overcrowding in 40 percent of black classrooms, compared to 12 percent of white classes; black schools employed higher percentages of teachers with temporary certificates and little experience; 73 percent of all portable classrooms were used at black schools. The Washburne Trade School was 97 percent white, since most unions in the city would not accept black graduates as apprentices.[10]

The Hauser report made 13 recommendations, including a modified open enrollment plan, free bus transportation from overcrowded to underused schools, and the integration of all school faculties. The board of education dutifully adopted the Hauser report in principle on April 8, 1964, but did nothing to implement it. The Havighurst report, a fuller survey of the whole Chicago school system also released in 1964, seconded Hauser's recommendations and concluded, "There is strong scientific evidence that growing up in a racially segregated school is harmful to Negro children." The board also ignored this evidence.[11]

Willis's contract as superintendent expired in the spring of 1965, and it was widely believed that the board would not rehire him. Yet by this time Willis had become the Bull Connor of the North, a symbol of white resistance to angry black demands, so a fearful board of education renewed his contract for four years, but secured an unwritten pledge that he would actually step down on his 65th birthday in December 1966. Willis's retention set off the largest, most sustained campaign against school segregation in the U.S. during the 1960s.[12]

Al Raby, convener of the CCCO, led daily marches to the board of education's downtown offices and to city hall during the summer of 1965. Martin Luther King, Jr., fresh from his acceptance of the Nobel Peace Prize, flew into town on a weekend in late July to lead a massive march the following Monday, July 26. Dr. King followed a killing schedule of rallies and meetings over the weekend, then checked into a hospital briefly on Monday morning, suffering from exhaustion. But at 3:30 that afternoon he stepped off from Buckingham Fountain, surrounded by priests and ministers, leading a crowd of 30,000 people. They marched 14 abreast in the streets from Grant Park to the LaSalle Street entrance of city hall, black and white linking arms and singing "We Shall Overcome," punctuated by shouts of "Willis Must Go." Police lined the sidewalks, and the rush hour crowds, deterred momentarily from their headlong dash homeward, stood curious and mostly silent. A few, however, sang the anthem of white Chicago resistance:

> Oh, I wish I was an Alabama trooper,
> That is what I'd really like to be-e-e.
> 'Cause if I was an Alabama trooper,
> I could kill the niggers legally.

The march broke up peacefully at city hall. Mayor Daley wasn't there; he was attending a mayors' conference in Detroit.

Martin Luther King, Jr., left town the next morning; Benjamin Willis remained in office, and the daily marches returned to their usual numbers of one hundred or so.[13]

While the anti-Willis campaign unfolded in Chicago's streets, Congress passed the Elementary and Secondary Education Act of 1965, the first large-scale, federal aid-to-education measure. The prospect of Chicago's Board of Education buying more Willis Wagons with federal money terrified federal officials; so in October, Commissioner of Education Francis Keppel deferred Chicago's $32 million share of federal aid. Title VI of the 1964 Civil Rights Act prohibited any federal assistance to agencies that discriminate on racial grounds, and Keppel believed there was evidence of "probable noncompliance" in Chicago. Mayor Daley, however, angrily complained to President Lyndon Johnson, who had not been consulted before the office of education acted, and within five days Keppel's order was rescinded and the money released. This action not only eased Washington's pressure on Chicago but halted any other federal desegregation initiatives in the North for several years.[14]

Willis finally resigned in August 1966, and the school board stayed true to form by replacing him with an outsider, James F. Redmond, a Kansas City native who had served as superintendent in New Orleans and in suburban Syosset, New York. Yet Redmond was an outsider with a difference, having earlier spent six years in Chicago as assistant to Herold Hunt. Moreover, his quiet, patient, tolerant personality was a refreshing change from Willis's imperiousness. Civil rights leaders, exhausted from the struggle against Willis, gave Redmond some leeway to develop his own policies, which he presented to the board in August 1967. The Redmond plan called for the building of magnet schools to attract students of all races, the offering of financial incentives to keep better teachers at inner-city schools, and some limited busing to preserve racial balance in changing neighborhoods. The board initially approved two busing proposals, for South Shore and Austin, but rapidly backed off in South Shore and changed the Austin plan to a voluntary one, when white opposition flared up explosively. Redmond attempted no further busing initiatives and few of his other proposals bore fruit either. Only one magnet school, Walt Disney on the north lakefront, was built during his administration.[15]

The federal government, however, had not permanently abandoned the desegregation struggle. From 1968 to 1973, a series of Supreme Court decisions swept aside southern delaying tactics and put an end to the South's dual school systems. By 1980 the 11 states of the South experienced the lowest level of segregation in the country. Then the Court turned its attention to de facto segregation in the North. The 1973 *Reyes* decision in Denver held that if proof were found of willful discrimination in some substantial portion of a northern school district, the courts could order desegregation of the entire district. Sweeping decisions by federal judges in Boston, Detroit, and other cities led to massive busing under court supervision.[16]

No sweeping busing plan was proposed for Chicago, but in 1976 the Department of Health, Education, and Welfare threatened again to use Title VI of the Civil Rights Act if teaching staff were not thoroughly integrated. A federal administrative law judge found the city schools guilty in February 1977, and the school board rapidly integrated its staff at all schools. Now the Illinois State Board of Education weighed in with a threat to cut off state aid unless new plans were struck for pupil desegregation. The board dusted off the Redmond plan for magnet schools and voluntary busing, renamed it Access to Excellence, and put it into effect in 1978. Nothing much changed. In 1980, Illinois's schools remained more segregated than any other state's on two out of three measures.[17]

The Department of Health, Education, and Welfare eventually ruled the Access to Excellence plan inadequate and referred the case to the Justice Department for possible prosecution in 1980. However, the Chicago Board of Education, the Justice Department, and a federal district court judge, Milton I.

Shadur, entered into a consent decree in September 1980, thus avoiding a long court battle. The board agreed to draw up a new desegregation plan, which it approved in April 1981 and began to implement the following school year.[18]

The number of magnet schools was expanded to 45 city-wide, each with a specialized program such as foreign languages, fine arts, math, or science. Principals at magnet schools were allowed to choose their teachers without regard to seniority; students were assigned by lottery in order to maintain racial integration. The magnet schools became the system's pride and joy, standing out, as a journalist aptly phrased it, "like a working elevator in a housing project." All remaining white schools were desegregated, that is, they admitted at least 30 percent minority students, but most of the black and Latino schools remained segregated. The worst of them received extra teachers and special help to raise the levels of academic achievement. Judge Shadur approved this plan in January 1983, even though its effect on racial integration would be minimal. The Monitoring Commission for Desegregation Implementation was established to watch over the accord, but it was granted little power and few resources.[19]

Throughout the era of the civil rights movement, theorists and activists had debated whether total integration of the races or so-called ghetto enrichment strategies were more realistic. After 20 years of agitation for integration had failed in Chicago, the consent decree finally recognized that the effort had been futile and the federal government acquiesced in a plan of ghetto school enrichment.[20]

Desegregation or integration of schools had become largely a dead issue by the 1980s. The courts refused to order busing across school district lines, so few metropolitan area busing plans including both city and suburbs were attempted. In Chicago and most other big cities, not enough whites remained in the city schools to produce any effective integration. Chicago settled for a two-track system of education in which a favored few of all races and ethnic groups enjoyed access to good teachers and facilities in the magnet schools, while the great majority remained stuck in second-class neighborhood schools.

The Politics of Bankruptcy

The Chicago Board of Education accepted a consent decree from the federal government in 1980 rather than fight desegregation orders because it could not afford a prolonged court battle. In a scenario similar to the highly publicized bankruptcy of New York City, the Chicago board had flirted with financial default in late 1979 and was only saved by a state and city bailout plan.[21]

The Illinois School Code requires that school districts in cities over five hundred thousand in population (i.e., Chicago) adopt a balanced budget each year. In the decade of the 1970s, however, the Chicago Board of Education balanced its budget in only 4 of the 10 years. Board financial officers employed various accounting gimmicks to make the budget appear balanced on paper, but in the years from 1970 to 1976 the schools actually accumulated a deficit of $85.2 million. Some progress was made in the next few years, reducing the accumulated deficit to $53.8 million by 1978, yet income still did not meet annual expenditures.[22]

Chicago schools relied on a relatively low tax rate for their support. The Educational Fund rate remained at $2.11 per $100 assessed value throughout the 1970s even as unprecedented inflation raged in the latter years of the decade. Though higher than most downstate Illinois districts, this tax rate was much lower than that paid by suburban Cook County taxpayers. The state government provided an increasing share of local school district revenues throughout the decade, but the state sometimes experienced cash-flow problems, so it often stretched out its school aid payments. As a result, the Chicago school board met its annual cash needs by issuing tax anticipation warrants. That is, they paid their bills by borrowing against money that was due them but not yet paid.[23]

Furthermore, the state and federal governments mandated

many expensive programs and studies, but they were often tardy in reimbursing the school district for these programs and sometimes they provided little or no additional funding. The Education for All Handicapped Children Act of 1975, for example, required elaborate and costly provisions for special education, yet Congress never paid more than one-eighth of the costs. School officials, too, concocted numerous desegregation plans and appeared in court frequently to defend them, and even though little meaningful desegregation resulted, the board still amassed high staff and legal costs.[24]

Probably the most significant factor leading to school board insolvency, however, was the increasing cost of teacher union contract settlements. Salaries and benefits made up a full 87 percent of the board's expenditures, so pay raises for teachers had a decisive impact on the system's financial health. Mayor Daley pushed through a collective bargaining agreement for the Chicago Teachers Union in 1966 over the protest of then-Superintendent Benjamin Willis, and in the very first contract negotiations, Daley set a dangerous precedent. As the *Chicago Tribune*'s veteran education columnist, Casey Banas, phrased it: "The Board of Education financial crisis...had its beginning on Sunday, January 8, 1967, in the City Hall office of Mayor Richard J. Daley." The teachers were threatening to exercise their newly acquired right to strike, but Daley pushed both sides until they reached an agreement granting a five hundred dollar pay raise. The board of education did not have sufficient revenue to pay this raise, but Daley wanted to buy labor peace at any price.[25]

This pattern continued until Daley's death in late 1976. The teachers struck four times for higher wages, in 1969, 1972, 1973, and 1975, and each time the board caved in under pressure from city hall. The 11-day walkout in 1975 proved the most costly. The board voted $79.6 million it did not have, producing such a cash crunch that schools closed early the following spring when the board ran out of money.[26]

The day of reckoning finally arrived when Friday the 13th

fell on a Tuesday, November 13, 1979. Moody's Investors Service announced that it was lowering its rating for the board's tax anticipation notes to Moody's Investment Grade Four, the lowest possible rating. This news took politicians and the public by surprise. Everyone knew about the New York bankruptcy, but Chicago was reputed to be "the city that works," and most observers thought Schools Superintendent Joseph Hannon had been making steady progress since taking office in 1975. The board had renewed Hannon's contract in September, granting him a hefty raise, and the Civic Federation congratulated him for whittling away at the accumulated deficit. Yet, the financial crisis had been building all during 1979 due to actions by the courts, the legislature, and the bankers.[27]

The Illinois Supreme Court triggered the immediate problem in March 1979 when it declared the personal property tax null and void under the new state constitution adopted in 1970. The personal property tax was an unpopular and much-evaded levy on all property except real estate, yet it furnished about 25 percent of the funds supporting local school districts in the state. The state legislature did not plug this fiscal hole until August, when it raised the corporate income tax as a replacement for the lost personal property revenues. Court challenges to the replacement tax were not finally dismissed until November 21. Thus, a huge chunk of school revenue had to be borrowed in 1979.[28]

When the board of education prepared a prospectus for its usual tax anticipation note sale in the fall, however, legal counsel for Continental Bank found some curious financial practices. The board wished to borrow $124.6 million, but much of this was needed to repay an earlier note issue of $84.6 million coming due on November 26. In short, the board was rolling over its indebtedness. A newspaper reporter tried to explain the practice this way:

> In layman's terms, the Board's action is like getting a $10,000 home improvement loan....Instead of using it for a home improvement, however, you use it for groceries, figuring you can

always get another loan to pay off the home improvement borrowing when it comes due.[29]

In addition, the board had been meeting some of its operating expenses by borrowing from special accounts established to retire long-term bonds. Not only was it spending the "home improvement loan" for groceries, it was dipping into the "mortgage money" as well. Bank officials brought these facts to the attention of the bond-rating agencies, triggering Moody's November 13 surprise. Superintendent Hannon spent all day on November 14 trying to sell the board's notes to local and out-of-state banks, but he received no bids. Then on November 16 the other major bond-rating agency, Standard & Poor's, dropped their ranking of school board bonds two full grades, from minus A to a very speculative BB. The board of education could not borrow anywhere in the nation, and it faced the prospect of either defaulting on its November 26 note repayment deadline or closing the schools, or both.[30]

Two months of frenzied political activity ensued in Chicago and Springfield, though, unlike New York's 1975 financial crisis, the federal government never became involved. The board did scrape up enough money to pay off its notes and meet its November 21 payroll, when Governor James R. Thompson advanced state aid payments to all Illinois schools. A second advance allowed the board to pay its teachers again on December 7, but Thompson warned that he could not legally move up any more payments. At the November 28 board of education meeting, Superintendent Hannon unexpectedly resigned without any explanation. The board's top two financial officers, Eugene Gutierrez and Robert Stickles, followed suit, as did Board President John D. Carey, who had held the presidency since 1970. The board elected Catherine Rohter—the only member who had consistently warned against devious financial practices—as its new president, and Mayor Jane Byrne engineered the appointment of Angeline P. Caruso, a 35-year veteran of the school system, as interim superintendent. Caruso was advanced over the head of her immediate superior, Deputy

Superintendent Manford Byrd, Jr. (who was black), thus angering black board members and community leaders.[31]

The board had not defaulted, for it fulfilled its obligation to pay off tax notes in November, but it could no longer meet its payroll or pay its other bills. On December 21, 1979, the board's 48,600 employees suffered their first payless payday since the Great Depression. The Chicago Teachers Union advised its members to return to classes on January 2 after the Christmas vacation, but not to work past January 4 if the board did not pay them on that day. January 4 turned out to be a second payless payday.[32]

Throughout this crisis the horrible example of New York's fiscal woes haunted the political leaders. In a time of rapidly escalating interest rates, neither the city nor the state could take its credit rating for granted. The *Chicago Tribune* editorialized, "If one tottering branch of government is allowed to drag others down with it, Chicago will soon find itself in the same plight as New York." Ominously, Moody's downgraded their bond rating for the Public Building Commission, a separate governmental body that engaged in construction for the city, the schools, and other government agencies.[33]

Finally, Governor Thompson assembled representatives from the board of education, the city government, the teachers' union, the Chicago banks, and the legislature for a summit meeting at the Executive Mansion in Springfield. The negotiators met all day and most of the night on Friday, January 4 and Saturday, January 5, emerging with an agreement in the wee hours of Sunday morning.

The bailout plan involved three phases. Phase 1, which needed no new legislation, would provide loans totalling $150 million to meet the immediate cash-flow problem and pay the teachers. This sum came from the following sources: $50 million dollars from the state; $25 million from Chicago banks; $25 million from major unions, including the teachers' union pension fund, and the remaining $50 million from the board's meager cash reserve.

Phase II was a $225 million "bridge loan" raised by a city of Chicago tax anticipation warrant sale. Finally, in Phase III, the state legislature established a five-person Chicago School Finance Authority that would sell five hundred million dollars in long-term bonds and exercise rigorous financial oversight and control over the board of education. This long-term solution was closely modeled on a similar control authority established in New York to guard that city's financial recovery. The mayor named two members of the authority and the governor, two members; the chairman, industrialist Jerome Van Gorkom, was jointly agreed upon by Thompson and Byrne.[34]

The school financial crisis petered out in a long and bitter aftermath. The short-term financing did not come together as rapidly as the bailout plan called for, so the teachers endured another payless payday in late January, then staged a wildcat strike during the week of January 28. Though they were finally paid on February 1, they stayed out for yet another week to protest $60 million in spending cuts ordered by the school finance authority. The bailout legislation did not require the school board to show a balanced budget until the 1981-82 school year, but finance authority chairman Jerome Van Gorkom insisted the board make a significant start at reducing its deficit. Finally, the teachers returned to work on Monday, February 11 after the school board restored 504 of the 2,244 jobs they were planning to eliminate. Teachers sacrificed one day's pay, instead of two as originally proposed.[35]

When the state legislature passed the enabling bills for the bailout plan on January 12, Senator Harold Washington added an amendment ending the terms of all Chicago Board of Education members on April 30. This permitted Mayor Jane Byrne to appoint a whole new board, if she wished, but also challenged her to satisfy black leaders' demands for more influence over school policy. Byrne got the message. She reappointed only one member of the old board, black minister Kenneth Smith, and named four other blacks, two Latinos, and four whites to serve with him. The new board elected Rev.

Smith as president immediately after they were confirmed by the city council, giving Chicago a minority-dominated school board and a black board president for the first time. Mayor Byrne, however, with the unerring knack for controversy that earned her the nickname Calamity Jane, denounced the board action as hasty and premature, since the board members had not been officially sworn in yet. Byrne had publicly advocated white, utilities official, Thomas Ayers, for board president.[36]

The Chicago School Finance Authority successfully marketed its first batch of long-term bonds at the end of April to put the schools on a firmer financial footing. Yet, the authority demanded another $50 million in spending cuts from the September 1980 budget. When both the school board and the teachers acquiesced, Jerome Van Gorkom concluded, "The crisis, for the moment, seems to be over." Interim Superintendent Caruso added wearily, "We're left with a stripped-down school system, but a viable school system."[37]

The financial crisis of 1979 had enormous consequences. It shattered forever Chicago's smug self-image as the "city that works" and decisively punctuated the end of the Daley machine era. *Chicago Tribune* editorialists concluded, "Chicago can no longer work just because the mayor shakes a few hands and tells it to work. The magic of past years has been exposed as the deception it was." State Senator Arthur Berman remarked, "The fact was that Daley wasn't around any more so the bean counters and pencil pushers on the Wall Street bond houses started to look at things that they probably should have been looking at from day one."[38]

Governor Thompson, on the other hand, earned much acclaim for saving the schools without a tax increase, and his actions set a precedent. With Mayor Daley dead, Chicago school authorities now looked to Springfield not city hall for decisive intervention. Yet Thompson set another precedent as well. Though the governor took credit for bailing out the Chicago schools, the state government did not provide any new money for the city's embattled system, merely loan authority.

Throughout the coming decade, Springfield would remain very frugal with its aid to Chicago.

The Harold Washington amendment requiring mass resignation of the school board also established a precedent that would be followed during the school reform drive later in the decade. More immediately, it led to increased minority influence on school policy. About one year after the financial crisis, the new board hired Ruth B. Love, the highly regarded black superintendent of Oakland, California schools, to replace Interim Superintendent Caruso. Though blacks and Latinos held a majority on the board and both the board president and the superintendent were black, many community leaders were still irritated since the local black candidate, Manford Byrd, had been passed over again.[39]

Most important, the power of the bond-rating agencies and the rigorous oversight of the school finance authority hung over the school system. The Authority had a legal obligation to approve each school year's budget and assure the bond agencies that it was balanced without accounting gimmicks. Strict fiscal controls and the memory of the 1979 crisis meant that new money was unlikely for any educational innovations.

The Chicago Board of Education entered the 1980s chastened by the federal desegregation consent decree and embarrassed by the financial mess. Two legally established watchdog panels, the Monitoring Commission for Desegregation Implementation and the Chicago School Finance Authority, scrutinized its every action. Blacks had acquired unprecedented recognition at the highest levels of school policy, yet the schools remained as segregated as ever and the black community bitterly distrusted the Byrne administration. No one expected much money from Reagan's Washington or Thompson's Springfield to meet the continuing problems of city schools. Indeed, Judge Milton Shadur, the guardian of the desegregation consent decree, had to issue repeated court orders forcing the Reagan administration to help pay for its implementation.[40] The school reform movement of the eighties could not have faced a less promising set of circumstances than it found in Chicago.

Notes

1. Mary J. Herrick, *The Chicago Schools: A Social and Political History* (Beverly Hills: Sage Publications, 1971), is the standard history. Julia Wrigley, *Class Politics and Public Schools, Chicago, 1900-1950* (New Brunswick: Rutgers University Press, 1982), provides a useful supplement for the first half of this century.

2. Wrigley, *Class Politics and Public Schools*, 222.

3. Paul E. Peterson, *School Politics Chicago Style* (Chicago: University of Chicago Press, 1976), 87.

4. Advisory Panel on Integration of the Public Schools, "Report to the Board of Education City of Chicago" (hereafter cited as the Hauser report), 31 March 1964, 6, 14.

5. Herrick, *Chicago Schools*, 309.

6. Ibid., 311-12.

7. Diane Ravitch, *The Troubled Crusade: American Education, 1945-1980* (New York: Basic Books, 1983), 114-44, 171; Gary Orfield, *The Reconstruction of Southern Education: The Schools and the 1964 Civil Rights Act* (New York: John Wiley & Sons, 1969), 1-32, 155.

8. The stormy saga of Ben Willis has been told many times. Herrick, *Chicago Schools*, 306-35, provides a low-key, balanced account. The early journalistic biographies of Mayor Richard J. Daley tell it more vividly: Bill Gleason, *Daley of Chicago* (New York: Simon and Schuster, 1970), 37-41; Len O'Connor, *Clout* (Chicago: Henry Regnery Company, 1975), 180-90; Mike Royko, *Boss* (New York: E. P. Dutton & Co., 1971), 138-39. Orfield, *Reconstruction of Southern Education*, 151-207 gives a thorough account in the context of federal desegregation policy. David J. Garrow, *Bearing the Cross: Martin Luther King, Jr., and the Southern Christian Leadership Conference* (New York: William Morrow and Company, 1986), 431-34, focuses on the brief involvement of King in the struggle. Alan B. Anderson, George W. Pickering, *Confronting the Color Line: The Broken Promise of the Civil Rights Movement in Chicago* (Athens, Ga.: University of Georgia Press, 1986) is a massively documented study of CCCO's composition and tactics.

9. Herrick, *Chicago Schools*, 318.

10. Hauser report, 14-23.

11. Herrick, *Chicago Schools*, 323-29; Hauser report, 25-38; Robert J. Havighurst, *The Public Schools of Chicago* (Chicago: The Board of Education, 1964), 373.

12. Orfield, *Reconstruction of Southern Education*, 163-67.

13. Gleason, *Daley of Chicago*, 37-41; Anderson and Pickering, *Confronting the Color Line*, 150-67.

14. Orfield, *Reconstruction of Southern Education*, 167-207; Anderson and Pickering, *Confronting the Color Line*, 178-82.

15. Peterson, *School Politics Chicago Style*, 36-37, 143-58; Herrick, *Chicago Schools*, 342-50.

16. Gary Orfield, *Must We Bus? Segregated Schools and National Policy* (Washington, D.C.: Brookings Institution, 1978), 16-36; Ravitch, *Troubled Crusade*, 174-78.

17. Orfield, *Must We Bus?*, 174-75; Gary Orfield, *Public School Desegregation in the United States, 1968-1980* (Washington, D.C.: Joint Center for Political Studies, 1983), 10.

18. *Chicago Tribune*, 25 September 1980, 1.

19. *Chicago Tribune*, 7 January 1983, 1, 2; *New York Times*, 7 January 1983, 1; 8 January 1983, 11; 20 January 1983, 22; Steve Bogira, "Whatever Happened to School Desegregation?" *Chicago Reader*, 29 January 1988, 1; Monitoring Commission for Desegregation Implementation, "Interim Report," (February 1983).

20. *Chicago Tribune*, 26 September 1980, sec. 3, p. 2; *New York Times*, 7 January 1983, 16. The *Chicago Tribune*, 7 January 1983, 2, presented a useful chronology of the whole Chicago school segregation struggle, dating back to 1961.

21. The 1975 New York financial crisis has been fully described by journalist Ken Auletta in *The Streets Were Paved With Gold* (New York: Random House, 1979). No similar account of Chicago's school crisis has been published, but two unpublished reports document it: Joint House and Senate Chicago Board of Education Investigation Committee, "The Chicago Board of Education's 1979 Financial Crisis and its Implications on Other Illinois School Districts," 81st General Assembly, 13 January 1981 (hereafter cited as Joint Legislative Investigation); Continental Illinois National Bank and Trust Company of Chicago, "The 1979 Chicago Board of Education Financial Crisis— A Continental Bank Review," 16 April 1980 (hereafter cited as Continental Bank study).

22. Joint Legislative Investigation, 10, 31, 57-58; Continental Bank study, 8-9.

23. Joint Legislative Investigation, 57-64.

24. Ravitch, *Troubled Crusade*, provides a brilliant survey and critique of these federal and state mandates in chapter eight, "The New Politics of Education," 267-320.

25. Joint Legislative Investigation, 66-68; *Chicago Tribune*, 5 December 1979, sec. 4, p. 2.

26. *Chicago Tribune*, 5 December 1979, sec. 4, p. 2; 4 February 1980, 1; State Senator Aldo A. DeAngelis, Republican cochairman of the Joint Legislative Investigation, appended a personal minority report to the study, emphasizing these political pressures by Mayor Richard J. Daley as a major factor in the board's financial problems, 215-22.

27. *Chicago Tribune*, 14 November 1979, 1. The Joint Legislative Investigation provides a detailed chronology of the crisis, 43-56.

28. Joint Legislative Investigation, 44-45; Continental Bank study, 11-14.

29. *Chicago Tribune*, 29 November 1979, 18.

30. *Chicago Tribune*, 15 November 1979, 1; 17 November 1979, 1, 25 November 1979, 8.

31. *Chicago Tribune*, 25 November 1979, 8; 29 November 1979, 1; 14 December 1979, 1; Joint Legislative Investigation, 52-53.

32. Joint Legislative Investigation, 54.

33. *Chicago Tribune*, 28 November 1979, sec. 4, p. 2.

34. *Chicago Tribune*, 3 January 1980, 1; 5 January 1980, 1; 6 January 1980, 1; Joint Legislative Investigation, 55-56; Continental Bank study, 26-28. The *Chicago Tribune* profiled the five finance authority members on 16 January 1980, 4.

35. *Chicago Tribune*, 28 January 1980, 3; 29 January 1980, 1; 4 February 1980, 1; 11 February 1980, 1.

36. *Chicago Tribune*, 16 April 1980, 1; 17 May 1980, 1. Profiles of the board members appear on 16 April 1980, 17.

37. *Chicago Tribune*, 1 May 1980, sec. 3, p. 2; 1 September 1980, 3; 3 September 1980, 5.

38. *Chicago Tribune*, 12 February 1980, sec. 3, p. 2; Arthur Berman, interview by authors, 30 September 1991.

39. Ruth Love was profiled in *Chicago Tribune*, 14 January 1981, 1.

40. *New York Times*, 1 July 1983, 6; 23 July 1983, 5; 16 August 1983, 12; 26 August 1983, 10; 27 September 1983, 18.

③

A Rage for Excellence, A Call to Power

Nonetheless, a movement for school reform engulfed the nation in the early years of the 1980s, and as it gained momentum, it spilled over into Chicago. In April 1983, the report of a presidential commission on education ignited a national rage for educational excellence and made political leaders extremely sensitive to calls for school reform. Chicago school officials had been arguing about race and money for two decades, but the quality of teaching in the schools was forgotten until the federal government focused a searchlight on it.

That same year, in fact during the very same month, the election of Harold Washington as Chicago's first black mayor inspired minority leaders, including Latino community groups, to believe they too could make a political impact. Two seemingly unrelated events in 1983, the national education debate and the election of Mayor Washington, came together to set the stage for the dramatic march on Clemente and to foster the school reform movement in Chicago.

The Year of the Education Report

On April 26, 1983, the National Commission on Excellence in Education (NCEE) released a 36-page report titled "A Nation at Risk." One education writer hailed it as the launch of a "paper Sputnik." Indeed, "A Nation at Risk" hit the national consciousness with as much force as the launch of the first Soviet satellite into space 25 years before. It touched off a national debate over educational policy that raged throughout 1983 and into the presidential election year of 1984.[1]

It was highly ironic that the Ronald Reagan administration initiated this great debate. Reagan came to the presidency determined to shrink the national government. In particular, he had campaigned on a pledge to abolish the federal Department of Education, recently established by his predecessor, President Jimmy Carter, with the strong support of the teachers' unions. Terrell H. Bell, the education secretary, was Reagan's last appointee to the cabinet. Bell, the director of higher education for the state of Utah and a former U.S. commissioner of education, came to Washington with his belongings in a U-Haul trailer, not expecting a long stay. In the first two years of Reagan's administration, he rarely saw the president, and he presided over a drastic reduction in his department's funding and staff.[2]

With little fanfare, Secretary Bell established the National Commission on Excellence in Education (NCEE) on August 26, 1981. He exhorted the commission to address a "nationwide problem of declining college entrance scores" and "the widespread public perception that something is seriously amiss in our educational system." Perhaps Bell, who was not so ideologically conservative as President Reagan, hoped the commission would make a strong enough case to save his department from the ax. Or he may simply have wanted to show that the federal government "can play a useful coordination and advocacy role," even without a Department of Education. Bell was known to favor a federally chartered education research foundation if the department were abolished. As it turned out, the NCEE would certainly demonstrate the power of federal advocacy.

Secretary Bell chose David P. Gardner, president of the University of Utah as chairman of the commission, and named 17 other educators, businessmen, and politicians to serve under him. The commission held hearings around the country, but its 16-member staff from the Department of Education, headed by Milton Goldberg, also surveyed the existing educational literature and commissioned several original studies as well. Eighteen months and $785,000 later, the NCEE released its report at a Washington news conference.[3]

Most commission reports make dry reading and are swiftly exiled to library shelves where they gather dust eternally. The authors of "A Nation at Risk," however, employed a lively style and caught the nation's attention with some exaggerated shock tactics. The report began with a dire warning, "Our nation is at risk....The educational foundations of our society are presently being eroded by a rising tide of mediocrity that threatens our very future as a Nation and a people." It then continued with rhetoric drawn from the depths of the cold war: "If an unfriendly foreign power had attempted to impose on America the mediocre educational performance that exists today, we might well have viewed it as an act of war. As it stands,...we have, in effect, been committing an act of unthinking, unilateral educational disarmament."[4]

True to its charge from Secretary Bell, the commission decried the national decline in test scores. "Average achievement of high school students on most standardized tests is now lower than 26 years ago when Sputnik was launched," it asserted.[5] Then the report focused on four areas where education needed drastic improvement: content, expectations, time, and teaching.

The commissioners exhorted school systems to revise their educational content or curriculum and emphasize what they called the "five new basics." They urged that all high schools require (a) four years of English; (b) three years of mathematics; (c) three years of science; (d) three years of social studies; and (e) one-half year of computer science. Indicting the permissive atmosphere of the 1960s for a lowering of expectations in the schools, they called for higher standards, both for graduation from high school and for admission to college. They noted that most other nations require students to spend more time in school and assign more homework than American schools do. Therefore, they raised the controversial issue of extending the school day to seven hours and the school year to 200 or even 220 days. Finally, they recommended that teachers should be paid more but that salary, promotion, and tenure should be tied more closely to performance.[6]

The National Commission on Excellence in Education touched several major nerves. Many Americans still felt uneasy about their country's role in the world a decade after the national traumas of Vietnam and Watergate. Ronald Reagan had skillfully played on this uneasiness by blaming his predecessor, Jimmy Carter, for spreading a feeling of malaise. By the time the NCEE reported, the nation had reached the bottom of the deepest economic downturn since the Great Depression of the 1930s. Economists were dolefully pontificating that Japan had usurped America's economic primacy.

A lively fear that the U.S. was no longer Number One in the world animated all the findings and recommendations in "A Nation at Risk." Dr. Ernest L. Boyer of the Carnegie Foundation quipped that the national response could not have been greater if the Japanese had launched a Toyota into orbit.[7]

Americans seemed ready to accept the NCEE's diagnosis. The *New York Times* editorialized, "The National Commission on Excellence in Education may dwell too obviously on the link between national security and good schools....But who can deny that public education's lost credibility creates a crisis?" Albert Shanker, president of one of the two major teachers' unions, the American Federation of Teachers, encouraged his members to cooperate with the reform movement. "Our response should not be a knee-jerk type of response," he warned. "This is an absolutely new situation."[8]

In the months that followed, a cascade of similar education reports rolled off the presses. The Education Commission of the States, led by Governor James Hunt, Jr., of North Carolina, had been working on a parallel track to the national commission. They titled their report, approved in May 1983 and published that summer, "Action for Excellence." Like "A Nation at Risk" it sounded an alarm "that the poor quality of American public schools was threatening the military, economic and social well-being of the country." Hunt and other southern state governors had particular reasons for alarm. They feared that the backward school systems of the South were hindering the economic renaissance of the Sun Belt. The states' report recommended higher salaries for teachers and longer school days. Another southern governor, Lamar Alexander of Tennessee, took the lead in devising a new career ladder for teachers in his state that would provide economic incentives for improved teaching and would closely monitor a teacher's progress toward improvement. After a long fight, Governor Alexander convinced the Tennessee legislature to approve his plan in February 1984.[9]

Prestigious think tanks, such as the Carnegie Foundation for the Advancement of Teaching and the Twentieth Century Fund Task Force on Federal Elementary and Secondary Education Policy, weighed in with reports that closely resembled those of the national and state commissions. Renowned educators John Goodlad and Theodore Sizer produced more reflective and thoughtful volumes on the quality of teaching in American schools. In all, eight highly publicized national education reports appeared between April 1983 and January 1984.[10]

This, in turn, set off a frenzy of activity at the state level. The Education Department issued a report card on the first anniversary of the NCEE report revealing that 275 state-level task forces had gone to work on education in the past year and that most were recommending a back-to-basics curriculum, higher standards for graduation from high school and for entry into college, and more math and science in order to compete better economically.[11] A rage for excellence had taken hold.

President Reagan, despite his initially minimal involvement with education policy, quickly seized the educational reform issue and reshaped it to his own agenda. Shortly before the NCEE report appeared, Democratic Senator Paul Tsongas of Massachusetts remarked offhandedly to a gathering of scientists and educators, "If the President had any political sense, he'd grab this issue and take it away from us and run with it."[12] That is precisely what the "Great Communicator" did.

At the White House ceremony on April 26, when the NCEE commissioners presented Reagan with his copy of "A Nation at

Risk," the president baffled journalists and surprised the commissioners by hailing the report for its call to end federal intrusion in education. Actually, the report said: "The Federal Government has the *primary responsibility* [emphasis added] to identify the national interest in education. It should also help fund and support efforts to protect and promote that interest." Reagan ignored the contradiction and continued to assert that no new federal money was needed for education. Instead, he called for action on his three pet education measures: tuition tax credits for private school students, a constitutional amendment to allow prayer in the public schools, and the abolition of the Education Department. The president took a verbal beating from the pundits for his harping on the dangers of federal involvement in education. The *New York Times* compared him to a robot: "For the third time in three weeks he was repeating the same message, as oblivious to contradiction and rebuttal as a tape cassette."[13]

Reagan, however, proved shrewder than his critics. He quietly shelved his plans to abolish the Education Department. All of a sudden, Terrell Bell became one of his most important advisers and a hot property on the lecture circuit. The president himself hit the trail in June for a series of education speeches in Hopkins, Minnesota; Knoxville, Tennessee; and Albuquerque, New Mexico. Reagan hit hard at the back-to-basics theme and called for greater effort and discipline from both teachers and students. The only specific reform he advocated was merit pay for superior teachers, a position vehemently opposed by the National Education Association and viewed warily by Albert Shanker's American Federation of Teachers.[14]

Walter Mondale, and the other candidates vying for the Democratic presidential nomination, ridiculed Reagan's stance as "voodoo education" and called for across-the-board increases in pay for teachers. This was all the opening that Reagan needed. From then on, he defined the issue as quality (excellence in education) versus quantity (more money, big spending, new taxes). Transforming the issue into a debate over money put the

Democrats, and their teacher union allies, on the defensive. Egged on by Reagan's attacks against big government and free-spending liberals and still smarting from the deep economic recession of the early eighties, many Americans were ready to accept a tough, hold-the-line-on-spending approach to education reform. Long before he won the Democratic nomination, Walter Mondale had lost the education issue to the Republicans.

The year of the education reports ended with a growing consensus that America needed education reform but that no new money should be thrown at the problems. This reinforced the frugality that Chicago's financial crisis had imposed on the board of education.

The national education debate seemed very remote from the concerns of black or Latino parents in the inner city of Chicago, and indeed it was. Critics of the education reports pointed out that they "failed to address the needs of the poor, the minorities, and inner city youth. Strategies to encourage dropouts to remain in school, for example, were not considered." A few critics even argued that, despite the inflammatory language of the reports and their conjuring up of crises, the reforms advocated were not radical enough.[15]

Perhaps the greatest failing of the education reports was their neglect of accountability and governance issues. None of the reports advocated a dismantling of the top-heavy bureaucratic structure of American education. Though most paid lip service to parental involvement, none envisioned any means of parental control over local schools or any devices to hold educators accountable. An education writer for *Esquire* summed it up best, "The reports are well-intentioned...but their promise of real, deep-down change is a hoax."[16]

Parents in the inner city of Chicago needed no one to tell them this. Their schools had the highest dropout rates and were crawling with gang members. Their sons and daughters often felt afraid to go to school. When a young interviewer commissioned by Aspira to explore the educational concerns of Latino teenagers began making her rounds, the father of one high school dropout interrupted her, screaming, "It's wrong to call that school after such a great man [Roberto Clemente], that school should be named after Al Capone."[17]

Yet the national education debate created a climate of opinion in which politicians were ready to listen. There would have been no National Commission on Secondary Education for Hispanics to witness the Clemente march in Chicago had the NCEE not stirred up such a furor. And both black and Latino leaders felt confident enough to try to capitalize on the education ferment, for they had been energized and challenged by the election of Chicago's first black mayor.

Here's Harold!

Harold Washington was the Happy Warrior of Chicago politics. A big bear of a man with an infectious grin and an impressive command of the English language, Washington loved the game of politics more than any power or money it might bring him. Inheriting the political bug from his father, Roy Washington, a minister, lawyer, and wardheeler on Chicago's black south side, Harold played the game of politics with gusto all his life. "Politics is like shooting pool or eating Cracker Jacks," he once remarked. "Once you start you just can't stop." A Washington aide made the same point with a sensuous metaphor: "He loved politics and he was the most faithful lover I ever knew. Twenty-four hours a day he had this mad passionate affair."[18]

Washington defeated Richard M. Daley, son of the late, legendary Mayor Richard J. Daley, and Jane Byrne, the incumbent, in the Democratic primary on February 22, 1983. Then, in a nasty, racially charged campaign, he barely edged out Bernard Epton, a Jewish Republican, in the general election on April 12.[19]

Byrne and Daley split the white vote in the primary, allowing Washington to win the Democratic nomination with just 36 percent of the ballots. He rode a massive mobilization of his black voting constituency, employing an 80-80 strategy (i.e., trying to produce an 80 percent turnout of black voters and to win 80 percent of their votes). He easily topped the 80 percent mark for black vote totals, though turnout fell a little short. Still the 73 percent black turnout was enough to over-match the divided white votes of his two opponents.

Bernard Epton, a little-known Republican with a liberal record, found himself unexpectedly at the head of a white crusade to prevent the election of Chicago's first black mayor. Though no Republican had come close to winning the mayoralty since 1931, Epton nearly made it. Some white Democratic ward bosses openly defected to Epton, others gave Washington only lukewarm support. The Republican candidate's campaign slogan, "Epton. Before it's too late," played on racial fears none too subtly. When Walter Mondale campaigned for the Democratic candidate on March 27, he and Washington faced an ugly white crowd at St. Pascal's Catholic Church on the city's northwest side that forced them to exit hastily. This incident made television news nationwide. Finally, Edward Vrdolyak, the Democratic party chairman for Cook County, admitted openly what everyone already knew, "It's a racial thing." Epton came within 48,000 votes of denying Washington election.

Race so dominated both the primary and general elections of 1983 that neither the gender issue (Byrne), the dynasty issue (Daley), nor anti-Semitism (Epton) received any attention. Polish-Americans, who had a long history of friction with Jews in the old country and a loyal Democratic voting record in the city, voted over 80 percent for the Jewish Republican. In the final analysis, Washington captured virtually all of the black vote, a majority of the Latino votes, and a sizeable minority of whites in the liberal lakefront wards. These combined to give him 668,176 votes (51.8 percent) to Epton's 619,926.[20]

To most white residents of the city, Washington seemed to come out of nowhere in 1983, but in fact, he had been in Chicago politics all his life, had held office for nearly 20 years, and had even run for mayor before. After returning from service in the air force during World War II, Washington attended

Roosevelt University on the G.I. Bill, then earned a law degree from Northwestern University. He worked political campaigns with his father, then, after Roy Washington's death, joined the organization of Third Ward alderman and committeeman Ralph Metcalfe. Washington won his first election campaign in 1964, when he went to the state legislature in Springfield; he moved up to the state senate in 1976.[21]

Despite an independent temperament that led to frequent arguments with his mentor, Metcalfe, and the boss, Richard Daley, Washington remained a reasonably faithful machine supporter in Springfield. He saw little alternative if he wished to remain a political player. He was cautious also to avoid most of the civil rights turmoil of the 1960s. He only marched in one demonstration, when Martin Luther King, Jr., came to town in July 1965. This march on the board of education to protest the policies of Schools Superintendent Benjamin Willis was the lowest common denominator for Chicago civil rights supporters. Just as all Jews, whether religious or not, observe Yom Kippur, anyone, black or white, with the slightest interest in civil rights turned out for Dr. King in 1965.[22]

Harold Washington never felt comfortable as a machine lackey, and he grew increasingly frustrated as the years went along. One of his biographers suggests that the carelessness about income taxes and personal finances that later blew up into a controversy during the mayoral campaign was due to Washington's depression, from bottling up his independence for so long.[23] In any case, he remained loyal to the Democratic organization until the death of Richard J. Daley in December of 1976.

State Senator Washington then made a quixotic bid for the mayoralty in the special election called in 1977 to fill out Daley's final term. He ran a distant third behind the machine-backed victor, Michael Bilandic, and a Polish challenger, Roman Pucinski. Washington won only 11 percent of the vote in his hastily thrown together, poorly financed campaign, but he did carry five black wards on the south side. The machine felt sufficiently worried to try to knife him in his 1978 reelection bid for state senator. Then in 1980, Washington finally broke decisively with the Democratic regulars, running for the U.S. Congress in the First District against three other candidates, each of whom had backing from powerful party factions. He won that contest handily and remained in Congress until his election as mayor. Washington was reluctant to bid for the mayoralty a second time after his decisive defeat in 1977, but the rising tide of black voter militancy finally swept him up and carried him to victory.

Black voters had traditionally been loyal followers of the Daley machine. In particular, the black proletariat living on welfare in public housing developments depended on the machine for their livelihood and produced substantial majorities for Daley in each of his six mayoral elections. From about 1970 on, however, the rapidly growing black middle class became disaffected from the Democratic machine. At first they showed their displeasure by simply dropping out of the electorate. Black turnout generally averaged 10 percent less than white turnout during the Daley years, but black middle-class turnout fell even lower. Upwardly striving black professionals and businessmen saw little benefit to themselves in the racist structure of the machine, but they also saw no viable alternative. Therefore, they stayed at home on election days.[24]

After the death of Richard J. Daley, this began to change. Michael Bilandic, a lackluster, caretaker mayor, seemed destined for reelection in 1979 until a fierce snowstorm stalled the city and breathed new life into the campaign of Bilandic's challenger, Jane Byrne. During the great snow, the city's forces proved unable to clear the streets, and Chicago Transit Authority elevated trains callously breezed past black patrons freezing on the platforms in inner-city neighborhoods. The black electorate rose up and delivered over 63 percent of their votes to Byrne, sweeping Bilandic and the remnants of the Daley machine from office. The turnout in black middle-class wards doubled between 1977 and 1979.[25]

Mayor Byrne swiftly alienated her newly aroused black followers with a series of insensitive political maneuvers. She appointed Richard Brzeczek, a Polish-American cop with a get-tough image, as police superintendent instead of the blue ribbon outsider she had promised to search for during the campaign. Then she turned around and snubbed black insider, Manford Byrd, Jr., for the post of schools superintendent during the financial crisis. Transit strikes and higher sales taxes on food and medicine during the Byrne administration hit the impoverished black community proportionally harder than others. Then, in the summer of 1982, Byrne replaced two controversial black appointees on the Chicago Housing Authority, naming two whites to take their places. This action, cementing a white majority on the board, incensed the black community. In protest, Rev. Jesse Jackson mounted a partially successful boycott of Byrne's favorite civic celebration, the youth-oriented Chicago Fest.[26]

At the same time that Calamity Jane was carelessly throwing aside her black support, the presidency of Ronald Reagan threatened even more damage to black political and economic interests. Reagan's cutbacks in federal aid to the cities hampered the ability of mayors like Byrne to satisfy the aspirations of minorities, even if they were inclined to do so. The twin threats of Reagan and Byrne produced a black voter registration drive that swelled the numbers of minority voters. Between 1979 and 1983, voter registration in Chicago rose from 1,423,476 to 1,594,253, an increase of 11.7 percent. In the 17 predominantly black wards, however, voter registration leaped forward 29.5 percent. Republican Governor James R. Thompson nearly fell victim to this upsurge. Expected to win handily over former senator, Adlai Stevenson III, Thompson squeaked through by fewer than five thousand votes in November 1982. Another 62,190 blacks registered between the November election and the mayoral primary; 30,000 more enrolled between the primary and the general election. The number of blacks eligible to vote reached nearly seven hundred thousand by the time of Washington's election.[27]

The unprecedented mobilization of black political power shocked white residents of the city and led to the infamous "Council Wars," an abrasive obstruction of Washington's administration. In May 1983, almost immediately after Washington's election, Alderman Edward Vrdolyak of the Tenth Ward seized leadership of the city council and forged a majority bloc of 29 aldermen that prevented Washington from passing any major legislative measures. The 29 could out-vote Washington's 21 council loyalists, but they could not override a mayoral veto if they passed legislation of their own. The city government, then, was locked in an impasse that would last for nearly three years. The Vrdolyak bloc also refused to approve numerous mayoral appointments, thus leaving major boards and agencies of city government leaderless.[28]

Though Council Wars temporarily stalled the black political upsurge before Harold Washington could take complete control of city government, Washington's election still marked a notable success for Chicago's black voters. It also served as a model and an inspiration to the city's second largest minority group, the Latinos.

Notes

1. *New York Times*, 27 April 1983, 1; George Leonard, "The Great School Reform Hoax," *Esquire*, April 1984, 47.

2. *New York Times*, 27 December 1983, 1.

3. *New York Times*, 25 August 1981, sec. 3, p. 5; 27 August 1981, 28; 27 April 1983, 1.

4. National Commission on Excellence in Education, "A Nation at Risk: The Imperative for Educational Reform" (Washington: Government Printing Office, 1983), reprinted in Beatrice and Ronald Gross, *The Great School Debate: Which Way for American Education* (New York: Simon and Schuster, 1985). Our references to "A Nation at Risk" are to the page numbers in the Gross book. The opening quotes are on page 23.

5. Ibid., 26.

6. Ibid., 34-43.

7. *New York Times*, 4 October 1983, sec. 3, p. 8.

8. *New York Times*, 2 May 1983, 18; 1 May 1983, 1; 11 April 1983, 18.

9. *New York Times*, 5 May 1983, 1; 26 February 1984, 25. Several years after leaving the governor's office, Lamar Alexander was named federal secretary of education by President George Bush.

10. The reports, in order of appearance, were: National Commission on Excellence in Education, "A Nation at Risk" (April 1983); Business—Higher Education Forum, "America's Competitive Challenge" (April 1983); The College Board, "Academic Preparation for College" (May 1983); Education Commission of the States, "Action for Excellence" (May 1983); Twentieth Century Fund, "Making the Grade" (May 1983); Carnegie Foundation, "High School" (September 1983); John I. Goodlad, "A Place Called School" (September 1983); Theodore R. Sizer, "A Study of High School" (January 1984). For a listing and comparison, see Gross, *Great School Debate*, 52-53.

11. U.S. Department of Education, "Responses to the Reports from the States, the Schools, and Others," in Gross, *Great School Debate*, 391-99.

12. *New York Times*, 22 March 1983, sec. 3, p. 7.

13. *New York Times*, 27 April 1983, 1; 28 April 1983, sec. 2, p. 15; 24 May 1983, 24.

14. *New York Times*, 9 June 1983, 1; 14 June 1983, 16; 16 June 1983, 25.

15. Lawrence C. Stedman, Marshall S. Smith, "Weak Arguments, Poor Data, Simplistic Recommendations," in Gross, *Great School Debate*, 94. See also, Paul E. Peterson, "Did the Education Commissions Say Anything?" *Education and Urban Society* 17 (February 1985): 126-44; and Carol Camp Yeakey, Gladys Styles Johnston, "High School Reform: A Critique and a Broader Construct of Social Reality," Ibid.: 157-70.

16. Leonard, "School Reform Hoax," 48.

17. Quoted in Charles L. Kyle, "'Los Preciosos': The Magnitude of and Reasons for the Hispanic Drop Out Problem in Chicago: A Case Study of Two Chicago Public Schools" (Ph.D. diss., Northwestern University, 1984), 52.

18. Robert McClory, "Up from Obscurity: Harold Washington," in *The Making of the Mayor: Chicago, 1983*, ed. Melvin G. Holli and Paul M. Green (Grand Rapids: William B. Eerdmans, 1984), 3; Harold Baron, interview by authors, 4 December 1990.

19. The best account of the primary is Paul M. Green, "The Primary: Some New Players—Same Old Rules"; of the general election, Don Rose, "How the 1983 General Election Was Won," both in Holli and Green, *Making of the Mayor*. See also, chapter one in Melvin G. Holli and Paul M. Green, *Bashing Chicago Traditions: Harold Washington's Last*

Campaign (Grand Rapids: William B. Eerdmans, 1989), and Paul Kleppner, *Chicago Divided: The Making of a Black Mayor* (DeKalb: Northern Illinois University Press, 1985).

20. For complete vote totals by ward, see Holli and Green, *Making of the Mayor*, 124.

21. McClory, "Up from Obscurity," is the best brief biographical sketch of Washington. Florence Hamlisch Levinsohn, *Harold Washington: A Political Biography* (Chicago: Chicago Review Press, 1983), and Dempsey Travis, *"Harold," the People's Mayor: The Authorized Biography of Mayor Harold Washington* (Chicago: Urban Research Press, 1989) are fuller accounts, both by personal friends of Washington.

22. Levinsohn, *Harold Washington*, 109.

23. Ibid., 159.

24. This revisionist interpretation of black voting behavior in Chicago has been developed by William J. Grimshaw. See his *Black Politics in Chicago: The Quest for Leadership, 1939-1979* (Chicago: Loyola University Center for Urban Policy, 1980), and "Harold Washington: The Enigma of the Black Political Tradition," in *The Mayors: The Chicago Political Tradition*, eds. Paul M. Green and Melvin G. Holli (Carbondale: Southern Illinois University Press, 1987). Michael G. Preston, "The Resurgence of Black Voting in Chicago, 1955-1983," in Holli and Green, *Making of the Mayor*, follows the same line.

25. Preston, "Resurgence of Black Voting," 46.

26. Ibid., 46-47; Green, "The Primary," 23-24.

27. Preston, "Resurgence of Black Voting," 47-48.

28. Milton Rakove, "Observations and Reflections on the Current and Future Directions of the Chicago Democratic Machine," in *The Making of the Mayor*, 137-39; Alton Miller, *Harold Washington: The Mayor, The Man* (Chicago: Bonus Books, 1989), 111-30.

④

4

The Latinos in Chicago

Chicago is unusual among big cities in the variety of Latin-American nationalities who have settled there. Nearly 75 percent of all Latinos in North America reside in just five states: California, Texas, Florida, New York, and Illinois. Yet in the other major Latino areas one nationality dominates, such as Puerto Ricans in New York, Cubans in Miami, or Mexicans in California and Texas. The Midwest's metropolis, however, has large numbers of both Mexicans and Puerto Ricans, as well as smaller populations of Cubans, Central Americans, and South Americans.[1]

This unusual diversity of populations made it difficult for Latinos to unite and exercise political influence proportional to their numbers. The election of Harold Washington marked one of the first times these various nationalities acted together in the political arena, and the mass movement of black voters that elected Washington served as a powerful example to Chicago's Latin-American communities.

There had been some instances of Latino consciousness and joint action in the decade before Washington's election. As members of the different Spanish-speaking nationalities faced similar problems in churches, schools, and the job market, they slowly realized that they might exercise more influence against discrimination and exploitation if they stuck together. The Spanish Coalition for Jobs mobilized community organizations in 1972 and 1973 to fight for more employment at Illinois Bell and Jewel Tea Co. After some success in this endeavor, however, the coalition narrowed its scope and became a local neighborhood organization for the Mexican community on the near southwest side. The Latino Institute, which opened in 1975 as a cultural resource and leadership training center, has been longer lived and has helped crystallize a sense of interethnic Latino consciousness. Significantly, the Latino Institute chose the neutral turf of a downtown location, rather than one of the Mexican or Puerto Rican barrios, for its headquarters.[2]

The U.S. Census and most of the English-language media employ the term *Hispanic* as the umbrella adjective for Spanish-speaking people in America. Yet, many community leaders prefer to call themselves *Latino*. The word Hispanic refers to the Spanish conquerors of Central and South America. Labelling Latin-Americans Hispanics is akin to calling Irishmen Britons, because they come from one of the British Isles. Obviously, one does so at his own risk. Latino is more inclusive than Hispanic, for it also encompasses the Portuguese-speaking Brazilians, and is a more neutral label for all migrants who come from south of the border. It is simply a shortened term for Latin-American.

Theoretically, the migrants from Cuba, Puerto Rico, and Mexico enjoy several options for forging an ethnic identity and mobilizing for political action. They could simply remain as separate nationalities seeking to gain their slice of the economic and political pie, or they could coalesce into a bloc with other Catholic ethnic groups, or they could form a coalition of the oppressed with blacks and other dark-skinned peoples. The relatively small numbers of each group and callous disregard from old-line political bosses made it impossible for them to function politically as just another ethnic group. Institutional neglect from the Catholic church and frequent discrimination by individual Catholics largely closed off the Catholic bloc option.

Forming a "rainbow coalition" of the oppressed remains a tantalizing possibility, and Harold Washington attempted to do just that. Blacks and Latinos often face similar problems, and the white community generally classifies Latinos as a nonwhite minority. One early Puerto Rican migrant recalls: "I went to a tavern with a friend and the owner of the bar refused to serve us....'We don't serve niggers here.' I replied that we were Puerto Ricans and he just said, 'That's the same shit.'"[3] On the other hand, Latin-Americans are relatively free of race prejudice. Indeed, Puerto Ricans, in particular, form an amalgam of Indian, black, and white races nearly unique in the Western Hemisphere. Three children in the same family might have black, white, or olive-colored skin.

Yet, generally speaking, *Latinismo* or Latino consciousness has been the most powerful unifying force among the Latin-American nationalities in America. A common language and many cultural similarities have combined with the common problems of economic and political discrimination to forge an interethnic political consciousness that has been growing in importance. As one community activist has phrased it, "I try to use Latino as much as I can. When I talk to people in my community, I use Mexican, but I use Latino when the situation calls for issues that have citywide implications."[4] In sum, Latino is an essentially political word, denoting a coalition of several Latin-American nationalities. The midwestern melting pot of Chicago has been a major crucible forging this unifying consciousness.

Neighborhoods and Churches

The first Mexicans settled in Chicago in 1916 when the railroad companies recruited 206 track laborers from the Texas-Mexico border. These workers settled near the rail yards south and west of Chicago's Loop forming a small community around Halsted and Roosevelt Road. Another Mexican community, a stopping off point for migrant farm workers in the Midwest, formed just south of the Burlington Railroad tracks along Halsted and 18th Street in the predominantly Bohemian neighborhood of Pilsen. Other Mexican laborers followed them during and after World War I to work in the steel mills of South Chicago and the stockyards on the southwest side. The 1920 census counted 1,200 Mexicans in Chicago. By 1930 their numbers had swelled to 20,000, about equally divided between the three primary working-class neighborhoods on the near west side, South Chicago, and Back of the Yards.[5]

Many Mexicans entered Chicago's heavy industries as strikebreakers, and when the labor strife ceased, employers often released them. In the 1930s, with the depression threatening the jobs of immigrant and native alike, the Immigration and Naturalization Service deported many Mexican laborers, reducing Chicago's Mexican population to 16,000 by 1940. Yet for those who managed to stay on, the steel mill jobs provided the highest pay and job status available to Mexican workers, with railway labor the most unstable and packinghouse work located somewhere in between.[6]

Seventy years after first settling in Chicago, Mexicans still remain concentrated in the same areas of the city.[7] Urban renewal, however, wiped out much of the housing on the near west side, so Mexicans moved south and made Pilsen a predominantly Latin barrio. Curiously, the community still retains the European name of a city in Bohemia. Mexicans also moved west from Pilsen into the South Lawndale neighborhood along 26th Street, west of California Avenue. This time they changed the name of the neighborhood as well, calling it *La Villita* or Little Village.[8]

The early history of Mexicans in the Chicago steel mills and stockyards resembles closely the experience of European immigrants. Yet, Mexicans faced a threat that earlier immigrants escaped, the constant fear of deportation. Seemingly in 20-year cycles, the INS zealously hunts down illegal immigrants. Not only Mexicans, but even Puerto Ricans, who are American citizens by birth, are frequently stopped by federal agents and asked for identification. This harassment has built an important link between these two Latino communities. Perhaps no other ethnic group has experienced the need to constantly justify its existence in America.[9]

Puerto Ricans did not begin to arrive in great numbers until after World War II. The 1960 census counted 32,371 Puerto Ricans in Chicago and by 1970 the population had grown to

78,963. By this time Chicago's heavy industries no longer needed increasing numbers of laborers, so Puerto Ricans tended to take low-paying jobs in smaller factories and in service industries. Not tied to the mills and the stockyards, they settled in a more dispersed pattern than the Mexicans, with small concentrations in several north lakefront neighborhoods, as well as on the west side and in Woodlawn. Urban renewal, however, posed a major threat to Puerto Ricans on the north side, as great a threat as deportation did to Mexicans. Development pressure and neighborhood change, often accompanied by arson (the poor man's urban renewal), shifted Puerto Ricans from one place to another. Gradually, however, Puerto Ricans concentrated along Division Street in the West Town and Humboldt Park neighborhoods where good transportation gave access to jobs downtown and in various industrial areas.[10]

Hundreds of thousands of Cubans fled to the U.S. in the early 1960s after Fidel Castro's revolution, and Chicago was one of the designated resettlement areas to decrease the congestion of Cuban refugees in Miami. Many settled in the north side neighborhoods of Uptown, Edgewater, and Rogers Park. Many of these refugees came from the educated and privileged classes of pre-revolutionary Cuba and were able to make rapid economic strides in America. Still, they often started in low-status jobs and faced some of the same linguistic and discrimination problems that other Latinos did. The 1980s saw further waves of Latino refugees, this time from Central America, where nearly constant warfare in El Salvador, Nicaragua, and Honduras sent many families and individuals northward.

All in all, Latinos numbered 422,063 in Chicago in 1980 and 508,609 in the five-county metropolitan area. These numbers swelled to 545,852 for Chicago and 836,905 for the total metropolitan area in the 1990 census count. Though diverse in nationality and social origins and geographically dispersed through the city and suburbs, Latinos do share many common characteristics. Seventy-six percent of Chicago's Latino population is under 35 years of age; one in eight (12.6 percent) earn incomes below the official poverty level; and approximately two-thirds (64.5 percent) have not completed high school. Seventy-nine percent speak at least some Spanish, and though most are bilingual, perhaps one in four speak no English. In sum, Chicago's Latinos are very young, poor, and poorly educated, and many face a language barrier as well.[11]

Though most Latinos profess the Catholic religion, the church in Chicago did not welcome them as openly as it had previous Catholic immigrants from Europe. European immigrants who settled in Chicago before World War I formed national parishes in the neighborhoods where they lived. Though the Catholic church in the city is generally organized geographically, with about one parish per square mile, close by these "territorial" parishes in the densely populated, multiethnic, working-class wards, stood several national parishes for the non-English-speaking groups. Thus many neighborhoods no more than a mile square might have four or five Catholic churches close together.[12]

Both Roman authorities and the local Chicago bishops, however, discouraged the expansion of the ethnic parishes after World War I. The codification of Canon Law in 1918 made the founding of national parishes a definite exception, requiring permission from Rome. In Chicago, Cardinal George Mundelein, an efficient business manager who came to the city in 1916 to consolidate the church's administration, found the numerous ethnic parishes side by side highly inefficient and overly expensive. Mundelein did not try to undo the past, but he made it very difficult for any ethnic group, particularly the city's large Polish population, to organize new national parishes.[13]

Mundelein showed some flexibility when an entirely new ethnic group, such as the Mexicans, entered the city. In 1925 he invited a Spanish religious order, the Claretians, to organize a Mexican parish in South Chicago. Worshipping first in a wooden chapel provided by the Illinois Steel Co., the Mexican community built the Church of Our Lady of Guadalupe in

1928, which became known colloquially as the "Mexican cathedral." At about the same time, Mundelein also handed over St. Francis of Assisi, an old German church on Roosevelt Road, to the Claretians as a second Mexican cathedral for the near west side. The Claretians later extended their religious work to the Mexicans living back of the yards; however, their storefront church in that neighborhood was not organized as a full-scale parish, but only as a mission outpost, known as Immaculate Heart of Mary vicariate. A decidedly second-class facility, Immaculate Heart looked like a garage with a church facade tacked onto it.[14]

Though the Archdiocese of Chicago officially recognized two and one-half Mexican national parishes, this fell far short of meeting the religious needs of the Mexican community. In some ways the existence of a few national parishes made the religious status of Mexican Catholics difficult. When Mexican parents found their way to the nearest Catholic church to arrange a baptism for their child, the English-speaking pastor often told them to "go to the Mexican parish," which might be miles away in a strange neighborhood. When large numbers of Mexicans moved into a new neighborhood, the local church finally would institute one Spanish mass on Sundays, but it was often scheduled at an inconvenient hour or in the school basement.

Puerto Ricans, as American citizens by birth, were not granted any national parishes at all. By the time they, and the other Spanish-speaking groups, arrived in Chicago after World War II, the Catholic church was building new parishes in the suburbs and seeking to close or consolidate many older ethnic parishes in the city. The last thing the Chicago bishops intended to do was build new national parishes for the Spanish-speaking.

Some older parishes, such as St. Mark's, where the candlelight march on Clemente began, became so heavily Latino that they were considered de facto national parishes. In fact, St. Mark's became known as the "Puerto Rican cathedral" by the 1960s. Similarly, the Cubans centered their religious life around the Spanish mass at St. Ita's in Edgewater. There they held devotions to Nuestra Señora de Carmen, the patroness of Cuba. But the Latinos enjoyed no official status at these parishes, and since urban renewal often forced them to move frequently, they felt no sense of ownership or belonging. Typically, in neighborhoods that were once settled by Polish or Bohemian immigrants but were now heavily Latino, the local church would conduct three masses on Sunday: one in English, one in Polish or Bohemian, and one in Spanish. The parish belonged to nobody in particular.

Years ago, the Polish Catholics of Chicago felt aggrieved because Cardinal Mundelein would not ordain auxiliary bishops of their nationality, and he attempted to assign some Polish priests to English-speaking parishes. Yet, they had a Polish league of 34 national parishes served by a numerous Polish-born clergy to fall back on. Polish pastors ruled over these parishes like feudal lords and reported only to a Polish monsignor designated by Mundelein as his delegate for Polish affairs. The Polish league could not have been more autonomous if it were a separate diocese. Latinos, by way of contrast, lacked sufficient priests in their home countries and they brought very few with them to the United States; they experienced very little autonomy in the Chicago Archdiocese.[15]

By the time that Latinos spread into numerous Catholic parishes of Chicago, parochial school education had been priced out of their reach. Before the Second Vatican Council, religious orders of sisters provided the teaching staff of parochial schools and the local parish subsidized most of the costs. The Archdiocese of Chicago built a string of parish schools that, at their peak in 1965, formed the third-largest school system in the nation, surpassed in numbers only by the public schools of New York and Chicago.[16] Tuition was free in many parishes, or at most a nominal dollar or two per month.

From the 1960s on, however, lay teachers replaced the teaching sisters and yearly school costs soared to five hundred dollars or more per child. Latino parents, with large families and yearly incomes near or below the poverty level, could not afford Catholic school tuition. Less than 10 percent of Latino Catholics send their children to parochial schools, a percentage far lower than most previous Catholic immigrant groups.

Latino Catholics, then, felt like second-class citizens in the Catholic church. Often turned away from English-speaking parishes or segregated in basement masses, they had few national parishes of their own. Furthermore, Latinos could not afford the hallmark of Chicago Catholicism, a Catholic school education, and thus had to rely on the overcrowded public schools.

The Catholic church in Chicago, potentially one of the Latinos' most powerful allies, instead conditioned Spanish-speaking people to feel inferior. A small, dedicated band of Catholic priests in Chicago, led by Fathers Leo Mahon and Donald Headley, did learn Spanish and dedicate their lives to the Latino community. The archdiocese established the Office for the Hispanic Apostolate in 1979, and in December 1983 Cardinal Bernardin consecrated Placido Rodriguez, a Mexican-American who grew up in the national parish of St. Francis of Assisi, as an auxiliary bishop. Yet all in all, the Catholic church, which could have been a support and an ally, has often been just another obstacle to the national aspirations of Mexicans, Puerto Ricans, and others. The net result of church policy has been to create feelings of inferiority in Latino parishioners and make them passive when facing social problems in the city and public schools.

Still, the common problems that Spanish-speaking Catholics faced in their neighborhood churches indirectly stimulated a wider Latino consciousness. Although the candlelight procession to Clemente High stepped off from the "Puerto Rican cathedral," it drew Mexican-Americans, including Bishop Rodriguez, and other Latinos as well.

Political Obstacles

Latinos arrived too late to share in the rich ethnic diversity of national Catholic parishes that flourished at the turn of the century in Chicago. They came too late, also, to help build the Democrats' ethnic coalition from the ground up.[17] Instead, Latinos confronted a Chicago Democratic machine that had been entrenched for decades and enjoyed a monopoly of political power, and they settled in neighborhoods where some of the most intransigent political bosses held sway.

Vito Marzullo, the ward boss of the Pilsen area, was an unlikely media darling who enjoyed folk hero status among city hall reporters. An elderly, crusty, Italian-born original, he was first elected to the city council in the 1950s and by the decade of the eighties had served longer than any other living alderman. Basing his power on a small Italian enclave along South Oakley Avenue, Marzullo made no attempts to naturalize and register the Mexican immigrants in his neighborhood; consequently, his 25th Ward had the lowest voter registration in the city during the late 1970s and early 1980s.[18]

When Puerto Ricans moved into the Division Street area, they encountered Alderman Thomas Keane of the 31st Ward, Mayor Richard J. Daley's finance committee chairman and floor leader, widely recognized as the second most powerful politician in the city. Since Keane's new Latino constituents were mainly Puerto Ricans, who are citizens by birth, he had to devise various stratagems to weaken their potential political power.

Keane inaugurated the practice of naming Latinos as assistant precinct captains. The old-time resident who was the real precinct captain would have a big city job like a deputy commissioner for streets and sanitation while the Latino would work for the city as either a garbage man or a park janitor. In the Democratic party, as in the Catholic church, Latinos were second-class citizens.

Keane instructed his assistant precinct captains to register only Latinos they could trust to vote with the Daley machine.

The machine used numerous tricks to produce the right vote total. For example, Spanish-speaking residents who used food stamps were told that the bell in the voting machine would not ring if they did not vote a straight Democratic ticket. If they didn't hear the bell, their food stamps would be taken away. Of course, the bell rang whenever a voter pulled the voting machine lever, but newly registered migrants didn't always know this.

Alderman Keane was known at city hall as the Map Wizard, for he drew the new city ward maps after each census. As a result of his efforts, the ward boundaries in Latino areas often resembled stars and asterisks as Keane gerrymandered the boundaries to ensure that Latinos never held a majority in any ward. Keane was convicted of mail fraud by U.S. Attorney James R. Thompson in 1974 and spent most of his declining years in federal prison, but his maps remained at large. Mayor Byrne even called on the 76-year-old Keane, out of office and out of jail, to help with the 1981 redistricting, which was later overturned in court.[19]

As Tom Keane exited the political scene, a younger Democrat entered: Edward Vrdolyak, boss of the 10th Ward in South Chicago. Vrdolyak started as a young Turk in the Daley machine, then rose to head the Cook County Democratic party during Mayor Jane Byrne's regime. After the election of Harold Washington, he led the city council opposition of 29 die-hard white aldermen. Washington once remarked of Vrdolyak, "I've known guys like Eddie all my life....He's not a racist. He's a bully....He'll use anything, he'll use his own grandmother to get what he wants."[20] Racist or bully, Fast Eddie was unlikely to grant any large measure of political power to the Mexican community in his ward.

Besides the opposition of Democratic party barons, Latinos faced several other major obstacles in the political arena. Their geographic dispersion resulted in low population concentrations in most wards. In 1979, for instance, Latinos constituted 5 percent or more of the electorate in 17 wards, but in only two wards did they form more than 30 percent of the electorate. Latinos did not comprise a majority in any ward. Tom Keane's maps aggravated the effects of population dispersion. A large Mexican population had been concentrated in the 10th Ward before 1971, but that year's redistricting divided it between the 7th, 8th, and 10th wards.[21]

The low rate of naturalization and the extreme youth of the Latino population combined to produce a low total of registered voters. In 1980, an estimated 70 percent of Chicago Mexicans and Cubans were not American citizens, and thus ineligible to vote. More than three-fourths (76 percent) of Chicago's Latino population were under 35 years of age. Those under 18, of course, could not vote, and those between 18 and 35 fell into the population group with the lowest voter turnout, regardless of their ethnic background.[22]

Occasionally a Latino independent, like Miguel Velasquez, remained undaunted by these political obstacles and ran for office anyway, so ward bosses and precinct captains would resort to their ultimate weapon. If they felt the independent candidate had a chance to win, they would pay off street gangs to terrorize his supporters and keep them from voting.

As a result, Latinos accounted for about 14 percent of the city's population in the early 1980s, but they comprised only 5 percent of the electorate. The four most heavily Latino wards (22nd, 25th, 26th, and 31st) were Chicago's bottom four in voter registration. Nine wards elsewhere in the city each contained more registered voters than the four Latino wards combined. As the 1980s began, Latinos were virtually shut out from political representation, with only one Cook County commissioner, a trustee of the University of Illinois, and two circuit court judges. There were no Latino aldermen, committeemen, or state legislators.[23]

The Washington Example

Not much had changed by the time Harold Washington launched his mayoral campaign in 1983. Edward Nedza, Tom

Keane's successor as boss of the 31st Ward, had slated Jose Berrios for state representative and Miguel Santiago for alderman, and independents Rudy Lozano and Juan Velazquez were preparing to run for alderman in Pilsen and Little Village. A few of the younger Latino professionals had noticed Congressman Harold Washington a year or two earlier when he spoke out against an Immigration and Naturalization Service sweep that resulted in over five thousand deportations from Chicago, but the bulk of the Latino community knew little or nothing about him.

Only 39 percent of voting-age Latinos registered in 1983, their 75,000 votes making up about 4 or 5 percent of the city totals. About 70 percent of those registered did turn out for the 1983 primary; however, they split their votes between the two white candidates, Byrne and Daley, and had little effect on the outcome. Led by the younger Latino professionals who had backed the black candidate from the beginning, Latinos then turned heavily to Washington once he had earned the Democratic nomination. An estimated 65 to 79 percent of the Latino voters marked their ballots for Harold Washington in the general election. This allowed them to claim (along with other groups) that they had provided the crucial 48,000 vote margin that sealed Washington's victory.[24]

Sure of his black voter base, Washington had campaigned heavily in the Latino community. Miguel del Valle stumped for him on the northwest side as did Rudy Lozano on the southwest; both shared Washington's vision of a "rainbow coalition," which clearly posed a threat to the established political order. Lozano narrowly lost his race in the 22nd Ward and was murdered shortly thereafter, a crime that remains unsolved to this day.[25]

The Democratic mayoral candidates staged the last of their four debates during the primary campaign at Roberto Clemente High School on Monday, January 31. A large, noisy audience showed up to see Daley, Byrne, and Washington in person. Latino parents turned much of the questioning to education issues, and both Daley and Washington attacked Byrne for politicizing the board of education. Washington stated, "Instead of fighting for quality education, Jane Byrne has fought to make the school board a racial battleground, despite the fact that the majority of students are black or Hispanic." One member of the audience called for the appointment of a Puerto Rican as district superintendent for the northwest side, but Byrne sidestepped the question.[26] After his narrow election, Washington returned to Clemente with his newly appointed cabinet for one of a series of town meetings he conducted to show that he was mayor of all the people. Again, the sharp questioning revolved mainly around education.

Washington's election proved that a hitherto slumbering minority could rouse itself, mobilize for action, and win a major victory. Yet it did more than this. The black voter registration drive also demonstrated *how* to mobilize a community, thus providing an example for others.

First of all, the remarkable unity of the black vote pointed out that ethnic solidarity was crucial. The Latino community was usually divided into several competing ethnic groups, but the large Latino vote for Washington in the general election marked the first appearance of a unified voting bloc. An exit poll conducted by the Midwest Voter Registration Education Project on election day showed Puerto Ricans voting 87 percent for Washington, Mexicans 68 percent, and even the Cubans, who were generally Republicans, 54 percent Democratic.[27]

The United Neighborhood Organization (UNO), started in 1980 by Mary Gonzales and her husband Gregory Galluzzo, typified the kind of group that learned this lesson from Harold Washington's election. Gonzales had long been involved with the Pilsen Neighbors community organization, but she and her husband, a former Jesuit priest, shared a wider vision of Latino unity throughout the city. They started church-based community organizations in South Chicago, Back of the Yards, and Little Village, and drew in Danny Solis, a former SDS radical, to transform the Pilsen Neighbors into a similar church-based group. In 1984 these four organizations came together in a federation named UNO Chicago. The acronym *UNO* means "one" in Spanish.[28]

Second, the mobilization of the black community came largely from the grassroots. Church ministers, welfare rights activists, and community organizers, such as Lu Palmer, took the lead, with black politicians playing a secondary role. Harold Washington benefited from the voter registration drive; he did not lead it. Latino community organizers noted all this, and for the first time, experienced some feelings of confidence and hope.

Finally, the election of Harold Washington was sparked by a movement—even a crusade at times—more than by a traditional electoral campaign. The final Washington rally at the Pavilion of the University of Illinois took on all the trappings of a revival meeting as 12,000 supporters chanted, "Harold, Harold." Resentment and anger drove the movement, resentment at Jane Byrne's highhanded patronage tactics and deepseated anger at the long exclusion of blacks from political power. The movement focused on the overriding issues of fairness and equity in the distribution of power and jobs.

Latinos were just awakening to the importance of this. The broadcasting manager of WOJO-FM, the Spanish-language radio station that carried the Clemente candidates' debate with a simultaneous translation, remarked, "When I got here 10 years ago, you didn't hear a word about the city government in the Hispanic media." But a *Chicago Tribune* poll before the 1983 election found a new awareness. "It is difficult to attach numbers to it," the *Tribune* reporter wrote, "but Hispanics in general put delivery from City Hall above all other categories. They want clout. 'What can you do for me?' is the most important factor in the choice for mayor."[29]

Latino politicians moved swiftly to claim their share of appointments and jobs in the Washington administration. The new mayor named Miguel del Valle chairman of his Advisory Commission on Latino Affairs and appointed Arturo Vazquez from Northeastern Illinois University as deputy commissioner in the Department of Economic Development. When the mayor ran for reelection in 1987, he slated Puerto Rican Gloria Chevere as his running mate for city clerk.[30]

Throughout the early 1980s a legal challenge to Tom Keane's final ward map, filed by the Mexican American Legal Defense and Education Fund in league with several black groups, was winding its tortuous way through the courts. Finally, in 1985, a federal judge approved a new map creating supermajorities of 65 or 70 percent of Latinos in four wards and blacks in three additional wards. The 1986 special elections in these newly drawn wards finally broke the Council Wars deadlock, allowing the mayor to break ties in his own favor and finally take full control of the city government.[31]

Important as these political gains were, the attainment of clout was not the only, or even the principal, concern of Latino voters during the Harold Washington years. Just before Washington's election, Spanish-speaking interviewers from the Midwest Voter Registration Education Project dug a little deeper and found that Latino voters were most concerned with unemployment, gangs, housing, and education.[32] This final concern, education, would prove to be the issue that Latino organizers used to mobilize their community.

Bilingualism and Beyond

As the decade of the 1980s began, Latino students outnumbered whites in the Chicago public schools for the first time. The ethnic and racial survey issued by the board of education in the fall of 1981 counted 86,755 Latino students, 19.6 percent of the 442,889 students in the system. Blacks still formed an overwhelming majority, 60.7 percent of the enrollment, but whites had fallen to third place with only 76,112 students (17.2 percent).[33]

Latinos faced enormous problems in the public schools, with overcrowding at the head of the list. In Pilsen, Little Village, Back of the Yards, and South Chicago, Latino students often attended classes in basements, cloakrooms, or recycled Willis Wagons. UNO focused attention on this issue in each neighborhood they organized. They marked their first success with the building of Niños Heroes Magnet School in South Chicago, named after the child heroes of the Mexican-American War, young cadets who held Chapultepec Castle for days against the American invaders. When some older residents of the neighborhood objected and demanded an American name for the school, Mary Gonzales silenced them by asking, "What's an American name? Pulaski?"

After years of lobbying by the Latino community, the state legislature authorized nearly $24 million in 1985 to alleviate overcrowding by constructing new school buildings. In August, however, Governor Thompson vetoed the appropriation. UNO organized a rally and demonstration in Springfield on October 31, Halloween. Parents and children, some in trick-or-treat costumes, surrounded the Executive Mansion until Thompson appeared. The governor solemnly promised to visit the Latino schools and assess conditions himself. Later the governor's staff tried to renege on the promise, but Mary Gonzales told them they were turning out two thousand people for a protest meeting and they had already hired 27 buses. They intended to pack people into the buses and hunt down the governor wherever he was, at home or office. Thompson attended the rally, visited the schools, and eventually released the funds.[34]

Severe as the overcrowding problem was, Latino students also harbored deeper discontents. The poet Richard Garcia, in his caustic poem "America You Lied to Us," widened the indictment of public education, deriding the "schools where human beings are dissected, injected and infected instead of frogs."[35] Because of their limited English ability, many Spanish-speaking students were held back in lower grades or incorrectly placed in special education classes for the mentally retarded. Bilingualism became the preferred remedy for educators, a rallying cry for hard-pressed Latino parents, and a major source of controversy.

The first bilingual education program for Spanish-speaking youngsters was organized in 1963 in a Miami elementary school serving recent refugees from Castro's Cuba. This experimental program, funded by the Ford Foundation, proved highly successful at training children to function in both English and Spanish and thus led to a wider demand for bilingual education. Congress held extensive hearings on the subject in 1967, largely at the instigation of Texas Senator Ralph Yarborough, then passed the Bilingual Education Act of 1968. Though the major impetus had come from Latinos, the act authorized bilingual education programs for all "children of limited English-speaking ability." The permissive and experimental programs of the Bilingual Education Act soon gave way to mandatory requirements when a group of Chinese parents in San Francisco won their case (*Lau v. Nichols*) before the Supreme Court in 1974. The *Lau* guidelines required school districts to provide special assistance to "limited English proficient" (LEP) students.[36]

Misunderstanding and controversy surrounded the issue of bilingual education from the very beginning. Congressmen had clearly meant for bilingual training to be remedial and temporary in nature, intended only to ease the transition of foreign students into the English-speaking mainstream. Many bilingualism advocates, however, viewed foreign language classes as permanent cultural maintenance programs that would improve the self-image of immigrant students and instill pride in their heritage. The sharp conflict between these two contradictory goals for bilingual education, assimilation versus bicultural maintenance, dogged the program at every step.[37]

Though Chinese parents had carried the major test case to the Supreme Court and literally dozens of language groups took advantage of bilingual schooling in the United States, Latinos dominated in the foreign language-speaking population, and bilingualism was widely viewed as a Latino issue. One study in 1982 found that "approximately 3.6 million school-age children in the United States have limited ability in English. About

73 percent of these children are Hispanic."[38]

In 1973, the Illinois General Assembly added Article 14C to the school code, mandating bilingual education for LEP students. Approximately 10 percent of the students in the Chicago public schools attend bilingual classes representing 19 different home languages, but over 75 percent of the bilingual students are Latino.[39] Bilingual classes have provided many jobs for Spanish-speaking teachers, though some have begun to see such jobs as dead ends.

Nevertheless, Latino parents and educators remain committed to bilingual maintenance programs. For Puerto Ricans, they are a virtual necessity. So many Puerto Ricans travel between the island and the mainland in the *va y ven* (back and forth) phenomenon that their children must learn to function in two monolingual societies, Spanish-speaking in Puerto Rico and English-speaking in the 50 states. Many Puerto Ricans maintain dual home bases with family networks and strong emotional attachments to two widely separated places of residence. Since Puerto Rico is part of the United States, it is hard to see how the bilingual skills needed to maintain these dual home bases can be denied. Just as the neighboring country of Canada contains a French-speaking province of Quebec and several English-speaking provinces, so the United States encompasses a Spanish-speaking commonwealth of Puerto Rico and a much larger English-speaking society in the rest of the country.[40]

Other Spanish-speaking families, however, particularly those from Mexico, also travel back and forth between the United States and their home countries, thus they too require bilingual education. The descendants of European immigrants often resent such special treatment for recent Spanish-speaking immigrants. Many educators also believe that bilingual education leads to lowered achievement in both languages. Numerous studies have not settled the question of how much educational benefit students derive from bilingual programs.[41]

Nevertheless, bilingualism is a sacred cow for Latinos in Chicago and throughout the nation. However controversial it may be among educators and however much resentment it may stir up among Anglos in America, its continued existence is legally solid and has been accepted as a fait accompli. One Latino educator has remarked, "Perhaps Hispanic minorities are so overwhelmingly in favor of bilingual education regardless of lack of evidence of its success because the experiences with past programs have been so negative that any alternative is a step in the right direction."[42]

Bilingual education was so firmly established in Latino schools that it did not become an issue during the school reform debates of the 1980s. Instead, the major concern of Latino parents was the dropout problem. Indeed, the dropout problem has been described, without exaggeration, as "so catastrophic at some schools that it almost resembles a student strike."[43]

Notes

1. The 1980 Census of Population enumerated 422,063 persons of Spanish origin in Chicago. Of these, 255,802 (60%) were Mexican; 112,074 (27%) were Puerto Rican; 11,513 (3%) were Cuban; and 42,674 (10%) were listed as other Hispanic. All Latinos comprised 14% of the city's 3,005,072 people. The 1990 census counted 545,852 Latinos in Chicago's population of 2,783,726 (20%). The numbers of Mexicans had grown markedly in a decade, to 352,560 (65%), whereas the number of Puerto Ricans remained virtually the same, 119,866 (22%), and the number of Cubans actually declined to 10,044 (2%). 63,382 people were listed as other Hispanics (12%).

2. Felix Padilla, *Latino Ethnic Consciousness: The Case of Mexican Americans and Puerto Ricans in Chicago* (Notre Dame, Ind.: University of Notre Dame Press, 1985), 89-137.

3. Felix Padilla, *Puerto Rican Chicago* (Notre Dame, Ind.: University of Notre Dame Press, 1987), 59.

4. Padilla, *Latino Ethnic Consciousness*, 62.

5. Louise Año Nuevo Kerr, "Mexican Chicago," in *Ethnic Chicago*, eds. Melvin G. Holli and Peter d'A. Jones (Grand Rapids: William B. Eerdmans, 1984), 270-71; Padilla, *Latino Ethnic Consciousness*, 20-21; Paul S. Taylor, *Mexican Labor in the United States: Chicago and the Calumet Region* (Berkeley: University of California Press, 1932), 34; Gerald W. Ropka, "The Evolving Residential Pattern of the Mexican, Puerto Rican and Cuban Population in the City of Chicago," (Ph.D. diss., Michigan State University, 1973; New York: Arno Press, 1980).

6. Anita Jones, "Conditions Surrounding Mexicans in Chicago," (Master's thesis, University of Chicago, 1928; Los Angeles: R and E Research Associates, 1971).

7. The Chicago Department of Planning estimated that in 1985, midway between the federal censuses, the community area called Lower West Side (Pilsen) had 40,220 persons of Spanish origin; South Lawndale (Little Village), 66,946; South Chicago, 17,241; and New City (Back of the Yards), 24, 757.

8. This entire section on Latino community areas relies heavily on Joanne Belenchia, "Latinos and Chicago Politics," in *After Daley: Chicago Politics in Transition*, eds. Samuel K. Gove and Louis H. Masotti (Urbana: University of Illinois Press, 1982), 118-28.

9. Ibid., 122-24.

10. Ibid., 124-27; Padilla, *Puerto Rican Chicago*, 78-98. The Chicago Department of Planning estimated the Spanish origin population of West Town and Humboldt Park at 86,340 in 1985. The majority of these would be Puerto Rican but there would be members of other Latino nationalities as well.

11. Henry Santiestevan and Stina Santiestevan, eds., *The Hispanic Almanac* (Washington, D.C.: The Hispanic Policy Development Project, 1984), 60-63.

12. Edward R. Kantowicz, "Church and Neighborhood," *Ethnicity* 7 (1980): 349-66; Edward R. Kantowicz, *Corporation Sole: Cardinal Mundelein and Chicago Catholicism* (Notre Dame, Ind.: University of Notre Dame Press, 1983), 65-66.

13. Kantowicz, *Corporation Sole*, 72-74; Charles Shanabruch, *Chicago's Catholics: The Evolution of an American Identity* (Notre Dame, Ind.: University of Notre Dame Press, 1981), 181-85.

14. Shanabruch, *Chicago's Catholics*, 210-11; Harry C. Koenig, ed., *A History of the Parishes of the Archdiocese of Chicago* (Chicago: Catholic Bishop of Chicago, 1980), 1: 285-86, 444-47, 691-95.

15. Kantowicz, *Corporation Sole*, 76-81; Edward R. Kantowicz, "Polish Chicago," in *Ethnic Chicago*, 232-36.

16. James W. Sanders, *The Education of an Urban Minority: Catholics in Chicago, 1833-1965* (New York: Oxford University Press, 1977), 183-204.

17. To see what the Latinos missed in Chicago politics, consult John M. Allswang, *A House for All Peoples: Ethnic Politics in Chicago, 1890-1936* (Lexington: University Press of Kentucky, 1971).

18. For a portrait of Marzullo, see Milton Rakove, *Don't Make No Waves, Don't Back No Losers: An Insider's Portrait of the Daley Machine* (Bloomington: Indiana University Press, 1975), 117-25; see also Mike Royko, *Boss* (New York: E. P. Dutton, 1971), 61-62.

19. Len O'Connor, *Clout* (Chicago: Henry Regnery, 1975), 237-38, 251-52; Rakove, *Don't Make No Waves*, 34-35; Milton Rakove, "The Message of the Ward Remap," *Illinois Issues* 8 (January 1982): 4-5.

20. The quote is in Alton Miller, *Harold Washington: The Mayor, The Man* (Chicago: Bonus Books, 1989), 122. For portraits of Vrdolyak, see Melvin G. Holli and Paul M. Green, *The Making of the Mayor: Chicago, 1983* (Grand Rapids: William B. Eerdmans, 1984), 112-13, 137-39; and Roger Simon, "Mayor Vrdolyak?" *Chicago*, December 1984, 176-82, 222-35.

21. Luis W. Salces and Peter W. Colby, "Mañana Will be Better: Spanish-American Politics in Chicago," *Illinois Issues* 6 (February 1980): 20.

22. Ibid., 19; David K. Fremon, "Chicago's Spanish-American Politics in the '80s," *Illinois Issues* 16 (January 1990): 18.

23. Fremon, "Chicago's Spanish-American Politics," 16, 18.

24. *Chicago Tribune*, 31 January 1983, 1, 11; 24 March 1983, sec. 2, p. 3; 14 April 1983, sec. 2, p. 2; Melvin G. Holli and Paul M. Green, *Bashing Chicago Traditions: Harold Washington's Last Campaign* (Grand Rapids: William B. Eerdmans, 1989), 16-17.

25. Fremon, "Chicago's Spanish-American Politics," 16-18.

26. *Chicago Tribune*, 1 February 1983, 1, 5.

27. *Chicago Tribune*, 14 April 1983, sec. 2, p. 2.

28. Wilfredo Cruz, "UNO: Organizing at the Grass Roots," *Illinois Issues* 14 (April 1988): 18-22; Mary Gonzales, interview by authors, 12 October 1990; Dan Solis, interview by authors, 17 October 1990.

29. *Chicago Tribune*, 1 February 1983, 5; 31 January 1983, 11.

30. *Chicago Tribune*, 16 November 1983, sec. 2, p. 1; Fremon, "Chicago's Spanish-American Politics," 17.

31. Fremon, "Chicago's Spanish-American Politics," 17; Holli and Green, *Bashing Chicago Traditions*, 27-33; Miller, *Harold Washington*, 257-81.

32. *Chicago Tribune*, 24 March 1983, sec. 2, p. 3.

33. Chicago Board of Education, "Racial/Ethnic Survey—Students," 30 October 1981, 2; cited in *Chicago Tribune*, 30 December 1981, 1. As the decade neared its end, the 1988 survey revealed that Latino students numbered 102,019, 24.9% of the total.

34. *Chicago Tribune*, 1 August 1985, sec 4, p. 6; 21 October 1985, sec. 2, p. 3; 26 November 1985, sec. 2, p. 4; 27 November 1985, sec. 2, p. 3; Mary Gonzales interview.

35. Quoted in Padilla, *Puerto Rican Chicago*, 69.

36. Pastora San Juan Cafferty and Carmen Rivera-Martinez, *The Politics of Language: The Dilemma of Bilingual Education for Puerto Ricans* (Boulder, Colo.: Westview Press, 1981), 16-22; Diane Ravitch, *The Troubled Crusade: American Education, 1945-1980* (New York: Basic Books, 1983), 271-80; Gary Orfield, *Must We Bus? Segregated Schools and National Policy* (Washington, D.C.: Brookings Institution, 1978), 206-23; Isidro Lucas, "Bilingual Education and the Melting Pot: Getting Burned," *Illinois Issues* 7 (September 1981): 19-22.

37. Ravitch, *Troubled Crusade*, 272-73.

38. Iris C. Rotberg, "Some Legal and Research Considerations in Establishing Federal Policy in Bilingual Education," *Harvard Educational Review* 52 (May 1982): 149.

39. "Chicago Public Schools Hispanic Agenda and Action Plan, 1990" (unpublished plan submitted to Superintendent of Schools Ted Kimbrough in March 1990). Though the agenda deals with issues current in 1990, its introduction perceptively comments: "Unfortunately, the Hispanic Agenda for the Chicago Public Schools has not progressed in the last ten years. The same needs are present" (p. 1). It can thus be used as a rough indicator of Hispanic educational concerns in the 1980s as well.

40. This need for bilingual education to fit Puerto Ricans for two monolingual societies, both forming a part of the United States, forms the theme of Cafferty and Rivera-Martinez's book, *The Politics of Language*. See also Marisa Alicea, "Dual Home Bases: A Reconceptualization of Puerto Rican Migration," *Latino Studies Journal* 1 (September 1990): 78-98.

41. Ravitch, *Troubled Crusade*, 277.

42. Jose A. Cardenas, quoted in Rotberg, "Some Legal and Research Considerations," 163.

43. "Hispanic Agenda and Action Plan," 3.

5

A Generation Too Precious to Waste

Early in 1984, Aspira Inc. of Illinois released a study of the Latino student dropout problem at two Chicago public high schools. The findings of the study rocked those communities like an earthquake, leading directly to the candlelight march on Clemente. Shortly after the march, the state legislature formed a Joint Legislative Task Force on Hispanic Student Dropouts to study the dimensions of the problem. Senate President Philip Rock, who pushed the task force resolution through the legislature, called the student dropouts "a generation too precious to waste," and the task force members adopted this phrase as the title of their final report, issued a year later. In the meantime, however, the controversy over dropout statistics shook the board of education and destroyed the superintendent of schools, who tried to minimize the problem.

The Aspira Dropout Study

In an earlier study, Dr. Isidro Lucas discovered that Chicago's dropout rates were underreported as early as 1971. Though Lucas was not a social scientist but rather a professor of Romance languages lecturing at St. Xavier's College, Aspira commissioned him to undertake a study of Puerto Rican dropouts in Chicago, and he was able to secure funding from the federal government. Lucas found that "the current drop-out rate for Puerto Ricans in Chicago is 71.2 percent." An unsigned, in-house analysis of the Lucas report by the board of education staff objected to his sample size and questioned the competence of his Puerto Rican interviewers. It also dismissed his use of a cumulative dropout rate, combining the percent of grade school dropouts (12.5 percent) with high school dropouts (58.7 percent), as "not comparable" with board of education statistics. The Chicago Board of Education ignored Lucas's findings, and his report gathered dust for 13 years.[1]

Parents and student leaders in the Latino community, however, knew they had a serious dropout problem. One year, the class valedictorian at Clemente High lamented that only one in four of her freshman classmates were on hand to hear her graduation address. So in 1979, Dr. Lucas asked one of the authors of this book (Charles L. Kyle), then a Catholic priest and a doctoral candidate in sociology at Northwestern, to undertake a new study that would test Lucas's 1971 conclusions. Aspira agreed to sponsor the research—they had also sponsored Lucas's study of Puerto Rican dropouts—and subsequently secured funding from the MacArthur Foundation and the Hispanic Policy Development Project (H.P.D.P.) of Washington, D.C. Carmelo Rodriguez, executive director of Aspira, put his personal reputation on the line to convince the H.P.D.P., which was already underwriting the National Commission on Secondary Education for Hispanics, to provide money.[2]

This Aspira study documented the dropout rates at two neighborhood high schools on the near northwest side. Though the pseudonyms West Town High School and Humboldt Park High School were employed throughout the work, the two schools were actually Roberto Clemente, 1147 N. Western Avenue, and William Wells, 936 N. Ashland Avenue. The Aspira study traced the freshmen who entered the two schools in 1979 and confirmed the shocking findings of the Lucas report. Of the 1,865 students enrolled as freshmen at Clemente and Wells in 1979, only 489 graduated four years later. This works out to a dropout rate of 75 percent.[3]

In 1984, the Chicago Board of Education used a dropout calculation formula that masked this reality. The school board reported the percentage of students enrolled each year who dropped out sometime during that year. For example, in the 1980-81 school year, 13,791 students dropped out from a total enrollment of 132,982 at the 67 public high schools, for a drop-out rate of just over 10 percent. Clemente High reported the highest number of dropouts that year, 693 out of an enrollment of 3,990 (17.4 percent).[4]

These figures sound serious enough in themselves, yet a single-year percentage is badly misleading: a student cohort should be tracked over the normal four-year span of high school attendance to determine the true dropout rate for the group. For example, if one thousand students enter a freshman class, and the school experiences a 17 percent dropout rate the first year, 15 percent the next year, then 16 percent, and finally 17 percent, only 491 students (49 percent) will graduate. The true dropout rate for the entering cohort of students is 51 percent, but the board of education would only report the lower annual dropout rates.

Official school board statistics were misleading in another way. It is possible that students leaving one school might trans-fer elsewhere and complete their high school education. The board of education reports 30 different "leave codes," or cate-gories, for each student, which makes it possible, in theory, to assess what happens to a departing student. When a student leaves school, the principal must record the reason, such as, transferred to another public school, transferred to a private school, went to work, returned to Puerto Rico, etc., assigning each reason a numerical code. These statistics, however, have little value because the leave codes rely heavily on the whims of the administrators and the students in the reporting process. No one checks the accuracy of the categories reported.

The principal of one of the schools in the Aspira study explained the process of assigning a leave code: "A youth comes to the counter and asks for a leave card. The youth is given a card for his/her parent to sign. The youth gives his/her own reason for leaving. The reason is not checked. The youth then brings the card with the parent's signature and is signed out. The youth may state the reason for leaving is to attend another school or to go to a school in Puerto Rico, but these reasons are not followed up on. We know many say they are leaving to move to Puerto Rico but never do." When school administrators were asked if the parent's consent was ever verified, they said they suspected that students forge their parents' signatures. As a result, many students reported as transfers or returning migrants, are really dropouts. Therefore, even the board's figures underestimate the annual dropout rate.[5]

The Aspira study used student identification numbers to trace the students throughout the system and thus check the accuracy of the leave codes. It found that few who left the two schools in West Town and Humboldt Park ever enrolled or graduated elsewhere. The final dropout rate for the cohort entering these two schools in 1979 stood at 73.8 percent. The study ran two other checks on the data. The 1979 freshman cohorts were followed over four years in the records collected for the annual Racial/Ethnic Surveys, mandated by the desegregation court settlement, and researchers also counted the pictures of 1983 graduates in the high school yearbooks. All three methods produced similar results, a dropout rate over 73 percent.[6]

Amazingly, even this figure is probably too low. Isidro Lucas had discovered that many students drop out in seventh or eighth grade and never enter high school at all. A later study, in 1989, confirmed that about 9 percent of eighth graders never go on to high school. "Eighth graders who never enter the ninth grade are designated by the school system as 'lost'....These young people are truly adrift somewhere between the records of the grammar schools and the high schools."[7]

Besides gathering these appalling statistics, the Aspira researchers conducted interviews with a random sample of 117 student dropouts and 84 student "stay-ins" at the two target schools (an attempt to interview one hundred students in each category failed because not enough students could be found who stayed in school). Since students were asked to state the reasons for leaving school in their own words, the pervasive fear of gangs emerged for the first time as a major cause of dropping out. Researchers did not use national survey questions or multiple choice forms, but rather an open-ended question about the conditions at school that lead to dropping out. The students mentioned gang activity spontaneously, without any prompting from the researchers or suggestions from the questionnaire design.

Respondents of both sexes indicated that gang pressure and the fear of violence stood out as the worst negative memory of high school—a memory that both dropouts and stay-ins shared. This finding was contrary to numerous statements made by administrators at the schools who said that "although street gangs claimed the territories surrounding the schools, they regard the inside of school buildings as 'neutral turf.'" Not so, according to the Aspira study. Fifty-six percent of the male youths interviewed stated they had been asked, on school property, to join a gang. More than half the respondents of both sexes said they feared physical harm at school.[8]

Table 1 (see p. 86) details the reasons given by the students interviewed who dropped out of school. Male students clearly considered fear of gangs the number one reason for dropping out, whereas pregnancy ranked number one for females.[9] School principals, however, consistently cited academic failings and student truancy as the main reasons for dropping out, ranking gang violence and student pregnancy well down the list.[10]

The Aspira research revealed a massive dropout problem at these two largely Latino high schools. A youth who entered their doors was much more likely to drop out than to graduate. Furthermore, Aspira reported figures gathered by the Illinois State Board of Education showing an "attrition rate" (the state board's jargon for a four-year dropout rate) in excess of 45 percent for the graduating classes of 1974 through 1983 at all Chicago public high schools—black, white, and Latino. Two wider studies by independent agencies, published one year after the Aspira report, confirmed this figure.[11] The misleading statistics published by the board of education prevented the public—and public policymakers—from recognizing the extent of the problem. Bogus statistics made a phenomenon that had become the norm appear to be merely an exceptional case.[12]

Table 1 Student Reasons for Dropping Out			
Reason Given for Dropping Out	Male	Female	Total
Gangs	30%	17%	24%
Told to leave	17%	16%	16%
Had a baby	0%	28%	14%
Cut too many classes	10%	9%	9%
Lost interest	7%	7%	7%
Behind in class	8%	5%	7%
Needed to go to work	7%	2%	4%
Too old	5%	3%	4%
Other	4%	9%	6%
No answer	13%	3%	8%
Total	100%	100%	100%
Number of responses	60	57	117

Dropping out of school led to far more serious consequences in 1984 than it did 15 or 20 years earlier. The state had not yet recovered from the depths of the "Reagan recession" in the early 1980s, and jobs remained scarce. Furthermore, the state's economy was buffeted by the forces of an emerging new international economy, as Third World countries with low labor costs captured many of the manufacturing jobs that had long been the Midwest's mainstay. Cook County lost 224,000 manufacturing jobs between 1972 and 1985. New service industries in the suburbs replaced lost manufacturing jobs in the city so that Cook County experienced a net job gain of 6 percent during the decade of the 1980s, but the city itself suffered a net loss of 4 percent.[13] Most entry-level service jobs, the only kind available to dropouts, paid only the minimum wage. Better-paying jobs in the service industries required higher skills and more education.

Due to these changes in the economy of Illinois the dropout problem took on new importance. Previously, when a youth dropped out of school, he or she could go to work in a factory or at the steel mills, usually with an older family member. Since Chicago was a union stronghold, factory wages were quite high, even for the unskilled and uneducated. Due to the widespread changes in the economy, however, dropping out and being unemployed became increasingly synonymous, and a large percentage of Chicago's younger generation was wasting its potential. As Roberto Rivera, head of the Network for Youth Services's (NYS) education task force remarked, "What else do young people without an education do, but hang out on street corners, join gangs, and start shooting each other? We bury kids, simply because we have not equipped them for a changing economy."[14]

Task Force Politics

Toward the end of 1983, the Aspira researchers shared their preliminary results with Roberto Rivera. Rivera, Father Kyle, and the staff members of Aspira huddled together for a weekend retreat at Felix Padilla's Latino Studies Center of Northern Illinois University; they vowed that the new findings would not suffer the same fate as the Lucas report. Heeding the example of Harold Washington's successful campaign, they decided to transform a report into a movement, social statistics into social action. NYS, a coalition of 30 social work agencies on the near northwest side, began planning the march on Clemente to publicize the Aspira study. This proved to be a crucial decision. Prior to the march on March 26, 1984, the new dropout statistics received only one press notice, an article in a neighborhood newspaper written by Aspira staff member Gabriel Lopez.[15] Without the march, the Aspira report would have been buried in oblivion.

While planning the march, Kyle and Rivera decided to cultivate their contacts in the state legislature. With Chicago politics paralyzed by Council Wars, Springfield looked like a more promising arena to stir up political concern for dropouts.

In early January 1984, Roberto Rivera and Father Kyle met with Senate President Phil Rock at Chicago's State of Illinois Building. A big, bluff Irishman with a jutting jaw, Rock took one look at the dropout figures from the two Latino high schools and bristled. The discrepancy between the official numbers and the actual 70 percent dropout rate jumped off the page. "I used to be a prizefighter, you know," Rock reminded them. "I like a good fight. I'll help you in any way I can."[16]

Because Rock was seeking the Democratic nomination for U.S. senator, Kyle and Rivera initially wrote off his interest to political expediency. Rock asked Father Kyle to accompany him on a campaign swing through LaSalle, Peru, and other towns in the Illinois River valley where local press had been labelling him a corrupt Chicago politician, indeed little better than a gangster. He hoped the appearance of a Catholic priest on the platform with him might dispel these misconceptions. The day of the campaign trip turned out to be the coldest day in 30 years, with the temperature dipping to 25 degrees below zero. Rock remarked at one point that if his car broke down they might literally freeze to death. As they drove home to Chicago that evening, grateful for surviving the cold and the downstate crowds, Rock turned to Father Kyle and said, "Let me know if there is anything I can do."

Kyle had been thinking that a legislative task force on Hispanic dropouts would make a logical follow-up to the Aspira study, giving the findings wider distribution and greater credibility. He, therefore, asked Rock if he would sponsor a resolution creating the task force. Rock shot back, with no hesitation, "Absolutely, I'll sponsor it." Unlike some politicians, when Phil Rock said "absolutely" he meant *absolutely*. Though Rock lost the Democratic nomination for U.S. senate to Paul Simon in the March 1984 primary, he pressed on with the joint resolution and stayed the course until the legislature established the task force.

Rock had assigned Steve Henriksen from his staff to draft Senate Joint Resolution 82, creating a 20-member task force, including several public members. He introduced the joint resolution on February 7, 1984, when the legislature convened, and had it referred to the Senate Executive Committee, which he controlled.[17] Rock then addressed the Parents' Leadership Conference at the Trina Davila Center in Humboldt Park on February 17 to explain the resolution.

This conference had been called to publicize the Aspira report and build up support for the upcoming march. Father Kyle and Carmelo Rodriguez told Spanish-language television reporters they expected 150 people at the conference, thinking to themselves that they really meant about 75. Instead, 500 turned out. The parents' advisory councils at schools with bilingual programs had done an effective job of spreading the word. Rock was impressed by the turnout. He said that most legislators blamed the dropout problem on parental apathy and neglect, but this outpouring of interest gave the lie to that argument. The audience was less impressed with Rock. In fact, they came close to booing him, for his remarks sounded like the same old political run-around. But Rock followed through.

Two days after the candlelight march at Roberto Clemente High School, Network for Youth Services capitalized on the momentum by planning a rally in Springfield to lobby for the joint resolution. Miguel del Valle recalls the new sense of purpose everyone felt after the march:

> We knew there was a correlation between the dropout problem and youth violence in the community; we knew that there was a correlation between the dropout problem and underemployment and unemployment; dropout problem and drug use; dropout problem and lack of family stability; dropout problem and the low self-esteem of entire families; dropout problem and the lack of respect from the powers that be, our powerlessness within the political process. We brought all that into focus.[18]

On April 25, over four hundred Latino parents and students filled the senate galleries. Senator Rock asked Father Kyle to deliver the invocation beginning the day's legislative session, then Rock pleaded eloquently for the resolution's passage. Pointing to the youthful faces in the galleries, he declared: "This is a generation too precious to waste. We dare not lose another generation as precious as these young people." Senators fell all over themselves to sign on as joint sponsors. SJR 82 passed the senate by a unanimous vote of 56 to 0. Miguel del Valle, who had only been in Springfield once before, was struck by the total absence of Latino faces in the well of the senate. As he left the capitol that day with his children, he turned to his brother and said, "I'm gonna sit in one of those chairs someday."[19]

The resolution stalled, however, in the house of representatives. House Speaker Michael Madigan was a cautious politician who earned his reputation as the second most powerful man in Illinois politics by tightly controlling the legislative agenda.[20] He routinely deferred action on most matters until the very end of the legislative session on June 30, using various bills and resolutions as bargaining chips right up until the last minute. Most probably, the Chicago Board of Education also lobbied him to kill the investigative task force. Schools Superintendent Ruth Love had announced her own dropout study commission shortly after the march on Clemente, and she must have viewed the legislature's involvement as unwelcome interference.[21] Everyone wanted to control the process of investigating and reporting dropout statistics.

NYS stepped up the lobbying campaign from the Latino community, however, and during the 1984 Memorial Day weekend, Speaker Madigan phoned Fr. Kyle at St. Francis Xavier rectory. "What's the problem, Father?" he asked. "I'm getting letters blaming me for the dropout problem." Kyle shot back, "You're the problem, Mr. Speaker, as long as you keep the investigation bottled up." Madigan asked Kyle to come down to Springfield and discuss the resolution, and in mid-June the Speaker sent him an amended version that he said he could support.

Madigan's amendment reduced the investigative task force to just eight legislators: two senators appointed by the senate president, two senators chosen by the senate minority leader, two representatives appointed by the Speaker, and two others selected by the house minority leader. The numerous public members authorized by Rock's original resolution were consigned to a Citizens' Advisory Board by the Madigan amendment.[22] The Velvet Hammer, as Madigan is called, intended to keep control of the task force investigation in the hands of the four legislative leaders. Phil Rock held out for the original resolution, however, and the legislature finally approved it on July 1.

Rock rendered another service during the legislature's final minutes on July 1. In the conference committee discussing the appropriation bill for the Illinois State Board of Education, he inserted a $50,000 appropriation to staff the Joint Task Force on Hispanic Dropouts.[23] This action was vital. Without money to pay staff, the task force could do little more than issue empty press releases. One final lobbying effort by Pete Wilson, who knew Governor Thompson's father, ensured that the governor signed the appropriation authorization on July 19. Wilson was a Springfield lobbyist, but he had formerly served as director of a Catholic Youth Organization program in Humboldt Park, and he had been deeply moved by the commitment of the students and parents who had packed the senate galleries in April. The appropriation changed SJR 82 from a motherhood resolution to an effective legislative instrument, enabling the task force to probe deeply into the dropout problem.

The Ruth Love Affair

Before the task force members were even appointed, however, the dropout controversy took an unexpected and bizarre turn with the firing of Schools Superintendent Ruth Love. Love appeared side by side with Board of Education President George Muñoz at the press conference announcing the state legislative task force held at Clemente High School on July 12. Less than two weeks later, however, the board of education voted, at Muñoz's urging, not to renew Love's contract.

Ruth B. Love had come to Chicago in March 1981 in the aftermath of the financial crisis. Though she was only the third choice of the board at that time (two other candidates were offered the job, but refused), she had impressive credentials and had climbed the educational ladder steadily in her native California. Born in Oklahoma, she grew up in Bakersfield, California, earned a bachelor's degree from San Jose State, a master's from San Francisco State, and a doctorate in human behavior from U.S. International University in San Diego. When she was named superintendent of the Oakland schools in 1975, she put her talent for public relations to good use. In particular, she attracted national attention with her Adopt-a-School program, which drew local business executives into partnership with inner-city schools.[24]

As Chicago's first black schools superintendent, Love faced a difficult situation, especially since the local black community resented her appointment over their own Manford Byrd. Due to the financial crisis, little money was available for innovative programs, and the superintendent did not have full authority over the budget. The bailout plan mandated that the chief financial officer of the schools report directly to the board of education, not to the superintendent, and each year's budget required approval by the finance authority before implementation. Finally, the $120,000 annual salary she negotiated before accepting the job made Ruth Love the highest paid superintendent in the country and Illinois's highest paid public official, virtually ensuring that her every action would prove controversial.[25]

Nevertheless, she announced several high-profile initiatives, including a High School Renaissance program and a new version of the Adopt-a-School plan. Taking into consideration the constant financial stringency, most observers thought Ruth Love was doing a creditable job in Chicago and that the renewal of her four-year contract would be a routine matter.[26]

Yet when the board of education met in a special executive session on July 6, 1984, to consider the renewal of Love's contract, the board members couldn't agree and thus postponed a decision. Someone privy to the board's deliberations leaked to the press that two straw votes had been taken. A 6-to-5 vote favored Love's retention, but a second 6-to-5 vote mandated a delay. Reportedly, Muñoz cast the deciding sixth vote in both cases; the board was split evenly on the Love contract and George Muñoz found himself in the swing position.[27]

The 11-member school board that deliberated the fate of Ruth Love was composed almost entirely of holdovers from Jane Byrne's administration. Council Wars had held up several Harold Washington appointments to the board; George Muñoz and William Farrow were his only appointees to win confirmation by the city council. Muñoz took office in February 1984, and was elected board president in May as a compromise candidate. The four whites on the board would not back a black candidate and the four blacks would not support a white, so both factions settled on the Mexican-American, Muñoz.[28]

Though Muñoz was not yet well known in Chicago, he was something of a boy wonder. Born in Brownsville, Texas in 1951, he was the fifth of 12 children. His father was a minimum wage laborer and his mother a housewife. George earned scholarships and worked his way through school, ultimately earning four degrees, including one from Harvard Law School. He came to Chicago in 1980 and joined the prestigious law firm of Mayer, Brown & Platt. At age 33 he found himself the youngest school board president in Chicago history and the center of a political firestorm.[29]

The school board debated Love's contract at their regularly scheduled meeting on July 18, but again deferred a decision. Then at a tumultuous, special session on the night of Monday, July 23, the board voted 6 to 5 not to rehire the superintendent, but to negotiate with Manford Byrd as her replacement. A sit-in by 14 black ministers demanding Love's retention delayed the meeting for one hour and 45 minutes. Then the board retired into executive session for three hours, emerging about 11:30 at night for a rapid public confirmation of the vote. The four black members plus one white member voted for Love's retention; three whites and three Latinos provided the majority against Love.[30]

Ruth Love reacted angrily to her dismissal, charging that Muñoz and Byrd had struck a political deal with Mayor Washington.[31] Actually, the role of black leaders, and of the mayor, was muddled, since both Love and her announced replacement, Byrd, were black. Black activists had picketed on Love's behalf when the board first began deliberating over her contract, and the four black members of the board gave her unwavering support. Yet the mayor himself remained unusually quiet throughout the controversy, not commenting at all until almost 24 hours after Love was fired. He later admitted that he had discussed the matter with George Muñoz before the vote but claimed that he had not dictated the decision. Muñoz has confirmed this. He says that the mayor warned him he was making a "very hot decision" and encouraged him to try to build greater support on the board so that he would not be the lone swing vote. The *Chicago Tribune* summed up the mayor's role: "If the Mayor didn't want...[her] fired, he appeared to have done little, if anything, to prevent it....He remained on the sidelines, expressing a public preference for Love but investing little political capital in her case."[32]

The board's plan to hire Byrd immediately, however, and perhaps to buy out the remainder of Ruth Love's contract, ran into court challenges by a number of board employees who hoped to succeed Love. On July 27, Judge Joseph Wosik issued a temporary injunction preventing the board from hiring Byrd and the matter remained in limbo for nearly two months.[33]

In the meantime, George Muñoz faced bitter condemnation by the media for causing the whole imbroglio. The *Tribune*

branded the affair "an ugly clash of wills and egos" and specu-
lated that Muñoz harbored soaring political ambitions, perhaps
even for the mayoralty. Twice in early August, the *Tribune*
editorialists called for Muñoz's resignation, concluding that he
was "part of the problem instead of part of the solution." The
Sun-Times concurred in equally strong terms on August 5:

> Three months ago, George Muñoz, the newly named president
> of the Board of Education, showed promise of guiding the
> school system with steadiness and firm resolve....Today, these
> hopes have come crashing down in the rubble that remains of
> the alley fight to dump School Superintendent Ruth B. Love
> and to replace her with Deputy Supt. Manford Byrd, Jr.[34]

Muñoz, however, refused to resign, and insisted that the
board would not reconsider its decision to dismiss Ruth Love.
He gave several reasons for Love's firing. She had repeatedly
failed to answer board inquiries about her policies, she had
been evasive and equivocal about the dropout problem, and she
released misleadingly positive standardized test scores showing
more progress in the schools than really existed.[35]

In September, the logjam in the courts broke and the Ruth
Love affair moved toward a conclusion. Judge Wosik finally
lifted the injunction on September 27, and the board of education voted unanimously the next day to offer a four-year term
as superintendent to Manford Byrd, effective March 25.[36]

Ruth Love dragged out the soap opera nearly a year longer
by filing a discrimination complaint with the Equal Employment Opportunity Commission and a companion lawsuit in
federal court. An out-of-court settlement awarded her no
money, but did require the school board to refrain from making
negative comments about her to future employers.[37]

In the final analysis, the board did not fire Love, George
Muñoz did. The board was evenly divided between pro- and
anti-Love factions. Muñoz first hesitated and delayed. Acutely
aware that he was a youthful newcomer in Chicago politics, he
wanted to give Superintendent Love every opportunity to build

support for her contract renewal. He encouraged her to consult with her opponents on the board of education and try to work something out. But Love refused and told him, "No more delays." So Muñoz informed the mayor of his decision and cast his vote against her.[38]

Was it just ambition and egoism on his part, as the *Tribune* alleged? Certainly, both Muñoz and Love possessed powerful intellects and enormous pride in their own accomplishments. A conflict between two such individuals is not hard to understand. Yet, Muñoz gained nothing from his role in the affair. In fact, if he were thinking only of his personal career he probably would have backed Ruth Love for she was popular with the media and with the business community. Muñoz states that he opposed Ruth Love's contract renewal because she had fabricated a rosy image of the public school system that was unsupported by the facts. She reported both the dropout rate and the results of standardized test scores in a misleading fashion. As a tax lawyer, George Muñoz felt that Ruth Love should be subject to "truth and disclosure."[39]

The circumstantial evidence supports the board president's account. Muñoz was almost as much of an outsider as Ruth Love, having arrived in the city only in 1980. As a bachelor, he had no children and was likely unfamiliar with the depth of problems in the schools when he accepted appointment to the board of education in February 1984. He took part in the Latino community's march to Clemente High School on March 26 and was visibly moved by the grief and sorrow of the parents whose children had dropped out or been murdered. When he tried to obtain accurate dropout statistics from Superintendent Love, she proved evasive, parroting the official 9 percent dropout figure. Her lack of candor on the major issue facing the Latino community was likely the decisive factor in Muñoz' decision to force her removal.

Latino activists took a leading role in the protests demanding Love's removal, and the Latino members of the board stood united against Love on every vote. The *Tribune* noted at one point that "the dismissal of Ruth Love...marks a turning point in the political visibility of the city's Hispanics." Yet, the established shapers of opinion found it hard to take the Latino role seriously. The *Tribune* concluded on another occasion, "There are complaints that Dr. Love neglected Hispanic schools, but this could not have been the essence of what brought her down."[40]

Much later, Walter Jacobson, WBBM-TV's award-winning commentator, reported that Love's lawyers had discovered the truth and were urging her to withdraw the discrimination lawsuit. "If the case now gets to court," Jacobson stated on the air, "there will be evidence presented that the reason Love was fired, or a major reason anyway, was that she was filling out and filing phony reports about the achievements of the students in the public schools. Evidence, for example, that she reported to the board of education that she lowered the dropout rate in the public schools to 9 percent, when the dropout rate was still more than 40 percent."[41] Jacobson was the only commentator who took Muñoz' concern over the dropout rate seriously.

In the short run, the Latino community gained little with Love's firing. Miguel del Valle commented, "In this case we've lost and won. We won because we brought our problems to the surface. We've lost because of what appears to be the appointment of Manford Byrd. The irony is Hispanics were strongly opposed to him four years ago."[42]

The problems of the public schools seemed as insoluble as ever when Ruth Love bowed out and Manford Byrd took office. Controversy over the dropout rate, however, and George Muñoz' principled stand against Ruth Love had established the Latino community as a significant player in school politics.

Notes

1. Isidro Lucas, "Puerto Rican Dropouts in Chicago: Numbers and Motivation" (Chicago: Council on Urban Education, 1971), 6 (hereafter cited as the Lucas report); Isidro Lucas, interview by authors, 26 September 1990.

2. Charles L. Kyle, "'Los Preciosos': The Magnitude of and the Reasons for the Hispanic Drop Out Problem: A Case Study of Two Chicago Public Schools" (Chicago: Aspira Inc. of Illinois, 1984); also submitted as a doctoral dissertation in sociology, Northwestern University, 1984 (hereafter cited as the Aspira dropout study or the Aspira report).

3. Aspira dropout study, 29.

4. *Chicago Tribune*, 25 November 1981, 9.

5. Aspira dropout study, 34.

6. Ibid., 35-42.

7. Charles L. Kyle, Joyce A. Sween, "Lost!: An Initial Study of the Magnitude of and Reasons for Early School Leavers from the Chicago Public Schools" (Chicago: Loyola University, Faculty Urban Seminar, 1989), 1.

8. Aspira dropout study, 54-55.

9. Ibid., 50.

10. Charles L. Kyle, John Lane, Joyce A. Sween, Armando Triano, Olga Reyes, "We Have a Choice: Students at Risk of Leaving Chicago Public Schools" (Chicago: DePaul University, Center for Research on Hispanics, 1986), 64-67.

11. Donald R. Moore, "The Bottom Line: Chicago's Failing Schools and How to Save Them" (Chicago: Designs for Change, 1985), reported that 53% of the students who entered Chicago public high schools in 1980 dropped out before graduation; G. Alfred Hess, Jr., Diana Lauber, "Dropouts from the Chicago Public Schools" (Chicago Panel on Public School Policy and Finance, 1985), tracked the entering class of 1978 and found that 43% dropped out and 9% transferred to other school systems. The Designs for Change and the CHIPs reports are much wider in statistical scope than the Aspira report, which only studied two high schools intensively, but the Aspira report includes important qualitative material lacking in the other two studies. The interviews with students who dropped out revealed that drugs and gangs were seriously eroding student motivation to stay in school.

12. Politics can affect how statistics are reported and this, in turn, can make a crucial difference in whether or not a problem is perceived. For example, when Everett C. Hughes studied the official statistics of Germany from 1932 to 1942, he discovered that in the statistics of the pre-Nazi years, a person was classified by religion but not by race while in the Nazi statistics a person was classified by race but not religion. The reason for this difference in recording was to "never show in a summary and graphic way the success of the program to rid the country and the folk of foreign (Jewish) blood." See Hughes, *The Sociological Eye* (Chicago: Aldine Atherton, 1971), 521.

13. Charles L. Kyle, Erica Sufritz, "Indivisible: Good Schools = Healthy Economy, Poor Academic Achievement = Increased Unemployment" (Chicago: Loyola University, School of Education, 1989), 23; *Chicago Tribune*, 19 August 1990, 1, 15.

14. Roberto Rivera, interview by authors, 20 September 1990.

15. *Logan Square Free Press*, 12 January 1984, 7.

16. This story is told largely from Kyle and Rivera's reconstruction of events. Tim Bannon reported part of the story in *Chicago Reader*, 17 July 1984, 3. Philip Rock, interview by authors, 27 August 1991. For profiles of Rock, see Charles N. Wheeler III, "The Democratic Primary for U.S. Senator," *Illinois Issues* 10 (March 1984): 10; Diane Ross, "Phil Rock: Holding Together a Raucous Caucus," *Illinois Issues* 11 (April 1985): 8-14.

17. The legislative history of Senate Joint Resolution 82 can be found in *Final Legislative Synopsis and Digest*, 83rd General Assembly, 1984 sess., 2: 1707-8; the text of the resolution is in *Journal of the Senate*, 83rd General Assembly, 1984 sess., 1: 28-29.

18. Miguel del Valle, interview by authors, 29 January 1991.

19. *Journal of the Senate*, 83rd General Assembly, 1984 sess., 1: 272; *Logan Square Free Press*, 3 May 1984, 4; *The Reporter*, 16 May 1984, 1; Rivera and del Valle interviews.

20. For a profile of and interview with Michael Madigan, see Diane Ross, "The Ascension of Michael Madigan," *Illinois Issues* 9 (May 1983): 6-11.

21. *Chicago Tribune*, 16 April 1984, sec. 3, p. 1; *Education Week*, 2 May 1984, 4. Love's 32-member task force produced a "Report on Dropout Reduction" in December 1984, but little action followed.

22. Madigan's amended text was labelled House Resolution 1178. See *Journal of the House*, 83rd General Assembly, 1984 sess., 3: 4900-4901. It was formally introduced on 1 July 1984 but Madigan allowed it to die and the original Senate Joint Resolution to be adopted.

23. Section 1-112.5 of HB 2546. See *Journal of the House*, 83rd General Assembly, 1984 sess., 3: 4962.

24. Robert J. McClory, "A Look at Love's Labors," *Illinois Issues* 9 (April 1983): 27-31; Ruth B. Love, telephone interview by author, 9 October 1990.

25. *Chicago Tribune*, 13 January 1981, 1; 14 January 1981, 1.

26. *Chicago Tribune*, 6 July 1984, 22; 29 July 1984, sec. 5, p. 1; McClory, "Love's Labors," 31.

27. *Chicago Tribune*, 7 July 1984, 1; 10 July 1984, sec. 2, p. 4. The Chicago Board of Education "Proceedings" provide no information on this special meeting. They simply report that the meeting convened at 11:05 A.M. with all 11 members present, and then went into private, executive session.

28. *Chicago Tribune*, 4 July 1984, sec. 2, p. 1; George Muñoz, interview by authors, 20 September 1990.

29. *Chicago Tribune*, 3 December 1984, 21, contains a good biographical sketch of Muñoz; *Chicago Sun-Times*, 29 July 1984, 6, profiles all three principals in the the drama: Muñoz, Ruth Love, and Manford Byrd.

30. *Chicago Tribune*, 24 July 1984, 1; *Chicago Sun-Times*, 24 July 1984, 1; New York Times, 24 July 1984, 1. "Official Report of the Proceedings of the Board of Education of the City of Chicago," 23 July 1984, 2415-19. The "Proceedings" do not report the deliberations of the board but do record the votes.

31. *Chicago Tribune*, 24 July 1984, 1; *Chicago Sun-Times*, 24 July 1984, 1. Ruth Love continues to make this claim. Though she would not discuss the details of the contract renewal controversy, she did state unequivocally, "It was pure politics." Love interview.

32. *Chicago Sun-Times*, 3 August 1984, 3; Muñoz interview; *Chicago Tribune*, 25 July 1984, 1.

33. *Chicago Tribune*, 28 July 1984, 1; *Chicago Sun-Times*, 27 July 1984, 1.

34. *Chicago Tribune*, 17 July 1984, 10; 25 July 1984, 12; 3 August 1984, 22; 9 August 1984, 26; *Chicago Sun-Times*, 5 August 1984, "Views," p. 3.

35. *Chicago Tribune*, 4 August 1984, 1.

36. *Chicago Tribune*, 13 September 1984, sec. 2, p. 1; 19 September 1984, sec. 2, p. 3; 28 September 1984, sec. 2, p. 1; 29 September 1984, 1; *New York Times*, 29 September 1984, 6.

37. *Chicago Tribune*, 18 October 1984, sec. 2, p. 1; 23 October 1984, 14; 25 October 1984, sec. 2, p. 1; 23 March 1985, 5; 26 September 1985, sec. 2, p. 1; 27 September 1985, sec. 2, p. 3; 1 October 1985, sec. 2, p. 1; 16 October 1985, sec. 2, p. 3.

38. Muñoz interview; Love interview. Ruth Love would not respond directly to Muñoz' account of events, but she suggested that she was asked to resign in 1984 in order to avoid a vote. She says she refused to resign because she did not want to tarnish her reputation.

39. Muñoz interview.

40. *Chicago Tribune*, 29 July 1984, sec. 3, p. 1; 25 July 1984, 12.

41. Walter Jacobson, "Perspective," WBBM Channel 2 News, 16 July 1985.

42. *Chicago Tribune*, 29 July 1984, sec. 3, p. 1.

6

The Folks and the People

Chicago's public schools suffered several sharp blows during the lame-duck months of Ruth Love's administration at the end of 1984. On September 26, 1984, a federal appeals court overruled Judge Shadur's orders compelling the Reagan administration to pay $103.8 million to carry out the desegregation consent decree. Though the decree remained in effect, the school board had to find the money to enforce it on its own. Then, the teachers walked out of class for the seventh time in 15 years on December 3, 1984, and stayed out for 10 days until they gained a 4.5 percent raise, a 2.5 percent one-time bonus, and a generous benefit package. These two events further constrained the tight budget facing Manford Byrd when he assumed office.[1]

The sensational murder of a high school basketball star two days before Thanksgiving, however, overshadowed these other misfortunes, riveting public attention on the open warfare between Chicago street gangs.

Seventeen-year-old Ben Wilson played basketball for state champion Simeon Vocational High School on the city's far south side. The 6' 8" senior, widely considered the number one high school player in the nation, hoped that his court prowess would win him a scholarship to college and possibly a ticket to the NBA. At lunchtime on Tuesday, November 20, 1984, Wilson was walking along the 8100 block of South Vincennes Avenue with his girlfriend and another girl when three gang members blocked the sidewalk and bumped him as he tried to pass by. In the shouting and pushing match that followed, one of the gang members pulled out a 22-caliber revolver and shot

Wilson twice, severing his aorta and puncturing his liver. Wilson died the next morning at St. Bernard's Hospital after losing 10 liters of blood.[2]

The murder of Ben Wilson shocked the city. Benji, as his family and friends called him, was not only a star athlete but a diligent student. He didn't live in a public housing project or a burned out slum, but a neighborhood that the *Tribune* referred to as "a well-kept community of bungalow homes." The Gresham police district where Simeon High School was located had not experienced a single gang killing the previous year and had one of the lower rates for other gang crimes.

Wilson's senseless slaying led to a flurry of antigang activities by police and politicians that inevitably became entangled in the ongoing Council Wars. The mounting concern over gang warfare also reverberated through the city's embattled school system, amplifying the clamor for school reform.

Gang Warfare in the Eighties

After a sharp decline in the mid-1970s, when many leaders of Chicago's street gangs were locked behind bars, gang warfare had heated up again during the early 1980s. In a major series analyzing Chicago's gang problem, the *Chicago Tribune* reported that 75 gang-related murders in 1983 accounted for about 11 percent of all homicides in the city that year. By comparison, five years earlier, in 1978, there were just 24 gang murders, about 3 percent of the city's homicides. At the end of 1984, after Ben Wilson's murder, the *Tribune* published pictures of 97 young people between the ages of 11 and 20 who fell victim to street violence during the year. Youth killings rose 27 percent in 1984, even though the total homicides for the city remained about the same.[3]

The leaders of Chicago's major gangs, such as Jeff Fort of the infamous Blackstone Rangers, had used their prison time to reorganize and strengthen their organizations. Gang members sent away to penitentiaries at Pontiac, Menard, or Joliet, feared for their lives in prison. In order to protect themselves, they reached out to leaders of other gangs and formed two large coalitions, the People and the Folks. Prison authorities quickly saw the stabilizing effect this could have on the inmate population and began separating incoming prisoners into two groups, assigning members of each gang nation or coalition to a different section of the prison. This kept the peace behind bars but helped solidify the organization of the two rival federations.[4]

Out on the streets there were other compelling reasons for forming alliances. The gangs of the 1970s and 1980s thrived on the sale of illegal drugs, so the coalitions between various components of the Folks and the People forged trade agreements, or cartels, that divided up markets for narcotics. Jeff Fort's Blackstone Rangers (who renamed themselves first the Black P Stone Nation, then the El Rukns) allied with groups such as the Vice Lords, the Latin Kings, the Gaylords, the Insane Unknowns, and the Insane Duces to form the People. The Black Gangster Disciples, Latin Jivers, Imperial Gangsters, Simon City Royals, Orchestra Albany, Latin Disciples, and Spanish Cobras formed the Folks. These alliances united black, white, and Latino gangs, and some of the individual gangs were mixed in race.

The one hundred or so individual gangs in Chicago during the 1980s ranged in size from 10 to 1,000 members. Each had its own symbols, colors, hand signals, and dress code. Most of the symbols identified the coalition that the gang belonged to. A crown or a five-pointed star indicated membership in the People, whereas a three-pronged pitchfork and a six-pointed star signified the Folks. A gang member affiliated with the Folks would often wear an earring in the right ear and tilt his hat to the right. The People wore an earring in the left ear and tilted their hats to the left.

The displaying of gang colors became an art form in its own right, with gang members often wearing professional sports regalia bearing the same colors as their gang. The Latin Kings, for instance, wore Pittsburgh Pirates caps with their black and gold colors; and the Black P Stone Nation favored black and red paraphernalia of the Chicago Bulls. Younger teens often displayed gang colors by wearing two different-colored shoe laces in their gym shoes.

Perhaps the most terrifying aspect of gang violence in the eighties was the large number of innocent bystanders killed when they inadvertently wandered onto gang turf with the wrong colors on their backs or with their hats tilted the wrong way. Eighteen-year-old Roosevelt Booker was shot in the head by a 15-year-old member of the Vice Lords in August 1982 on a street corner near Division and Western because he had his hands folded across his chest. His assailant thought he was flashing the signal of the Black Gangster Disciples. Booker, however—like basketball star Ben Wilson—had no gang affiliation.[5]

Gang warfare plagued the Latino community, particularly on the near northwest side. The two police districts encompassing West Town, Humboldt Park, and Logan Square accounted for more than 25 percent of the gang-related homicides in 1983, more than in the Cabrini-Green and Robert Taylor Homes housing projects combined.[6]

These bare statistics of gang warfare in Latino neighborhoods require some historical perspective for an accurate interpretation. The near northwest side has always been an immigrant receiving-area with high levels of social disorganization and youth crime. In the 1920s, Frederic Thrasher, a sociologist at the University of Chicago, wrote, in a classic study of street gangs, that "along Milwaukee Avenue, the great Polish business street...there is a gang in almost every block. The majority of gangs in Chicago are of Polish stock." The sociologist then summed up the causes of immigrant crime, "The gang...is one manifestation of the disorganization incident to cultural conflict among diverse nations and races gathered together in one place and themselves in contact with a civilization foreign and largely inimical to them."[7] Gang crime was endemic among Poles in the 1920s and Latinos in the 1980s not because of their ethnic backgrounds but because of recent immigration, poverty, and family disorganization.

Despite the similar causes leading to gang activity, however, gangs of the eighties differed from those of the past in some important respects. They exceeded earlier gangs in size and in the sophistication of their organizations, and they regularly crossed racial and ethnic lines. Most important, gangs of the past decade possessed a lethal arsenal of weaponry, for gang members found knives and guns as easy to buy as a pair of shoes. They did not resemble the Sharks and the Jets in the movie *West Side Story*, a handful of toughs engaging in fisticuffs. The Folks and the People waged all-out, heavily armed warfare for territory and drug profits.

Gangs and Politics

After the Ben Wilson killing, Mayor Washington and the city council produced competing antigang programs. The mayor addressed the thousands of people who jammed into Operation PUSH's headquarters for Wilson's funeral on November 24. "We have heard you, Ben," he said. "Nothing can stop us from making our streets safe." Yet Washington fell sick with the flu shortly after the funeral, so the white city council majority struck the next rhetorical blow. On November 29, the majority bloc, led by Ed Burke and Ed Vrdolyak, announced a plan to increase police presence in gang-infested neighborhoods by reassigning officers from other duties, and they proclaimed their steadfast opposition to a budget-cutting move, previously announced by the mayor, that would reduce the police force from 12,000 officers to 11,500. The aldermen also called for an auxiliary force of three thousand citizens to keep watch in their neighborhoods and assist the police. The mayor finally announced, on December 3, his antigang initiative, a two-pronged assault involving stepped-up police activity and the involvement of community groups. Washington also made it clear that he would withdraw his planned reductions in total police manpower.[8]

Both initiatives seemed little different from earlier "gang crackdowns"; an expert on gangs from the University of Chicago, Irving Spergel, criticized the mayor's program "for not paying enough attention to the grassroots component and for failing to recognize the important role that former gang members have played in antigang programs in other cities." Spergel had conducted a nine-month pilot program in the Humboldt Park area that paired six former gang members with University of Chicago students in a crisis intervention network. The Crisis Intervention Services Project (CRISP), funded by the Illinois Department of Children and Family Services, was modeled on a highly publicized program that former gang leader Bennie Swans had started in Philadelphia. Spergel claimed that CRISP's endeavors in Humboldt Park greatly reduced gang violence, but the program had lapsed at the end of July, 1984 when its state grant ran out. Now at the end of the year, the newspapers picked up Spergel's call for a more extensive intervention network to fight gangs. The professor seemed to have an answer, and the mayor looked indecisive.[9]

The Bennie Swans-Philadelphia model, however, contained a political trap for Mayor Washington. The reliance on former gang members to carry out crisis intervention called up echoes of a notorious incident in Chicago's earlier gang history. Jeff Fort of the Blackstone Rangers had obtained War on Poverty grants for his gang in the 1960s and 1970s. Acting on the advice of some University of Chicago professors, the Rangers virtually took over the First Presbyterian Church of Woodlawn with their government money and used it as a legitimate cover and front for their continuing illegal activities. Mayor Richard J. Daley had vehemently protested the channeling of federal funds to street gangs and had constantly blamed the university academics for misleading the federal government.

Now if Harold Washington paid former gang members to fight gangs, the Burke-Vrdolyak bloc would find themselves in a no-lose situation. Should the program succeed, the city council majority could take credit for prodding the mayor to adopt it; if it failed, they could blast the city's black mayor for funnelling money to known gang bangers.

Washington handled the situation with deft footwork. At his December 3 press conference, he announced the creation of the Mayor's Task Force on Youth Crime Prevention, under the direction of Michael Holewinski, one of the few white ethnics he had been able to recruit for his administration. Holewinski named three cochairmen for the task force—one white, one black, and one Latino—and put together a blue ribbon membership of political, civic, and religious leaders, including aldermen from the white majority bloc faction, who could hardly afford to refuse.[10]

In January 1985, the task force scheduled community meetings in all 25 police districts of the city to hear what the people most affected by gangs wanted done. They got an earful. About 2,200 people turned out in Pilsen, Humboldt Park, Logan Square, Robert Taylor Homes, and even in other areas less affected by gang crime. Over eight hundred came forward to testify. They wanted more police protection, of course, but they also emphasized the need for new sports programs and social services to keep young people out of trouble. Most seemed decidedly cool to the idea of former gang bangers running these programs.[11]

As a result of the task force hearings, Washington's administration devised a more extensive antigang program. The mayor proposed spending $3.9 million to train and support crisis intervention teams in nine high-crime areas of the city. The city council majority stalled the program by sneaking in an amendment requiring council *approval*, rather than simply *review*, of all funds granted to community groups for antigang efforts. The newspapers blasted the politicians for stalling on this high-profile issue: the *Chicago Tribune* editorialist called the aldermen "a street gang in pin-stripes." Cardinal Joseph Bernardin, usually the most cautious of religious leaders, chided both the mayor and the aldermen for stalling, and a delegation of community and religious leaders pressured Ed Vrdolyak personally at Democratic party headquarters. The mayor finally broke the logjam by committing one million dollars of city funds on May 28, on his own authority, without council approval. On May 30, the council majority proposed a face-saving compromise, substituting the word *concur* for *approve*, and the full program passed.[12]

The Crisis Intervention Network (CIN) formed the centerpiece of the new program. Organized within the city's Department of Human Services, CIN set up a central hotline for youngsters or parents threatened by gangs and nine field offices, each administered by a neighborhood advisory council and staffed by numerous volunteers. Washington hired Roberto Rivera, from Aspira, as the first executive director. Rivera had spent more than one year of his life fighting the school dropout problem, but in his new position he learned to appreciate even more the dire consequences of dropping out and joining a gang. During the two and one-half years that Rivera served with CIN he attended over 60 funerals, including Freddy Mercado's. The average age of the deceased was 17.[13]

Though at first glance the CIN appeared much like the Philadelphia project championed by Irving Spergel, and the newspapers made very little distinction between the two, it was actually different in subtle but important ways. CIN did hire some ex-gang members and occasionally engaged in vigilante-style intervention in gang wars, but most of its activities were more mundane. Mayor Washington, on the advice of his task force, consciously adopted a youth worker model for his anti-gang program. In years past, when the Irish, the Poles, and other European immigrants had suffered from high crime and youth gang activity, religious and social service agencies such as the YMCA, the Catholic Youth Organization (CYO), and the Back of the Yards Neighborhood Council had offered young people recreational activities to keep them off the street. In the 1930s, Bishop Bernard Sheil even started a boxing tournament to compete directly with the macho appeal of gangs. Over the years, many of these programs had become moribund. Parents who attended the task force's hearings trumpeted "the need to more fully use schools and parks, as well as other institutions, to offer constructive activities, especially recreational in nature."[14]

The Philadelphia project, which Spergel urged Chicago to adopt, employed a diplomatic model, attempting to convert hard-core gang members and use them as ambassadors to the gang leaders, as if they were heads of sovereign states. Many youth workers, however, doubted the sincerity of the hard-core gangsters' conversions; they suspected that many were double agents. With the example of the Blackstone Rangers always in mind, they feared the diplomatic model bestowed too much legitimacy on the gangs. The youth worker model, on the other hand, tried to detach the marginal gang members through competitive activities and leave the hard core to the police.

Though Mayor Washington gained little credit for it at the time, his antigang program was a political tour de force that provided an important preview of how he would handle the school reform issue. He avoided hasty measures that promised a quick fix, such as the booby-trapped Philadelphia project, and tried to build a consensus instead. The neighborhood hearings of the task force held throughout the city, not just in high crime areas, revealed that drug dealing, graffiti, and youth vandalism were prevalent in nearly every ward. The hearings produced a mass base for action, but they also served to educate the elite of the city. Religious leaders, police officers, aldermen, and youth workers sat down together to listen to the outraged citizens and suffered a baptism of fire. Afterwards, a priest in Logan Square could pick up the phone and call Fred Rice, the police commissioner, with a gang problem; a YMCA director could get access to a mayoral aide, such as Michael Holewinski, or a top city administrator, such as Judith Walker, when trouble broke out.

When the hearings concluded, Mayor Washington adopted a tried-and-true, traditional strategy: the youth worker model that had worked well with previous waves of immigrants and was well received across racial and ethnic lines. He emphasized the social service nature of the program by placing it under the jurisdiction of Judith Walker, his commissioner of human services. Though controversial from the start, often wracked by internal faction fights, and always underfunded, the Crisis Intervention Network outlived Mayor Washington and continued to function under his successors. His slow, subtle marshaling of community consensus during the gang crisis foreshadowed the approach he would take three years later when public concern for Chicago's schools reached crisis proportions.

Gangs in the Schools

Rival gangs fought each other, and communities sometimes fought back on many fronts, including the city's schoolrooms. Though public school principals and administrators denied that gangs posed a major problem, the high schools were actually major centers of recruitment and drug dealing. In a sense, this shouldn't be surprising. Where else could the gangs find a couple thousand potential recruits and/or customers in one place?

The Aspira dropout study documented the pervasive gang activity in the high schools of the near northwest side.[15] Fifty-six percent of the male youths interviewed stated that they had been asked in or around school to join a gang. The potential recruits narrated a common scenario. Two or three gang members would stop a youth in the halls and ask him, "Who you be about?" This interrogation is referred to as representing. The accosted youth is expected to answer the name of the right gang, such as, "I be about the Disciples." If he doesn't belong to any gang, he replies, "I be about myself." Yet this answer may prove nearly as dangerous as claiming membership in the wrong gang. Gang bangers don't believe in neutrality. They mark the innocent youth down as a suspected rival gang member; if they find evidence confirming this, they will threaten to kill him.

An assistant principal commented that if a stranger walked the halls of the high schools, he would think some kind of comedy was playing. "These kids walk around signalling each other with gang signs. Actually they look like third base coaches. But it's not so funny because kids come to me and say that they are afraid to go home because they've been signaled that they'll be jumped." More than half the youths interviewed by Aspira claimed that they had been afraid of physical harm in or around school; 40 percent reported actually suffering physical violence.

Students who didn't drop out of school had to learn certain tricks to survive. One youth stated that he would never wear two colors of clothing at school, since each gang had a different two-color scheme, "You had to wear only one color." Another reported that he acted like he was homosexual so the gangs would leave him alone. Thirty percent of all respondents admitted that they brought guns or knives to school for protection.

Faced with the reality of gang dominance, school authorities sometimes adopted the same policy as prison guards, keeping rival gangs apart. During the school year of the Aspira study, the district superintendent of the two schools approved 12 student transfers out of the district to shield the students from gang violence. These 12 youths, who belonged to the Latin Kings, found their lives in jeopardy since the schools were in Disciples territory. The principal of one high school took up a collection to buy a winter coat for a needy student. Raising the money was easy, but it took two days of meetings to decide what color coat to buy lest the student fall prey to gangs.

The Aspira researchers asked students how long it would take to buy a variety of drugs at school, such as marijuana, speed, cocaine, or heroin. The majority indicated that they could purchase hard drugs in less than an hour. One youth affirmed bitterly, "Drugs are all through the school like candy in a store." An assistant principal confirmed this and added, "The kids will not tell you anything about where they got drugs. They are much more close-mouthed about this than the gangs. They are more afraid about what can happen to them on the street if they talk about the source of the drugs than they are of anything that

I could do to them." As a result, only nine students were suspended for drug possession in the two schools during the 1983-84 school year; no one was suspended or arrested for selling drugs. One gang leader concluded, "They better not fool with the drug trade; it will really anger our suppliers. They don't want to lose a spot with four thousand kids in one place and have to go back to the street corners."

Yet it is not impossible for schools to keep gangs out. Most of the Catholic schools in Chicago remained gang-free in the eighties. These schools had a long tradition of harsh discipline and they regularly expelled students who caused trouble. Since most of them required students to wear uniforms, this cut down on the gang colors problem. Finally, a Catholic principal did not hesitate to call police if serious trouble broke out. The average public school principal, on the other hand, would consider it an admission of failure if he called the police and filed a report of gang violence with the school administration.

Some public schools, however, did fight the gangs. At DuSable High School, in the shadow of Robert Taylor Homes, the nation's largest public housing project, Parents United to Save DuSable volunteered to monitor hallways, call parents of troublemaking students, and even keep track of gang members after school. When gangsters met persistent resistance, they went looking for an easier market. Brenda Holmes, president of the group, told newspaper reporters, "That's the whole thing in a nutshell—taking control."[16]

Many educators agreed and pointed the finger at the school principal as the one who must take control. George Simms, chief of security for the Chicago public schools, stated, "If you have a strong principal, you'll have a safe school, even in the middle of a battlefield." New York school reformer Ronald Edmonds, who initiated the "effective schools" movement, emphasized "a strong principal who spends most of his time out of his office" as the first and foremost characteristic of an effective school.[17]

The Hispanic Dropout Task Force

The Hispanic Dropout Task Force, which Illinois Senate President Phil Rock had worked so hard to authorize, established a clear link between gangs and the dropout problem.

When the task force conducted public hearings in Chicago and Geneva, Illinois, early in February 1985, the continuing controversy over dropout statistics necessarily dominated the testimony and discussion. Isidro Lucas, who had first unearthed the magnitude of the Chicago dropout problem in his 1971 study, delivered a moving address to the task force and concluded that the problem was "a failing system, not failing students." Lucas employed a simple metaphor to drive his point home. If a factory experienced a 70 percent rate of defects on its assembly line, it would change the system, not fire the workers. Frank Llano, a Cuban-American educator serving as a staff member for the task force, confirmed the accuracy of the catastrophic dropout statistics for Latinos in Chicago. His candor and honesty was gratefully acknowledged by task force members. Finally, Doug Hoeft, a truant officer in the far suburbs of Kane County, lightened the atmosphere a bit, remarking that official statistics were so illusory he sometimes felt he was dealing with "evaporated students."

Yet with the murder of Ben Wilson still fresh in the minds of many, the gang problem kept breaking into the discussion. Mark Ballard, a youth worker in the Humboldt Park area, testified that Clemente High School "looked like the Audy Home (the juvenile detention center) on the outside, and felt like the Audy Home on the inside." Linda Martinez Roman, one of the interviewers in the Aspira dropout study, related that one of her informant's parents referred to Clemente bitterly as Al Capone High School.[18]

The task force spent little time probing for causes of gang warfare; they were more interested in solutions. Guillermo Gomez, a social worker with the Network for Youth Services, called for policies that would make schools into safe, neutral zones. Angela Miller, the assistant principal of Benito Juarez

High School, explained some of the methods that kept Juarez relatively safe. Juarez had been built in the late 1970s after community protests of overcrowding in the Mexican neighborhood of Pilsen, and from the very beginning, the community showed a strong sense of ownership. Mexican-American teachers and principals served as role models for the students and they did not tolerate any gang activity within the school walls.

The final task force report, "A Generation Too Precious to Waste," included a strong statement of the gang problem: "Gangs are known to control the campuses of many schools.... Also drug sales within schools are rampant. A purchase of alcohol, marijuana, pills, speed, cocaine, and heroin can be consummated in one hour." Drawing on the testimony of truant officers, the task force sketched out a strong connection between truancy and crime: "A study...showed that out of 127 chronic truants, 76 percent were caught in non-school-related crimes within two years after leaving school. In another study...it was found that 95 percent of the inmates at the Stateville Correctional Facility, Joliet, were high school dropouts." The task force recommended that "laws regarding possession and use of drugs and weapons on or near school grounds must be strengthened" and that "school officials must work with parents, community groups and law enforcement officials in order to create a safe school environment."[19]

Not everyone saw the connection between gangs and dropouts. At the height of the dropout controversy surrounding Ruth Love in August 1984, award-winning journalist Mike Royko published a column blaming the parents for letting their children drop out of school. After Ben Wilson's death, he penned another commentary reiterating the same point, parental responsibility. In his August column, Royko quoted Bernie Epton, of all people, "They are *your* children. It's your responsibility to keep them from dropping out of school." The columnist added his own conclusion, "So don't point at Ruth Love about the dropout rate. Go look in a mirror."[20]

A gifted satirist who assumes the pose of a working-class,

European ethnic spokesman, Royko touched a sensitive nerve with these columns. Casual readers of a newspaper always find it easier to blame the victim than probe for causes of a problem.

Certainly, no one can deny the importance of parental responsibility; this point surfaced repeatedly at the public hearings of the Mayor's Youth Crime Task Force. Yet the citizens who testified at those neighborhood hearings also emphasized the "lack of opportunity for training, education, and employment" and the "absence of alternative constructive activities available to occupy youth."[21] When young people have nothing to do with their free time and the schools look like dead ends, there is not much parents can do to keep them in school and out of trouble. A 16-year-old male feels invincible and you cannot tell him anything.

More important, Royko missed the point that struck the Hispanic Dropout Task Force so powerfully: many youths in Chicago drop out, not because they are lazy or behind in school, but because they are scared. After the murder of Ben Wilson, many politicians and educators began to understand that fear of gangs was a potent element of the dropout problem.

Notes

1. *Chicago Tribune*, 27 September 1984, 1; 2 December 1984, 1; 17 December 1984, 1; *New York Times*, 27 September 1984, 16; 9 December 1984, sec. 4, p. 3; 17 December 1984, 16.

2. *Chicago Sun-Times*, 21 November 1984, 1; *Chicago Tribune*, 21 November 1984, 1; 22 November 1984, 1.

3. *Chicago Tribune*, 8 January 1984, 1; 30 December 1984, 14.

4. The following background on gangs in Chicago is based on the *Tribune* series by Nathaniel Sheppard, Jr., and William Recktenwald, which appeared on the front page of the paper between 8 January and 12 January 1984 and was later published as a booklet titled *Gangs*. Other information came from the proceedings of the Gang Crimes Coordinating Conference, 6 July 1983, and the Gang Crimes Training Seminar, 26-27 March 1984, both conducted by the Gang Crimes Coordinating Council of Metropolitan Chicago in conjunction with the Chicago Crime Commission. See also the 1983 annual report of the State of Illinois's Gang Crimes Study Commission.

5. *Chicago Tribune*, 9 January 1984, 1.

6. Summary Report 1 for the Mayor's Task Force on Youth Crime Prevention (hereafter cited as Summary Report, Mayor's Task Force), reported crime statistics for the city's 25 police districts. Out of a citywide total of 72 gang-related homicides, district 13 (Wood) reported 7 and district 14 (Shakespeare), 12. District 2 (Wentworth) reported 5 homicides and district 18 (East Chicago), 8.

7. Frederic M. Thrasher, *The Gang: A Study of 1,313 Gangs in Chicago* (Chicago: University of Chicago Press, 1927; abridged edition, 1963), 9, 131, 153-54.

8. *Chicago Sun-Times*, 25 November 1984, 3; 3 December 1984, 1; *Chicago Tribune*, 30 November 1984, 1; 4 December 1984, 1.

9. *Chicago Tribune*, 2 December 1984, sec. 4, p. 1; 5 December 1984, 1.

10. *Chicago Tribune*, 4 December 1984, 17.

11. Summary Report, Mayor's Task Force; *Chicago Tribune*, 8 January 1985, sec. 2, p. 4; 10 January 1985, sec. 2, p. 3.

12. *Chicago Tribune*, 31 May 1985, sec. 2, p. 1; 4 June 1985, 18.

13. *Chicago Tribune*, 25 June 1985, sec. 2, p. 1; 5 August 1985, 1; Roberto Rivera, interview by authors, 20 September 1990; Dan Cohen, "Our Gang," *Chicago Reader*, 4 March 1988, 1, provided a long, in-depth look at CIN three years after its founding.

14. Summary Report, Mayor's Task Force.

15. All data in this section, Gangs in the Schools, (unless otherwise indicated) is taken from Charles L. Kyle, "'Los Preciosos': The Magnitude of and the Reasons for the Hispanic Drop Out Problem: A Case Study of Two Public Schools" (Chicago: Aspira Inc. of Illinois, 1984), 52-62, 72-82.

16. *Chicago Sun-Times*, 1 December 1984, 17.

17. *Chicago Tribune*, 5 May 1985, sec. 3, p. 8; James Traub, "A School, and a Principal, with Character," in *The Great School Debate: Which Way for American Education*, eds. Beatrice Gross and Ronald Gross (New York: Touchstone, 1985), 163.

18. Illinois State Task Force on Hispanic Dropouts, "Transcript of Public Hearings" (Chicago: 6-7 February 1985; Geneva: 8 February 1985).

19. Illinois State Task Force on Hispanic Dropouts, "A Generation Too Precious to Waste" (March 1985), 3, 11, 17.

20. *Chicago Tribune*, 10 August 1984, 3; 13 December 1984, 3.

21. Summary Report, Mayor's Task Force.

7

The Year of Education

Three streams of education reform fed into the Illinois state legislature to make 1985 the Year of Education. The first stream came directly from the "Nation at Risk" report, by way of the state's own "excellence commission." State Senator Arthur Berman and Representative Richard T. Mulcahey, the Democratic cochairmen of the Illinois Commission on the Improvement of Elementary and Secondary Education, filed their final report, "Excellence in the Making," on January 9, 1985. A cautious, consensus-building document, the Berman-Mulcahey report laid out the mainstream of education reform in Illinois. Its 57 recommendations, the product of 14 public hearings statewide, featured a no-frills, back-to-basics approach and a series of measures to increase accountability at all levels, from the individual students and teachers up to the top administrators.[1]

The heightened concern over school dropout rates in Chicago fed the second stream of education reform. The Illinois State Task Force on Hispanic Dropouts, established after the march on Clemente, held its public hearings during the first two weeks of February 1985, then issued its final report, "A Generation Too Precious to Waste," on March 15. Coincidentally, the Designs for Change research project issued its own report confirming the astounding dropout rates in Chicago public high schools during the week that the Hispanic Dropout commission was conducting hearings. Donald Moore, the director of Designs for Change, came directly from his own press conference on February 6 to testify before the commission at the State of Illinois Building. Two months later, yet another research report, from the Chicago Panel on Public School Policy and Finance (usually referred to as the CHIPS report), also revealed a systemwide dropout rate approaching 50 percent in Chicago.[2]

The accumulated evidence about dropouts in Latino and black high schools prompted the *Chicago Tribune* to conclude in a series of editorials, "The political climate is right for change now, even if it means insisting on concessions from the powerful teachers' unions and finding additional taxes. Public dismay over school problems and the enormous numbers of young people leaving school without an adequate education is acute." Joan Jeter Slay, a field organizer at Designs for Change, concluded more sharply in a teachers' newsletter, "The three independent studies paint a shocking picture of institutional failure for Chicago's school children. 'Educational genocide' is the right term."[3]

The public hysteria over gang warfare, which followed the slaying of Ben Wilson, fueled the third push for education reform. State Senator William A. Marovitz, chairman of the Judiciary Committee, adopted the antigang issue and proposed a series of "safe schools" bills on January 27. Senate President Phil Rock deftly tied the dropout and gang problems together at his press conference releasing the Hispanic Dropout report on March 24: "Where do you think these youngsters [the dropouts] go?" Rock asked rhetorically. "Straight to the street."[4]

Due to the nationwide ferment of education reform, the comprehensiveness of the local research reports, and a promise of support from Governor Thompson, some form of education legislation was a virtual certainty for 1985. The local concern about gangs and dropouts in Chicago, however, imparted a sharp sense of urgency that provided additional pressure for action.

The Omnibus School Reform Bill

Though all agreed that 1985 would be the Year of Education, the final shape of school reform legislation remained very uncertain as the year began. Senator Berman, the chairman of the Senate Education Committee, seemed rather pessimistic about the chances for significant reform. He had asked participants in an education conference the previous year to help him out by broadening the political coalition behind education bills. "Only 27 percent of taxpayers have children in public schools. [Politicians will say] there's no reason to upset 73 percent of constituents to help 27 percent."[5]

The two Democratic leaders of the legislature both made predictions early in the year that turned out to be wrong. Mike Madigan, the Speaker of the house, told reporters on February 8 that it looked unlikely the legislature would find any new money for the Chicago public schools that year. Yet when the final legislation took shape, it contained significant new funds for education. Senate President Rock remarked offhandedly during a long interview in April that raising the minimum teachers' salary from $10,000 to $20,000 looked like a near certainty. Yet that measure fell on the cutting-room floor when the education laws were spliced together at the end of the session.[6]

Governors in other states, particularly those in the South, had seized the initiative by advocating high-profile changes in their state education systems, but Governor James R. Thompson lagged behind and let the Illinois legislature and its excellence commission take the lead. Yet, with an eye on his upcoming race for an unprecedented fourth term, Governor Thompson finally decided to highlight education in a special joint session of the legislature on February 27. Though he had already delivered his annual State of the State address, proposing a massive public works program called "Build Illinois," and he was planning to outline his detailed budget requests in March, Thompson called both houses together in an extraordinary session so that the education issue wouldn't get lost.[7]

Referring to his previously announced construction program, Thompson began his education address by stating:

> The strongest and most efficient infrastructure we can construct
> will be of little use...if we are not, at the same time, willing to
> reform elementary and secondary education in this state....If
> this General Assembly enacts the Build Illinois and the educa-
> tional reform and financing programs I will propose today it
> will send the single most powerful signal to the business com-
> munity of the world that in Illinois we are ready, willing, and
> able to do business.

The specific measures Thompson recommended were a potpour-
ri of the education reforms advanced across the country in the
previous two years since the "Nation at Risk" report was
published. He omitted some of the more controversial proposals
that had surfaced, such as state aid to private schools, "leaving
it up to the Democrats," as the *Tribune* remarked, "to take the
lead on the politically sensitive matters." The only measure
Thompson proposed that did not have consensus backing was
merit pay for teachers, President Reagan's favorite school
reform. Political leaders from both parties greeted the governor's address with cautious applause, but they also agreed with
the newspaper editorialists that the Thompson proposals were
"only a beginning" and "a framework, but not the final blueprint."[8]

Over the next two months, individual legislators staked out
small pieces of education reform to appeal to their own constituencies, introducing nearly four hundred different education
bills in the 1985 legislative session. Representative Larry
Bullock, for example, a black legislator from Chicago's south
side, introduced a bill to abolish the Chicago Board of Education and carve it up into 20 smaller school districts, each with
its own elected school board. Such a radical decentralization
measure would give individual black neighborhoods community
control over school budgets and teacher jobs. Other legislators
discussed a plan to retain the present citywide board of education but change it from an appointive to an elected body. These
measures evoked a good deal of hand wringing by editorialists
and posturing by politicians, but neither gathered enough
support to pass.[9]

Senator William Marovitz and Representative Carol Moseley Braun, Democratic allies of Mayor Harold Washington,

introduced a less radical decentralization measure borrowed from the state of California. The Urban School Improvement Act, as it was called, proposed that each Chicago school establish a school improvement council made up of equal numbers of parents and school staff. The legislature would provide a per-student sum of money to each council to devise a school improvement plan and then grant the council limited authority to monitor the plan's implementation. A much-amended version of this plan did survive in the final legislation.[10]

On Friday, May 10, Phil Rock cut through the legislative confusion and called for a summit meeting of the four legislative leaders, the governor, and state education officials to hammer out an omnibus bill. The governor was spending nearly all his time that weekend at televised hearings on the Gary Dotson rape case. Dotson's alleged victim, Cathy Crowell Webb, had recanted her testimony and insisted that the jailed Dotson was innocent. Thompson, who never saw a camera he didn't like, conducted his fact-finding hearings in the glass-enclosed atrium of the State of Illinois Building. At one point during the circuslike proceedings, the governor waved a key piece of forensic evidence, Cathy Webb's semen-stained panties, at the TV cameras. After finally commuting Dotson's sentence, Thompson returned to more mundane matters of state government and eventually huddled with the legislative leaders. Their conclave was irreverently dubbed "Big Jim and the Four Tops."[11]

To the surprise of most observers, the Illinois State Board of Education (ISBE), and its new superintendent, Ted Sanders, proved to be significant forces in molding a consensus behind the omnibus bill. ISBE was created in 1975 as an appointive body with a professional staff to replace the partisan, elected superintendent of public instruction, but without any constituency of its own, the new board had never carved out a position of power and influence for itself. The previous superintendent, Donald Gill, had made matters worse when he publicly contradicted Governor Thompson at a 1984 press conference where the governor announced new graduation requirements for state high schools. Gill and ISBE wanted to stress "outcomes," that is, a specific body of knowledge each student should master in high school, whereas the governor's graduation requirements followed the traditional, union-backed system of required courses and hours. Gill resigned in late 1984 and Thompson lobbied for Gene Hoffman, a powerful Republican legislator from Elmhurst, to replace Gill. The state board, however, ignored the governor and hired John Theodore "Ted" Sanders, the superintendent of instruction from Nevada and a former candidate for national secretary of education, instead.[12]

Sanders, who was, incidentally, the only public figure in Illinois taller than Governor Thompson, showed remarkable political astuteness and got on well with the governor. He jettisoned his predecessor's unrealistic request for almost one billion dollars in new school funding and downplayed some other controversial ISBE proposals, such as raising the mandatory school age from 16 to 18 years of age. Sanders lined up the major education organizations and the two teachers' union federations behind the omnibus bill that the legislative leaders were hammering out, and he insisted to the legislators that some new funding was necessary to make any education reform work. When the Year of Education finally came to an end, the governor's chief of staff remarked admiringly to the members of ISBE, "When you are in the ballpark, people will listen to you. For the first time in years, you have a superintendent who knows where the ballpark is."[13]

As always, the final shape of legislation didn't become clear until the last days of June. The compromise version of Senate Bill 730 emerged from round-the-clock drafting conferences about 1:30 A.M. on June 26, then the governor and the four legislative leaders gave it their imprimatur on Friday, June 28. Senator Berman, who had started the tortuous process by heading the Illinois excellence commission, remarked, "There were 47 provisions of Senate Bill 730, and I haven't counted them up yet, but I would estimate 90 percent of them originated with the commission."[14]

Most of the major accountability measures remained in the bill: a requirement that school districts test all pupils in reading, math, and language at the 3rd, 6th, 8th, and 10th grade levels; a test of basic skills for all new teachers (referred to in the press as a bar exam for teachers); provisions for periodic evaluation of experienced teachers; and an innovative requirement that each school district issue a report card on itself, reporting the standardized test scores of students on a school-by-school basis.[15]

The omnibus bill also contained many other measures desired by educators, such as the creation of an Illinois Mathematics and Science Academy. Modeled on a high-tech school for the gifted established in North Carolina as part of that state's excellence reforms, the new Math and Science Academy would be a three-year residential school located in Aurora, Illinois. Educators also secured pilot programs for handicapped preschool children, new funding for summer school programs throughout the state, and an easing of the requirement of four years of physical education in high school if students chose to enroll in more rigorous academic programs. These measures helped keep the teachers' unions' support for the bill, even though it did not contain the minimum wage provision. As Robert Leininger, the chief lobbyist for ISBE remarked, the unions got jobs "up the gazoo" from all the new programs in the omnibus bill.[16]

The glue that held the whole bill together was the nearly $400 million in increased education funding: $100 million specifically aimed at the new programs, over $200 million in increased formula funding for local districts, and $75 million earmarked for categorical programs such as bilingualism and vocational education. This 12.5 percent increase in education spending over the previous year, the largest percentage raise in 10 years, was financed by new taxes on telephone calls and cigarette sales and by economic growth in the state's tax base. Educators wanted money for reform, but legislators insisted on reform for money. Accountability and increased funding were decisively linked.[17]

One necessary compromise enraged the professional education lobby. The Illinois Catholic Conference had long been seeking state aid to pay for transportation of students to Catholic schools. Governor Thompson did not mention this politically explosive proposition in his education address to the legislature, but he quietly slipped funding for it into his proposed 1985-86 budget. Meanwhile, the Catholic conference's lobbyist broadened the appeal of the transportation bill by including public school students whose districts did not provide free bus transportation. Though teachers' unions and educational associations howled at this diversion of funds from mainstream education proposals, Thompson, Madigan, and Rock insisted on including the transportation reimbursement provisions in order to win the support of Catholic legislators. By rolling the entire education package into one omnibus bill, the leadership forced the education establishment to hold their noses and accept transportation reimbursement or else kill the whole bill. Thompson told the public school educators bluntly, "We will not see an increase in money for the public schools without some kind of parochiaid."[18]

The state legislature stayed in session beyond its legal deadline of midnight June 30 for the 15th consecutive year. Years ago, the legislative leaders would simply stop the clock at midnight then carry on for hours or even days after the deadline. The state constitution adopted in 1970, however, ended this charade and required any measures passed after the June 30 deadline to obtain a 60 percent supermajority if they were to take effect immediately. In 1985, the house passed the education omnibus bill by a 77-to-41 vote shortly after midnight, but the bill stopped dead in the senate on July 1, when Republican legislators discovered a new tax on business telecommunication messages and a shortfall in formula funding for suburban schools. The leaders went back to the drawing boards, deleting the offensive tax provision and revising the formula funding process to funnel an extra $11.5 million to suburban school districts.[19]

Education reform was not the only issue stalling the legislature. The lawmakers also differed fiercely over division of the Build Illinois spoils. The education omnibus bill finally cleared the senate by a 56-to-2 vote after all the compromises were hammered out on July 2, but the legislature lurched into a holiday July Fourth session for the first time in history to work over the Build Illinois bond plans. Most voters probably missed these early July fireworks. News of the 39 hostages held captive aboard TWA flight 847 by Islamic terrorists in Beirut blanketed the newspapers for days, both before and after their

release on July 1. Then by July 3 and 4 when news reports of
the education omnibus bill appeared, most people were absorbed in family fun and fireworks of their own.[20]

Senate Bill 730 was an insider's bill from the beginning.
Responding to a widespread, but unfocused, public outcry to
improve the schools, Senator Berman and the legislative leaders
produced a law with something for everyone. Teachers did not
receive the higher minimum salary they had sought and were
unhappy with the private school transportation reimbursement,
but they gained many new experimental programs and the jobs
that went with them. Every educational special interest won
something: the Math and Science Academy for the gifted, summer school for remedial education, new money for handicapped
children, and increased funding for bilingual and vocational
education. The Illinois State Board of Education received the
legislature's encouragement to begin a program of consolidating
smaller school districts in the state. Chicago's mayor and his
allies obtained the first step toward decentralizing the city's
board of education and granting parents more control over the
schools.

The Illinois education reforms of 1985 were not, perhaps,
path-breaking measures, but they were about as comprehensive
as any passed since "A Nation at Risk" touched off the great
education debate two years before.[21]

Dropout Prevention and "Safe Schools" Bills

Despite the breadth of the omnibus education bill, the legislature also enacted two additional packages of education
measures in 1985. Seven bills emerged from the legislature
during the last week of the regular session that responded
directly to the dropout-rate controversy of the previous year.[22]
The first bill (HB 2158) provided a realistic definition of a
dropout for the first time and required that school districts adopt
a standard formula for calculating the dropout rate and report
the figures annually to the governor, the legislature, and the
state board of education. Routine and bureaucratic as this
sounds, it actually cut right to the heart of the dropout controversy. For 13 years since the Lucas report, the Chicago Board
of Education had been publishing bogus dropout statistics that

masked the enormity of the problem in black and Latino high schools. Now the new law slapped a criminal penalty on the falsification of dropout statistics. As one bureaucrat remarked when he heard about the new provision, "It's not worth going to jail for a number." Finally, legislators and educators alike would have access to reliable and comparable statistics statewide.

Following a recommendation of the Hispanic Dropout Task Force, the second bill (HB 2165) encouraged school districts to hire more counsellors and reduce the student-counsellor ratio to 250 to 1 by July 1, 1990. Quoting directly from the task force recommendation, the new law enjoined, "Each counselor shall spend at least 75 percent of his work time in direct contact with students." This bill was not as strong as it might have been, however, for it did not include an appropriation of additional money to meet the mandated student-counsellor ratio.

House Bill 2167 finally righted an ancient wrong in the Latino community, the wholesale assignment of non-English-speaking youth to special education classes for the retarded. The law required the Illinois State Board of Education to devise nondiscriminatory assessment tests for determining eligibility for special education and it specifically singled out Latino students as the group most affected. Another law (SB 1215) addressed an additional problem facing many Latino immigrants: the difficulty of obtaining official student transcripts from schools previously attended. The new law stated flatly that "no public school may refuse to admit a student for failure to present records." It further mandated schools within Illinois to provide such records within 15 days of receiving a request. Senate Bill 1212 created a 17-member advisory council for bilingual education. These three laws (HB 2167, SB 1215, and SB 1212) together went a long way toward ameliorating long-standing grievances of Spanish-speaking youths and their parents.

The sixth dropout prevention bill seemed so simple and full of common sense that it made one wonder why a specific law was necessary. The act (SB 210) required school authorities to notify parents by phone within two hours if their elementary school child was absent without cause. Critics often tried to blame the dropout crisis on apathetic parents, yet before this law passed, many parents of even small children would not know their children were playing hookey.

The final law in this package, titled the Educational Partnership Act (SB 1218), enlisted the aid of Illinois colleges and universities in the fight to prevent high school dropouts. It authorized institutions of higher education to set up tutoring programs for elementary and secondary students and provided grants to colleges that would conduct studies of the dropout problem. This law marked a first step toward overcoming the radical discontinuity between the levels of education in Illinois, each with its own governing bodies and vested interests. Some educators believe that the dropout problem will be more amenable to solution if Illinois education, from kindergarten through college, is considered all one system.[23]

None of these dropout prevention laws sounds very earth-shaking; indeed they almost seem like motherhood bills. This was intentional, for their sponsors sought to make them non-controversial. Yet the educational establishment tried to stop them before they were even drafted. When the Hispanic Dropout Task Force completed its hearings and was rushing to meet the March 15 deadline for producing its finished report, task force members discovered that Tom Grayson, the chief staff member of ISBE assigned to write the report, had stripped out its most controversial observations and most pointed recommendations. In particular, Grayson's draft omitted all statistics from the Aspira dropout study that had embarrassed the Chicago Board of Education.

Senator Rock sent his education staffer, Steve Henriksen, to intervene with Grayson, and Senator Nedza, the chairman of the task force, spent a whole day with various task force members reinserting the specifics that Grayson had deleted. Even so, when the task force held its final meeting in Chicago, each member found a copy of the toned-down text sitting at his or her place. Every *must* in the report had been changed to *should*. Nedza instructed Grayson to throw out all of these copies, and the task force voted unanimously to change the wording back to its stronger form. Bureaucratic caution might have prompted Grayson's initial softening of the task force's language, but Chicago Board of Education lobbyists likely spurred his unusual persistence.

Though the dropout prevention package received no publicity in the general news media, it provided direct proof of the Latino community's newfound political clout. Each measure corresponded directly to some portion of the Hispanic Dropout Task Force report. Without the march on Clemente, there would have been no task force, and without the task force, none of these bills would have even been written.

A final bit of lobbying proved necessary before the dropout prevention bills became law. Governor Thompson did not sign these measures along with the omnibus education act, and as the deadline for gubernatorial action approached, Latino community leaders feared he would not sign them at all. Isidro Lucas, who handled public affairs for Spanish-language television on Channel 60, decided to use the station's popular Saturday night movie as a vehicle for political pressure. Lucas invited legislators and educators to film 30-second spots urging the governor to sign the dropout prevention bills. The station aired these spots during the commercial breaks of the Saturday movie along with two phone numbers that allowed viewers to express their opinions. Viewers urging the governor to sign the bills were instructed to call one number, those who opposed the bills could call the other. Over four thousand people phoned in, with an overwhelming majority favorable to the laws. The station sent a certified tally of the call-in numbers to the governor's office. Governor Thompson not only signed the dropout prevention bills, he staged a signing ceremony for them at Roberto Clemente High School on September 20.[24]

The final package of education reforms in 1985 received considerably more attention in the press, due to the public outpouring of grief and fear following Ben Wilson's murder. The Aspira report had first revealed the role of gang warfare in adding to the dropout problem, and the Hispanic Dropout Task Force underlined the need for new laws against drugs and weapons in the schools. At the press conference announcing the task force report, Senator Nedza emphasized the reciprocal relations between gangs and dropouts. Fear of gangs keeps students away from school, but once the student drops out he becomes a prime candidate for either gang recruitment or gang violence. Ninety-five percent of the inmates at Stateville penitentiary were high school dropouts, Nedza asserted.[25]

Before the task force had even completed its work, however, the safe schools subcommittee organized by Network for Youth Services had floated a trial balloon. Police from the gang crimes unit, prosecutors from the state's attorney's office, and social workers from the schools felt they needed stronger laws to protect school property from the incursions of gang recruiters and drug dealers, so they proposed that the streets and sidewalks within one thousand feet of any school building in the city be designated "safe school zones." Certain specified crimes, especially the sale or possession of weapons and drugs, within these zones would have increased penalties attached to them. The Hispanic Dropout Task Force adopted the idea as one of its legislative initiatives and politicians swiftly jumped on the bandwagon. Senator William Marovitz, the chairman of the Judiciary Committee, and Senator George Sangmeister grabbed the safe school zone idea and announced in January 1985 that they would introduce legislation embodying the concept.[26]

Marovitz and Sangmeister introduced a package of six bills when the legislature opened in February, then conducted hearings on gang crime during a student assembly at Clemente High on March 12. Jaime Rivera, a social worker at the school, explained that "students might not come right out and tell you that they're afraid but if you take them aside and talk to them alone, they'll tell you horror stories." Senator Marovitz declared that the safe school zones were aimed at making schools "a haven for learning, not for gangs....We must restore each student's basic right to a good education....The schools themselves are the best place to start."[27]

The safe school zone proved a popular idea, indeed a politician's dream, so the Marovitz-Sangmeister bills attracted numerous cosponsors and little significant opposition. A house-senate conference committee combined several of the antigang bills into one omnibus piece of legislation that passed overwhelmingly on July 1. Senate Bill 207 provided that juveniles caught selling drugs or weapons in school zones would automatically be charged and tried as adults and that adults committing these crimes would be charged with a Class-X felony, a category of crime carrying a 6- to 30-year sentence. Recruiting for gang membership on school property and all drug and weapons possession charges within the school zone were also upgraded to higher classes of felonies with enhanced penalties. A second bill in the antigang package changed the penalty for selling a weapon to a minor from a misdemeanor to a felony. A third bill created a state Department of Alcohol and Substance Abuse to devise educational programs for students and training programs for teachers. The law provided an initial $1.6 million appropriation.[28]

Governor Thompson signed the school zone bills at the climax of an education conference in Chicago on September 24, using his amendatory veto to make a few minor changes in the various crime penalties. The legislature concurred with his changes during its veto session at the end of October.[29]

As the legislative Year of Education came to an end, Governor Thompson crowed, "We have moved to the head of the class in the United States in educational reforms." The *Chicago Tribune*'s education reporter congratulated the state's lawmakers with the same cliche, "In the national rush to learn how to improve schools, Illinois has moved to the front of the class....It took two years, reams of reports, four hundred bills, political horse-trading of the highest order and last minute deals." He then concluded soberly, "Now the hard part begins."[30]

Indeed, so many education laws flowed out of the legislature in 1985 that it took school superintendents, principals, and teachers some time to digest them all. Eventually, it became clear that the legislature's handiwork had stressed the imposition of tests, standards, and law-and-order measures rather than curriculum reform or experimental classroom procedures. State Superintendent Ted Sanders begged for time to assess the results, "So by the end of five years, we ought to see significant ground being covered."[31]

As it turned out, parents and taxpayers couldn't wait five years, for the 1985 laws produced no startling improvements in Chicago's troubled schools. Yet three of them proved significant in the long run. The adoption of a standard dropout reporting formula and the school report card provision, requiring school districts to publicize the results of standardized test scores, kept the low achievements of Chicago schools in the public eye. The Chicago Board of Education could no longer conceal the schools' shortcomings with bogus statistics. As Michael Bakalis has pointed out, the 1985 laws "should be viewed first and foremost as an accountability package."[32] Illinoisans began to hold their educators accountable, with a vengeance. A third measure, the local school improvement councils created by the Urban School Improvement Act, though woefully weak in their first incarnation, eventually pointed the way toward a more radical and effective means of accountability: local school councils with real power.

Notes

1. Illinois Commission on the Improvement of Elementary and Secondary Education, "Excellence in the Making" (January 1985); *Chicago Tribune,* 10 January 1985, sec. 2, p. 5; 13 January 1985, 1.

2. Illinois State Task Force on Hispanic Dropouts, "A Generation Too Precious to Waste" (March 1985); Donald R. Moore, "The Bottom Line: Chicago's Failing Schools and How to Save Them" (Chicago: Designs for Change, 1985); G. Alfred Hess, Jr., Diana Lauber, "Dropouts from the Chicago Public Schools" (Chicago Panel on Public School Policy Finance, 1985); *Chicago Sun-Times,* 7 February 1985, 3; 24 April 1985, 1.

3. *Chicago Tribune,* 17 February 1985, sec. 5, p. 2; 18 February 1985, 10; 19 February 1985, 10; *Substance,* February-March 1985, 6.

4. *Chicago Sun-Times,* 28 January 1985, 5; 25 March 1985, 16; *Chicago Tribune,* 28 January 1985, 12; 25 March 1985, sec. 2, p. 2.

5. Cynthia Peters, "Madigan's Conference on Education Reform," *Illinois Issues* 10 (May 1984): 5.

6. *Chicago Tribune,* 9 February 1985, 6; Diane Ross, "Phil Rock: Holding Together a Raucous Caucus," *Illinois Issues* 11 (April 1985): 8.

7. *Chicago Tribune,* 14 February 1985, 1; 25 February 1985, 13.

8. The text of Thompson's address is in both the *Journal of the House,* 84th General Assembly, 1985 sess., 1: 167-72, and *Journal of the Senate,* 84th General Assembly, 1985 sess., 1: 102-8. See also *Chicago Tribune,* 28 February 1985, 1; 1 March 1985, 22.

9. *Chicago Tribune,* 18 March 1985, sec. 2, p. 4; 23 March 1985, 10; 27 June 1985, 2.

10. Carol Moseley Braun, interview by authors, 5 February 1991; *Chicago Tribune,* 17 April 1985, sec. 2, p. 3; 18 April 1985, 18. The Urban School Improvement Act was passed as PA 84-935 (SB 1321) on 28 June 1985. See *Laws of Illinois,* 84th General Assembly, 1985 sess., 3: 5936-48. Portions of the original proposal were also included in the omnibus school reform bill described below in note 22.

11. *Chicago Tribune,* 11 May 1985, 5.

12. Don Sevener, "Education Reform and the Powerbrokers," *Illinois Issues* 10 (March 1984): 18-19.

13. Don Sevener, "Education Reform: The Outcome," *Illinois Issues* 11 (August-September 1985): 29; *Chicago Tribune,* 28 January 1986, sec. 2, p. 2.

14. *Chicago Tribune,* 27 June 1985, sec. 2, p. 1; 29 June 1985, 4; Sevener, "Education Reform: The Outcome," 29.

15. PA 84-126 (SB 730), passed on 2 July 1985. See the text in *Laws of Illinois,* 84th General Assembly, 1985 sess., 1: 1351-1470.

16. *Chicago Tribune,* 5 July 1985, 18; 8 July 1985, 15; Sevener, "Education Reform: The Outcome," 30.

17. *Chicago Tribune,* 4 July 1985, 8.

18. *Chicago Tribune,* 1 February 1985, sec. 2, p. 2; 28 February 1985, 2; 28 June 1985, sec. 2, p. 2; 30 June 1985, sec. 2, p. 1.

19. *Chicago Tribune,* 1 July 1985, 1; *Chicago Sun-Times,* 2 July 1985, 21.

20. *Chicago Tribune,* 3 July 1985, 1; 4 July 1985, 8; *Chicago Sun-Times,* 3 July 1985, 3; 4 July 1985, 2.

21. *Chicago Tribune,* 5 July 1985, 18; 8 July 1985, 15; *Chicago Sun-Times,* 7 July 1985, 4-5.

22. PA 84-662 (HB 2158), passed 24 June 1985, defined a dropout and required annual reports of dropout statistics; PA 84-663 (HB 2165), passed 30 June 1985, called for increased hiring of student counsellors; PA 84-664 (HB 2167), passed 24 June 1985, required non-discriminatory testing of special education students; PA 84-682 (SB 210), passed 24 June 1985, required phone notification of student absences; PA 84-710 (SB 1212), passed 29 June 1985, created a statewide advisory council on bilingual education; PA 84-711 (SB 1215), passed 26 June 1985, provided that no public school could refuse to admit a student for lack of records; and PA 84-712 (SB 1218), passed 29 June 1985 and titled the Educational Partnership Act, authorized grants to colleges and universities to conduct tutoring programs in the high schools aimed at preventing dropouts. See *Laws of Illinois,* 84th General Assembly, 1985 sess., 2: 4260-77, 4321-23, 4477-81.

23. "Open the Doors—Illinois Universities: Report of the Joint Committee on Minority Student Access to Higher Education" (submitted to the Illinois General Assembly, Spring, 1989).

24. The only press notice of the signing ceremony was in a neighborhood newspaper, *Logan Square Free Press*, 26 September 1985, 11; Isidro Lucas, interview by authors, 26 September 1990.

25. *Chicago Tribune,* 25 March 1985, sec. 2, p. 2.

26. Paul G. Vallas, "Legislative Initiatives" (Illinois State Task Force on Hispanic Dropouts, n.d.); *Chicago Sun-Times,* 28 January 1985, 5; *Chicago Tribune,* 28 January 1985, 12. The safe schools laws, described below in note 28, defined a school zone thus: "in any school, on the real property comprising any school, or on any public way within 1,000 feet of the real property comprising any school."

27. Press release from Senator William A. Marovitz, 12 March 1985.

28. *Chicago Tribune,* 14 July 1985, sec. 3, p. 1. PA 84-718 (SB 202), passed 27 June 1985, created the Department of Alcohol and Drug Abuse. PA 84-1074 (SB 206), passed 1 July 1985, upgraded the charge for selling a firearm to a minor from a misdemeanor to a felony. PA 84-1075 (SB 207, which incorporated SB 201, 204, 205, and 208), passed 1 July 1985, toughened the penalty for gang recruitment, selling of firearms, or selling drugs in a school zone, and provided for the transfer of juvenile weapons offenders in school zones to adult felony courts. See *Laws of Illinois,* 84th General Assembly, 1985 sess., 2: 4491-4500, 3: 7114-22.

29. Press release from Governor Thompson, 24 September 1985; *Chicago Tribune,* 25 September 1985, sec. 2, p. 3.

30. *Chicago Tribune,* 4 July 1985, 8; 5 July 1985, sec. 2, p. 1; 19 July 1985, 6.

31. Sevener, "Education Reform: The Outcome," 32.

32. Michael Bakalis, "Illinois School Reform: After the Cheering Stopped," *Illinois Issues* 12 (May 1986): 16.

8

A C.U.R.E. for Chicago's Ailing Schools

For the next two years, education receded from the public consciousness and the political agenda in Illinois.[1] Educators pleaded for time and sufficient state funding to implement all the new programs authorized in 1985. The state legislature provided about $250 million in new funds for education in 1986 on top of the hefty increases voted the previous year. This was less than the Illinois State Board of Education requested, but enough to keep the new educational programs alive, if not fully funded.[2]

Under the direction of Manford Byrd, Chicago's massive school system experienced much less controversy than during the Ruth Love years. The teachers went out on strike again in September 1985, but Governor Thompson stepped in after only two days with an advance of state funds and a promise of more money the following year, and the teachers signed a two-year contract. In 1986, the *Chicago Tribune* awarded Superintendent Byrd a "pass" grade on a pass-fail scale. "He has eased tensions in the administration....The air of constant crisis is gone...." A few months later, the newspaper congratulated Chicago's schools for a year without a strike. 1986 marked the first year of the 1980s with neither a school strike nor the cliff-hanging threat of a strike.[3]

The publication of the first statewide school report cards in October 1986 temporarily broke the calm. The uniformly low achievement of Chicago's schools reminded the voters that nothing fundamental had changed, and the school report cards drew many suburban educators into the school reform debate for the first time. The newspapers did what they do best: they published detailed score cards assessing winners and losers.

Governor James R. Thompson gave himself a lot of credit for school reform during his successful campaign for an unprecedented fourth term in 1986. Thompson delivered a moving inaugural address early in 1987 calling for increased attention to early childhood education, but the state legislature did not oblige him with a tax increase to fund any new programs.[4]

Education did not figure prominently in Harold Washington's successful reelection campaigns against Jane Byrne in the February 1987 primary and Ed Vrdolyak in the April 1987 general election. School Board President George Muñoz accurately summed up Mayor Washington's approach to educational policy: "He told me he intended to appoint school board members and not give them any direction from city hall. He has kept to that commitment."[5] When Muñoz stepped down from the board presidency in May 1987 to devote more time to his law practice, the board elected a key Washington supporter, businessman Frank Gardner, as his successor. For the first time ever, Chicago had a black school board president, a black schools superintendent, and a black teachers' union president. Mayor Washington and his main constituency, the black middle class, saw little reason to rock the educational boat.

The Latino leadership was similarly engaged in consolidating their political gains after the court-ordered redistricting of city ward boundaries. With Mayor Washington's backing, Luis Gutierrez defeated the Vrdolyak candidate, Manny Torres, in the aldermanic race that broke the Council Wars deadlock in April 1986. Miguel del Valle deposed a veteran state senator, Edward Nedza, in the Democratic primary that year, then won election as the first Latino state senator in Illinois.

Latino organizations did not abandon education issues. Network for Youth Services used new money generated by the reform law to open an alternative high school for dropouts. Operated at three different sites so students would not have to cross gang boundaries, the alternative school provided about 60 young people who had dropped out of school a second chance to earn a diploma. The school soon had a long waiting list and about two-thirds of those who enrolled eventually graduated. NYS also organized a media campaign called "Operation Graduation" to cut down on the dropout rate. Mr. Diploma-man, a cartoon figure drawn by high school students, was emblazoned on the sides of CTA buses and spoke out on Spanish-language television, urging young people to stay in school. Still, the high-profile political races of 1986 captured far more attention than these education initiatives.[6]

The calm atmosphere surrounding education, however, proved deceptive. The same *Tribune* editorial that hailed the "year without a strike" also warned prophetically, "as usual, the budget for the new school year was balanced only by resorting to patchwork and temporary solutions....So relief from school budget problems will be only temporary." When the teachers' two-year contract expired in 1987, the longest teachers' strike in Chicago history blew the lid off the educational calm.

Fortunately, a group of educators and community organizers convened by Michael Bakalis had been working quietly and with little publicity during the two-year lull to seek a remedy for Chicago's chronically ill school system. Calling themselves C.U.R.E., Chicagoans United to Reform Education, this group followed the school report cards like a fever chart, while testing a bold plan to cure the disease. When the fever rose to acute levels during the 1987 teachers' strike, Bakalis's group was ready with a C.U.R.E.

The School Report Cards

The notion of a school report card, assessing the strengths and weaknesses of individual schools and school districts, grew out of the movement for greater accountability in education that marked the early 1980s. A number of states mandated minimum competency tests for all students before they could be promoted from grade to grade, and some took the next step of publishing the results so the public and the politicians could judge which schools were succeeding and which failing. U.S.

Education Secretary Terrell Bell advocated a 50-state education ranking system. A few bold educators proposed that state governments declare "academic bankruptcy" for individual schools whose report cards revealed widespread failure to educate their students.

In Illinois, this idea emerged during the formative period of the Hispanic Dropout Task Force. Miguel del Valle suggested to members of the task force that a school report card would highlight the problems of minority schools in Chicago. In January 1985, Roberto Rivera and Father Charles Kyle were gathering data for the task force at the Illinois State Board of Education. They knew that the dropout statistics from the Aspira report were subject to challenge since they covered only two high schools, so they were searching for a "smoking gun," accurate dropout data for the entire Chicago system. Dr. William Humm, ISBE's chief statistician, showed them a printout revealing a 50 percent systemwide dropout average in Chicago public high schools.

Rivera and Kyle rushed to the office of Nelson Ashline, deputy superintendent of education, who virtually ran ISBE before Ted Sanders took the helm later that month. They showed Ashline their statistics and mentioned del Valle's suggestion of a published report card to inform the public about the schools' failings. To their surprise, Ashline liked the idea. He commented that he had just read an article in the national education magazine, *Phi Delta Kappan*, explaining the school report card and that he supported the concept.[7]

Ashline incorporated the school report card into the package of reforms that Governor Thompson submitted to the legislature in February 1985. The governor told the lawmakers:

> I propose the development of a school report card to accompany the pupil report card by which we now measure pupil achievement. If schools must, and are able to grade students, then parents and taxpayers must, and must be able to grade schools.[8]

Republican legislators firmly supported the school report card throughout the legislative maneuverings of the Year of Education, for it harmonized well with their dictum, "no money without reform, no reform without accountability." The measure survived intact as part of the omnibus school reform bill.[9]

The Better Schools Accountability program mandated that the 997 school districts and the 3,986 individual public schools in the state publish a wide range of achievement statistics between September 15 and October 31 of each year, beginning in 1986. The state board of education provided a standard 12-page form to report achievement test scores, college aptitude test scores, grade-to-grade promotion rates, daily attendance, and high school graduation rates. In order to help assess these performance figures, schools also had to report the percentage of students from low income families, student-teacher ratios, average teacher salaries, and the amount of money spent on each student.[10]

This sunshine measure initially caused more consternation in the suburbs than it did in Chicago. The Chicago public schools had been under the microscope for years and the school board annually published reading scores and many other achievement statistics. Chicago parents were well aware that most of their public schools were rotten. Suburban educators, however, unaccustomed to the glare of publicity, lobbied to delete or change the reporting requirements before they went into effect, but they did not succeed.[11]

When the first report cards came out in October, many suburban schools, such as New Trier and Deerfield high schools on the affluent North Shore, ranked at the top, and Homewood-Flossmoor High School in the far less wealthy southern suburbs trumpeted its achievements as "the New Trier of the South." Other schools, however, such as Proviso and Morton in the near western suburbs, were embarrassed and tried to dismiss the report cards as inaccurate or misleading. Suburban politicians became even more discomfited when real estate boards revealed that they were using the school report cards to rank communities on a desirability scale.[12]

The Chicago public schools, however, provided the really shocking statistics, as usual. When the Chicago Board of Education released its reports on October 15, they revealed that the city's schools fell below the statewide average on all the performance indicators. Chicago students recorded lower test scores in reading and math at the 3rd, 6th, 8th, and 10th grade levels. Daily attendance stood at 91.2 percent, slightly lower than the state average of 93.6 percent, and the dropout rate of 48.1 percent doubled the statewide percentage of 23.7 percent.[13]

Only two of Chicago's 64 public high schools—highly selective Lane Tech and the Whitney Young Magnet School—reported ACT college entrance tests higher than the state average. These widely used exams, devised by the American College Testing service, record student scores on a scale from 0 to 36. The average test score of 20 at Lane Tech was the highest in the city, but still ranked only 67th statewide; Whitney Young's score of 19.3 barely fell above the state average of 19.1. Dozens of segregated schools on the south and west sides of Chicago fell at the very bottom of the statewide rankings, with average scores as low as 8 on the ACT scale.[14]

Schools Superintendent Manford Byrd defended the Chicago schools' record by pointing out that Chicago enrolled nearly twice the state average of low income pupils, that more students transferred in and out during the year, and class sizes were larger than average. Critics, however, countered that the Chicago Board of Education spent nearly $4,182 per pupil compared to a statewide average of $3,526 and that Chicago teachers earned an average salary of $31,050 per year compared to a statewide average of $27,014. Clearly some school districts in the state managed to do more with less than Chicago did.[15]

Chicagoans United to Reform Education

Even before the state's figures were released in 1986, Michael Bakalis, newly installed as dean of education at Loyola

University, had been making some calculations of his own.

A remarkable combination of scholar and politician, Bakalis had earned a Ph.D. from Northwestern University in 1966, but he had spent nearly as much time in public service as in academia. Elected state superintendent of public instruction in 1970 on the Democratic ticket, he was the youngest individual ever elected to that post, and also the last. The 1970 state constitution transformed the office from an elective to an appointive position. After Bakalis's term as chief educational officer for the state expired in 1975, he served a two-year term as state comptroller from 1977 to 1979 and ran an unsuccessful campaign for governor against James R. Thompson in 1978. He served a short stint in the federal Education Department during the waning months of the Jimmy Carter presidency in 1980, then returned to the academic ranks as a professor of education and public management at Northwestern. In August 1985 he assumed the deanship at Loyola's school of education.[16]

Bakalis believed that the 1985 education reforms were superficial and incomplete. In particular, they did not address the special problems of the Chicago public schools. In the spring of 1986 he culled negative statistics about Chicago's schools from the public record and the numerous education reports published in previous years, and the picture that emerged horrified and depressed him. He sent a fact sheet to every state legislator and to a selected number of business executives with a cover letter asking them how in good conscience they could tolerate such a dismal educational performance. The politicians answered evasively, and the businessmen replied that they agreed with him but that they chose not to get involved.

Bakalis concluded that fundamental change could only come from the grassroots. It would not come from the board of education, the teachers' union, or the superintendent, whose selfish interests would be threatened by true reform, and sadly, it looked like reform would not come from the corporate community either. He knew that ultimately the legislature must act, but they would not go beyond the 1985 legislation until substantial pressure built up.

Chicago had a rich tradition of neighborhood activism, harking back to the legendary community organizer Saul Alinsky. A tough Jewish criminologist from the University of Chicago, Alinsky had organized the stockyards neighborhood in the late 1930s according to the principle that power is never given, it can only be taken. He built the Back of the Yards Neighborhood Council on the strong base of neighborhood institutions he found in the area, particularly ethnic Catholic churches. Alinsky later founded the Industrial Areas Foundation to teach his organizing principles to others, and Chicagoans were his best pupils. One veteran activist has called Chicago "the Harvard of community organizing, or maybe the Notre Dame of organizing since the Catholic Church has played such an integral role."[17] Fighting city hall was as typically Chicagoan as patronage or Polish sausage. So Bakalis sent his letter to every community and neighborhood organization he could locate, from large established groups, such as the Urban League, to small block clubs and parents' organizations.

His letter contained a long litany of educational failures:

- Almost 50 percent of students who enter Chicago public high schools never graduate; in many schools the noncompletion rate is closer to 70 percent.
- Less than half (18,500) of the 39,000 students who entered high school in 1980 graduated in 1984. Of those 18,500... only 6,000 were able to read at or above the national 12th grade level.
- In 1982, the average Chicago public high school student had a composite ACT score of 13.6...compared to a national average of 18.2.
- Only 25 percent of the 1983 Chicago public school freshmen were reading at or above the national average....
- In three separate and independent polls, Illinois taxpayers graded the Chicago public schools at about a D+ level.[18]

Bakalis invited the neighborhood leaders to a meeting at Loyola on June 23. Several dozen attended, and others showed up for subsequent gatherings in July and August. Most of those attending were sympathetic to the cause, but at the end of the summer only two groups were willing to join Bakalis in forming a permanent reform organization: the Save Our Neighborhoods/Save Our City coalition (SON/SOC), and Designs for Change (DFC).

SON/SOC was a coalition of neighborhood organizations on Chicago's northwest and southwest sides. After the election of Harold Washington in 1983 had polarized the city along racial lines, white ethnic organizations convened a conference at the Hyatt Regency Hotel on April 29, 1984, to proclaim their own agenda and make sure it wasn't neglected in the acrimony of Council Wars. SON/SOC delegates avoided overtly racist rhetoric but they made it clear they didn't want their neighborhoods neglected now that power was passing to black politicians. The "white ethnic agenda" that came out of the conference featured economic development proposals, such as a linkage plan that would require developers of downtown highrises to contribute funds for neighborhood development and a home equity neighborhood stabilization proposal. Under the home equity plan, areas of the city threatened by economic decline or racial change would tax themselves to form a home equity insurance pool to guarantee that participating homeowners would not lose money when they sold their homes. The "white ethnic agenda" also included some very general and sketchy proposals to improve the public schools.[19]

Bob Gannett, a codirector of SON/SOC's operations, also served with Michael Bakalis on the board of directors of *Illinois Issues*, an academic magazine devoted to state politics and policy issues, so Bakalis included Gannett in his initial recruiting for a school reform organization. Gannett and his partner, Mike Smith, attended all the meetings at Loyola during the summer of 1986 and found Bakalis's reform thrust congenial. The Loyola dean believed that only a decentralization of the public school system into 20 or 30 districts, such as New York City had achieved two decades earlier, held out any hope for improving the schools. Gannett and Smith, as followers of Saul Alinsky's organizing principles, felt comfortable with the idea of neighborhood-based, decentralized schools. They already had an adversarial relationship with the local politicians and a controversial reputation, so they had nothing to lose by championing a radical plan.[20]

SON/SOC's participation in a school reform movement seemed, at first glance, rather surprising, since a majority of their constituents on the northwest and southwest sides did not send their children to the public schools. The heavily Catholic ethnic groups had long supported their own parochial schools and traditionally opposed any increases in funding for the public school system. The northwest and southwest side neighborhoods were also the home of an increasingly aging population, whose children were grown and gone.

Yet SON/SOC had analyzed the city's tax base by community areas and found that the areas they represented paid a significant portion of the school taxes in the city. Whether their constituents sent their children to public schools or not, they helped pay for them and thus deserved a say in how they were run. Anything else would amount to taxation without representation. Furthermore, Smith and Gannett realized that viable public schools were a major anchor of successful, livable neighborhoods and that their communities could ill afford to let them continue failing. Too many young parents told them they were thinking of moving to the suburbs where they would get their money's worth for school taxes.

SON/SOC's presence at the Bakalis gatherings posed some thorny political problems for black, Latino, and white-liberal leaders who might be interested in joining the school reform coalition. The "white ethnic agenda" proclaimed by SON/SOC had received generally negative press notices and the group was widely, though mistakenly, perceived as a racist organization. Black leaders apologetically admitted that they could get in trouble back home if their constituents learned they were meeting with SON/SOC. Bakalis, however, wanted to have representation from every part of the city in his fledgling organization, and SON/SOC had a large base of operations on the northwest and southwest sides, and were willing to sign on for the long haul, at a time when no one foresaw any immediate results.[21]

The other organization that joined Mike Bakalis in the summer of 1986 also suffered from frequent misperceptions. Designs for Change was sometimes considered a downtown, white organization, an educational think tank cranking out research reports. Yet it was actually a multiracial group, with deep roots in the south side housing projects, and it devoted as much time to action and advocacy as it did to research.

Don Moore came to Chicago in 1969 with a doctorate in education from Harvard to start an experimental "high school without walls" for the Chicago Board of Education. He then organized a consulting group called the Center for New Schools and obtained a Carnegie Foundation grant to study children's advocacy organizations. When the Center for New Schools fell apart from internal disagreements in 1977, Moore took his Carnegie grant and started Designs for Change as a children's research and advocacy organization, along the lines of the groups he had been studying.[22]

Designs for Change turned out some first-class research reports, most notably "Caught in the Web," which documented the systematic misclassification of minority students as retarded, and the landmark dropout study, "The Bottom Line." The latter report, issued at the same time that the Hispanic Dropout Task Force was conducting hearings, had far more public impact than the previous Aspira dropout study, because it documented the dropout rate for all public high schools in Chicago, not just a selected sample. Furthermore, the study showed that students who did persist and graduate were receiving an inferior education. Only one-third of public high school graduates could read at the average 12th grade level. In Moore's words, "Producing literate graduates is the school system's bottom line."[23]

Yet Designs for Change did not just churn out reports. Earl Durham, a veteran community organizer from the black south side, worked with Moore from the very beginning, and in 1981 they hired Joan Jeter Slay as a full-time organizer. Slay had established an innovative alternative school on the west side and she was the mother of a handicapped son, so she knew firsthand how difficult education could be in Chicago. "At every step of the way, I looked for support in this school system," she reports, "and it was not to be found."

Slay's first assignment with Designs for Change ranks among the most difficult jobs ever attempted: organizing black welfare mothers with autistic children. "We sat and cried together a lot," is all she will say about this experience. Then she and Durham began organizing public school parents in the south side housing projects. These parents harbored dreams for their children, just like any parents would, but if they asked questions at school meetings, the principals reacted "as if dogs suddenly spoke." In the first half of the 1980s, Designs for Change organized about five hundred to six hundred parents from 25 to 30 schools into an organization they called South Side Schoolwatch. Their main constituency, then, was in Ida B. Wells, Robert Taylor Homes, Stateway Gardens, and other Chicago Housing Authority projects.[24]

During a summer planning retreat in 1986, Slay, Durham, and other DFC staffers vented their frustrations. It was becoming clear that no matter how many parents they organized, they would never have much impact on the public school system as presently constituted. Drawing on research from across the country, Don Moore then called for a total restructuring of the school system. In his opinion, even a radical decentralization into 20 or 30 school districts, as Mike Bakalis advocated, wouldn't go far enough. Unless parents could exercise power at the individual school level, they would continue to be discounted by the bureaucrats.[25]

Designs for Change staff member, Sue Davenport, had been attending Mike Bakalis's monthly meetings at Loyola all summer and reporting back to Moore and the others. Now at the end of the summer, Moore met with Bakalis, Mike Smith, and

Bob Gannett for lunch at La Tour, a restaurant in the Park Hyatt Hotel, famous for its "power lunches." Moore presented his ideas for a radical restructuring and argued that decentralization into several districts would prove inadequate. He said that Designs for Change would be willing to make a long-term commitment to the fledgling reform group only if they agreed to push for powerful local school councils. Bakalis, who had an almost mystical feel for "town hall" democracy, readily complied, and Bob Gannett and Mike Smith from SON/SOC found the new orientation compatible with their organizing philosophy as well.[26]

So in the summer of 1986, far from the glare of media publicity, the Loyola School of Education, the Save Our Neighborhoods/Save Our City coalition, and Designs for Change signed on for what looked like a quixotic quest. They brainstormed to find a meaningful name with a catchy acronym. Among the candidates they rejected were CASE (Citizens Active to Save Education), RSCUE (Returning Schools to Communities United for Excellence), and CURE (Citizens United to Rescue Education). They liked the C.U.R.E. acronym, but finally settled on an alternative formulation: Chicagoans United to Reform Education.[27]

The C.U.R.E. Plan

C.U.R.E. was a multiracial organization from the start. The regular members in its early months were Michael Bakalis and Art Safer from the Loyola School of Education, Bob Gannett and Mike Smith from SON/SOC (all white), Earl Durham and Joan Jeter Slay (black), Renee Montoya (Mexican-American), and Don Moore (white) from Designs for Change. They intended to expand the coalition as soon as possible by drawing in more black and Latino organizations, but they wanted to perfect their plan first and be sure that whoever they recruited was willing to make a long-term commitment.

During the winter of 1986-87, members of C.U.R.E. began the long, slow process of becoming comfortable with each other and learning to trust each other. They drafted and discussed a detailed reform plan for the public schools, which was eventually published as a nine-page brochure (the "blue sheet") in April 1987.

The C.U.R.E. plan briefly summarized the problem, which was becoming all too familiar to Chicagoans who were aware of the numerous dropout studies and the school report cards. Then it outlined a solution based on seven fundamental principles:

1. Make every school an effective school.
2. Schools must be accountable to their neighborhoods.
3. Attract creative principals and teachers.
4. Reduce the central board to a few key powers in limited areas.
5. Drastically cut the bureaucracy.
6. Increase parent and student choice.
7. Link local schools with businesses and universities.[28]

Much of the C.U.R.E. plan looked familiar to anyone who had followed the education reform movement since 1983, and some aspects of it had already been tried in Chicago. Ruth Love's Adopt-a-School program, for example, and the 1985 Educational Partnership Act were both variants of the seventh principle, linking local schools with businesses and universities. What set the C.U.R.E. plan apart from other reform proposals, however, was its clear call for parent and community voice and choice.[29]

The second principle, making schools accountable to their neighborhoods, formed the active ingredient in the C.U.R.E. for ailing schools. Much of the control over educational decisions would be shifted from the central board of education and its bureaucracy to local school governing councils composed of parents, community representatives, and teachers.

> Under the C.U.R.E. plan, School Governing Councils...will have power over hiring and firing, money, curriculum, and school improvement....One of their most important powers will

be to hire the school's principal, who will play the key role in running the school day-to-day and will be held accountable for improvement.

C.U.R.E.'s original proposal for school governing councils remained vague about the exact composition of the councils, because the C.U.R.E. membership was itself divided. SON/SOC representatives insisted upon equal representation of parents and community taxpayers who did not have children in school, whereas the minority members of C.U.R.E. wanted parents of schoolchildren to hold control. All agreed, however, that in order to be an effective voice from the grassroots, the local councils should be elected and that they should enjoy substantial power, not merely an advisory role.

The original C.U.R.E. plan also contained a proposal for parent and student choice. The blue sheet stated:

> The C.U.R.E. plan will increase family choice within the public school system, so that parents and students can "vote with their feet" about which schools should continue to operate. Students who live in a specific neighborhood will have the first opportunity to attend their local school. Then on a space available basis, other students will be able to apply.[30]

The limited system of choice already available in Chicago had created a two-track system of elite magnet schools and dreadful neighborhood schools. The C.U.R.E. plan envisioned a more sweeping choice that would put the dreadful schools out of business and transform the rest into effective urban training centers.

Besides the blue sheet, C.U.R.E. also printed an attractive pocket-sized brochure in Spanish and English, titled "Kids First—*Los Niños Primero*."[31] More than just a slogan, "Kids First" became the North Star of the C.U.R.E. reform movement. In the many battles, both public and private, which lay in the future, all parties eventually lowered their voices and searched for a compromise because they genuinely wanted to put kids first. Employing the medical metaphor implicit in the word C.U.R.E., we can say that the plan for a new Chicago school system was patient centered.

C.U.R.E. Goes Public

On March 7, 1987, Earl Durham chaired a one-day conference at the John Marshall Law School in the South Loop. Members of C.U.R.E. who organized this meeting felt both excited and fearful as the date approached, for this would be the first time that large numbers of white ethnic homeowners would sit down with black welfare mothers to discuss education reform. Tentatively at first, the 50 or 60 people in attendance began to share their frustrations with the system. They broke down into small groups to discuss the C.U.R.E. plan and to stage simulated school council meetings.[32]

Over lunch at Berghoff's they began to relax and realize how much they had in common. Joan Jeter Slay overheard a mother from Ida B. Wells Homes talking to a retired homeowner from the northwest side. While complaining how hard it was to make ends meet on a fixed income, the white pensioner showed her the huge plumbing bill he had to pay when a pipe burst the previous week. The woman from the projects had never understood that in the bungalow belt, a homeowner can't just call up the CHA and complain when something breaks. For possibly the first time, she began to realize that all white folks aren't rich. On the other hand, the passionate hopes of the south side parents that their children would do better in life than they had surprised and enlightened the white homeowners.[33]

Everyone involved felt that this meeting was a pivotal moment. If they couldn't sell the C.U.R.E. plan to this gathering, they might not be able to mount a citywide movement. The small-group simulations, however, showed that ordinary people of diverse backgrounds could understand the issues and work together. They could make local school governance work with simple common sense. At this first public meeting, C.U.R.E. passed a crucial test.[34]

The following month, Mike Bakalis hosted a larger and more elaborate conference at Loyola's Lake Shore Campus to kickoff the citywide campaign for school reform. Aiming for maximum media coverage, C.U.R.E. staged preliminary press briefings on April 16 and 21 and a preconference reception on Friday, April 24. Nearly five hundred people from over 80 schools and organizations attended the main conference on Saturday, April 25. Earl Durham again wielded the gavel as those in attendance listened to a keynote speech from M. Donald Thomas, the former deputy superintendent from South Carolina, who was a consultant on local school governance. Participants then broke into small groups for role-playing and simulated school council sessions.[35]

C.U.R.E. hoped to use this conference to involve one or more Latino organizations on a permanent basis. Bob Gannett and Mike Smith met privately with Mary Gonzales and Dan Solis from the United Neighborhood Organization (UNO), but the meeting did not go well. Ironically, SON/SOC and UNO were too much alike in some ways to get along together. Both were Alinsky-style organizations more comfortable with confrontation than cooperation. Saul Alinsky had often used a stock phrase to describe the style of organizations that followed his principles: "Change means movement; movement means friction; friction means heat; and heat means controversy." Alinsky's biographer has summed up his tactics as "rudeness, ridicule, and imagination."[36]

Apparently, UNO had been distributing the C.U.R.E plan under its own name. With a bit of rudeness and imagination they claimed credit for it. The minutes of the March 27 C.U.R.E. meeting frankly commented, "We had a few guffaws over the 'blue sheet' ripoff caper....This was not an in-depth, nor politically sophisticated discussion." At the same meeting, C.U.R.E. members hotly debated whether to make the April conference bilingual. The minutes stated, "Don [Moore] seemed somewhat hurt, and after he mentioned that Renee [Montoya] made a big point of this I could also see the fear in his eyes having to go back and face her!!" Ultimately, key portions of the conference were conducted bilingually.[37]

Dan Solis attended the April conference with a large delegation, but UNO did not join C.U.R.E. at this time. As an Alinsky organization, UNO tried to avoid abstract issues and unwinnable causes, and in early 1987 school reform looked like a decided long shot. Solis and company remained interested in education, but they devoted their attention to smaller demonstration projects that didn't require a long-term commitment such as C.U.R.E. demanded.[38]

The April conference gained C.U.R.E. its first public attention. In a shrewd move guaranteed to make any newsman salivate, C.U.R.E. opened the Saturday morning session by rolling out gigantic five-foot tall report cards. Selected delegates then trooped to the podium and awarded letter grades to the Chicago public schools. Flashbulbs popped as the Chicagoans United to Reform Education covered the report cards with a generous number of *F*s. One parent scrawled a large *S*, for *stinks*, on her card.[39]

Despite the theatrics, media coverage of the conference was spotty and few observers believed that C.U.R.E. would succeed where other school reform attempts had failed. Cynical reporters may well have dismissed it as just a stunt to keep Mike Bakalis's name in the news in anticipation of another race for governor. As it turned out, C.U.R.E. never did become a household name in Chicago, but ultimately the plan they unveiled in April 1987 proved to be just what the doctor ordered for Chicago's sick schools.

Notes

1. The *Chicago Tribune* index contained 354 entries under Education, Chicago and Education, Illinois in 1986, compared to 608 references the previous year, the so-called Year of Education.

2. Nora Newman Jurgens, "State of the State," *Illinois Issues* 12 (April 1986): 4-6, and 12 (November 1986): 4-6; *Chicago Tribune,* 3 July 1986, sec. 2, p. 7.

3. *Chicago Tribune,* 1 April 1986, 14; 22 July 1986, 10.

4. Charles N. Wheeler, "Governor's Vision for Illinois Children: A Dream Worth a Tax Increase?" *Illinois Issues* 13 (February 1987): 4-5; Michael D. Klemens, "The State of the State 1987: A Long, Long Time from February to July," *Illinois Issues* 14 (February 1988): 6-7.

5. *Chicago Tribune,* 11 February 1987, sec. 2, p. 6.

6. David K. Fremon, "Chicago's Spanish-American Politics in the '80s," *Illinois Issues* 16 (January 1990): 17; Tomas Sanabria, executive director of the Network for Youth Services, interview by authors, 5 October 1990.

7. This account is written from the recollections of Kyle, Rivera, and del Valle. The article Ashline referred to was probably Beverly Anderson and Chris Pipho, "State-Mandated Testing and the Fate of Local

Control," *Phi Delta Kappan* 66 (November 1984): 209-12, which gives a good overview of the movement for minimum competency testing.

8. Address of Governor James R. Thompson to a joint session of the General Assembly, 27 February 1985. *Journal of the House,* 84th General Assembly, 1985 sess., 1: 170.

9. Article 4 of PA 84-0126 amended Chapter 122 of the School Code by adding a new paragraph 10-17a, titled "Better Schools Accountability," which mandated that the school report card be submitted "to parents, taxpayers of such district, and the Governor, the General Assembly and the State Board of Education."

10. *Chicago Sun-Times,* 4 September 1986, 1; *Chicago Tribune,* 22 September 1986, sec. 2, p. 1.

11. *Chicago Tribune,* 3 May 1986, 1.

12. *Chicago Tribune,* 21 October 1986, sec. 2, p. 1; 22 October 1986, sec. 2, p. 6; 24 October 1986, sec. 2, p. 7; 30 October 1986, sec. 2, p 2; 2 November 1986, sec. 3, p. 1.

13. *Chicago Tribune,* 16 October 1986, sec. 2, p. 1.

14. *Chicago Tribune,* 4 November 1986, sec. 2, p. 1.

15. *Chicago Tribune,* 16 October 1986, sec. 2, p. 1.

16. Michael Bakalis, interview by authors, 13 July 1990; his career is profiled briefly in *Illinois Issues* 11 (October 1985): 36.

17. John McDermott, quoted by Ben Joravsky, in "Community Organizing: Alinsky's Legacy," *Illinois Issues* 19 (January 1988): 11. For further background on Saul Alinsky, see the massive biography by Sanford D. Horwitt, *Let Them Call Me Rebel: Saul Alinsky, His Life and Legacy* (New York: Alfred A. Knopf, 1989).

18. Michael J. Bakalis to Robert T. Gannett et al., 19 June 1986. Robert Gannett, co-executive director of the Save Our Neighborhoods, Save Our City coalition (SON/SOC), allowed us to inspect a complete run of minutes and correspondence from Bakalis's reform group C.U.R.E. (hereafter cited as C.U.R.E.-SON/SOC papers).

19. "Save Our Neighborhoods, Save Our City Convention Agenda," 29 April 1984, C.U.R.E.-SON/SOC papers. See also Paul M. Green, "SON/SOC: Organizing in White Ethnic Neighborhoods," *Illinois Issues* 14 (May 1988): 24-28.

20. Robert Gannett, interview by authors, 19 July 1990; Michael Smith, interview by authors, 19 September 1990.

21. Smith and Gannett interviews.

22. Donald R. Moore, interview by authors, 1 August 1990.

23. Donald R. Moore, "The Bottom Line: Chicago's Failing Schools and How to Save Them" (Chicago: Designs for Change, 1985).

24. Joan Jeter Slay, interview by authors, 2 August 1990; Earl Durham, interview by authors, 6 August 1990.

25. Moore, Durham, Slay interviews.

26. Bakalis, Gannett, Moore, and Smith interviews.

27. Handwritten notes from a meeting on 21 July 1986, C.U.R.E.-SON/-SOC papers.

28. Draft, "Needed: A New School System for Chicago," 8 October 1986; "The C.U.R.E. Plan for a New Chicago School System," April 1987, C.U.R.E.-SON/SOC papers.

29. Don Moore has organized a retrospective history of the reform movement around these two ideas: "Voice and Choice in Chicago" (paper delivered at the Conference on Choice and Control in American Education, University of Wisconsin-Madison, 17-19 May 1989); for the philosophical underpinnings of voice and choice in education, see David S. Seeley, *Education Through Partnership* (Washington, D.C.: American Enterprise Institute, 1981).

30. The C.U.R.E. Plan.

31. The Spanish rendering of the brochure title was not quite accurate. *Primero Los Niños,* which we have adopted as our book title, captures the nuance of "Kids First" more accurately.

32. "Conference Agenda," 7 March 1987, C.U.R.E.-SON/SOC papers; Gannett, Durham interviews.

33. Slay interview.

34. Gannett, Slay, Durham interviews.

35. "City-Wide Conference Agenda," 25 April 1987, C.U.R.E.-SON/SOC papers. Bakalis, Gannett, Moore, Slay, Durham interviews.

36. For background on UNO, see Wilfredo Cruz, "UNO: Organizing at the Grass Roots," *Illinois Issues* 14 (April 1988): 18-22; the quotes about Alinsky are in Horwitt, *Let Them Call Me Rebel,* 523-24.

37. "Notes on School Meeting," 27 March 1987 (these minutes appear to have been written by Bob Gannett), C.U.R.E.-SON/SOC papers.

38. Moore interview.

39. *Chicago Tribune,* 26 April 1987, sec. 2, p. 3.

9

From Community Control to
School-Based Management

The decentralization plan that Mike Bakalis, Don Moore, and the other members of C.U.R.E. hammered out in 1986 and 1987 had a long and tangled political lineage. In the nineteenth century, nearly all agencies of government, including the public schools, were small, local, and decentralized. The city ward, which sometimes formed a natural geographic and ethnic community, was the primary focus of all government services. As a result, the alderman, the cop on the beat, and the school principal reflected the community they came from. Irish and German immigrants controlled government institutions in their own neighborhoods, Anglo-Saxon Protestants controlled their own, and so on.[1]

Decentralized government meant democratic control by distinctive communities. On the other hand, it opened the door for corruption and patronage by local politicians. So around the turn of the century, progressive reformers centralized and professionalized government institutions, including the schools. Their explicit goal was to remove the schools from the clutches of politicians and place them in the hands of impartial experts. Yet an unstated motive, to reduce the power of newer ethnic groups, also impelled the reformers. As one educational historian has phrased it, "The reformers were white Protestants reasserting their dominance over the city's educational system, seeking to shape the rude immigrant masses in their own image."[2]

Centralized, professionalized, bureaucratized education remained largely unchallenged until the 1960s. In the ferment of that decade, however, student activists and civil rights leaders attacked the downtown educational bureaucracies as insensitive, racist institutions that stifled the creative impulses of teachers and frustrated the legitimate aspirations of minority communities. The activists demanded community control of the schools, a phrase often understood as a code for black power.

New York City experienced the most abrasive community control controversy and the most thoroughgoing experiment in school decentralization. When the passions of the sixties finally cooled, the community control movement lost much of its ideological charge. Yet the New York system remained decentralized, and many educators picked up where the activists left off. Some felt that even the New York system did not go far enough. Instead of community control, they now advocated school-based management or school-site management. Centralized bureaucracies generally remained entrenched, but a strong reaction was slowly gathering strength.

Community Control and Black Power

The innocent-sounding phrase *community control* has been forever marked by the time and place in which it arose: New York City during the black power phase of the civil rights movement. The efforts of civil rights leaders to integrate New York's school system had clearly failed by the mid-1960s, frustrated by white resistance and ultimately stymied by white flight that left black and Puerto Rican students as a majority in the public schools. Unable to integrate the schools, New York's black leaders determined to take them over and mold them to the cultural and educational needs of black children.

The movement for community control began in 1966 at Intermediate School 201, a newly constructed school building in the heart of Harlem. Educator Preston Wilcox proposed that IS 201 become an experimental school with "the responsibility for educational and administrative policy in the hands of the local community." An ad hoc parent council at IS 201 demanded the right to hire a black or Puerto Rican principal to serve as a role model for the children. Though liberal mayor John Lindsay and noted black psychologist Kenneth Clark looked favorably on the Harlem experiment, the teachers' union opposed it vociferously and the board of education rejected it.[3]

The following year, the chairman of the Ford Foundation, McGeorge Bundy, released a lengthy report recommending decentralization of the New York school system along the lines proposed by the parents at IS 201.[4] The foundation also made money available to test the concept in three demonstration districts while the board of education contemplated the full report. After much pressure and picketing by black power advocates during the summer of 1967, the board established the three demonstration districts, including IS 201 in Harlem, Ocean Hill-Brownsville in Brooklyn, and the Two Bridges district on the Lower East Side of Manhattan.

A steering committee of parents and teachers moved swiftly in Ocean Hill-Brownsville to hold elections for a district governing board and to hire radical activist Rhody McCoy as the district administrator. In April 1968 McCoy courted a confrontation with the predominantly white teachers' union by firing 13 teachers, five assistant principals, and one principal in the district. The governing board hired a full roster of black teachers to replace the white educators they had dismissed, so Albert Shanker led the United Federation of Teachers (UFT) out on strike in September 1968. A hasty compromise was patched together, but the Ocean Hill-Brownsville board refused to restore the white teachers to classroom duties, assigning them busywork instead. The UFT walked out again and stayed out until they won most of their demands. In mid-November a state trustee took over the Ocean Hill-Brownsville district and suspended the local governing board.[5]

Though community control advocates lost the Ocean Hill-Brownsville battle, liberal public opinion still favored a decentralization plan for the schools. Some conservatives had also realized that if blacks could control their neighborhood schools under decentralized management, whites could also control theirs. Thus, on April 30, 1969, the New York state legislature overwhelmingly passed a bill authorizing the board of education to divide the city into 30 to 33 districts, each with an elected community school board. The three controversial demonstration districts, however, were abolished and carved up.[6]

Black and Puerto Rican leaders had advocated decentralization expecting that they would control the majority of local school districts, but it did not turn out that way in New York. Though blacks and Latinos formed a clear majority of public school students, the parents of schoolchildren were not the only ones allowed to vote. All registered voters in the city, whether they had children in the schools or not, were eligible to vote or run for office in the community school board elections. In the first trial of the new system in 1970, the teachers' union and other special interest groups mobilized their constituencies, but some radical militants boycotted the elections, and many minority parents simply stayed home. Overall turnout averaged only 14 percent in 1970, and went even lower in subsequent elections. Slates of candidates endorsed by the teachers' union won control of a majority of the local school boards, an astounding result considering the origins of the plan in the black power movement. Ten years later, UFT candidates still controlled all but six of the 32 local school districts.[7]

Lessons from New York and Elsewhere

Community control turned out to be a major disappointment for the advocates of black power in New York City. Many other observers also considered the experiment unsuccessful. In June of 1980, the *New York Times* published a major series evaluating school decentralization a decade after its implementation. The very titles of the articles screamed failure: "Community-run schools leave hopes unfulfilled" "Achievement lagging in community-run schools" "Politics and patronage dominate community-run school districts." The *Times* quoted a disillusioned Kenneth Clark, a major advocate of community control in the sixties:

> I don't care how much the new structure has given people a sense of control over their own destiny. The schools are no better and no worse than they were a decade ago. In terms of the basic objective, decentralization did not make a damn bit of difference.[8]

David Rogers, the leading academic expert on the New York school system, published a more balanced appraisal of decentralization in 1983. He pointed out that the New York decentralization legislation was a watered-down plan passed after a long, exhausting political battle. It preserved considerable power for the central board of education and left ambiguous the relationship between the central board and community boards. Furthermore, an acute financial crisis hit New York shortly after the community boards were established so cutbacks in funding limited the amount of educational innovation possible at the local level. Rogers concluded that "any positive educational developments that may have taken place in New York...might well be magnified under a stronger plan."[9]

Rogers did indeed find many encouraging developments in his case studies of local school districts in New York. Despite much political turmoil in the first local district elections and the surprising power of the UFT slates of candidates, most local school boards enjoyed considerably more legitimacy in their communities than the central board ever did. Most boards were hard working and they hired younger, more energetic superintendents and principals who would have had to wait many years for promotion under the old system. These new administrators often exercised creative entrepreneurship, encouraging alternative school programs and hustling to obtain federal government and foundation grants to finance them.[10]

In retrospect, it is possible to isolate several important flaws in New York's community control experiment. First of all, it is unfortunate that the most thoroughgoing test of community control occurred in the nation's largest city at a turbulent time under the influence of black power rhetoric. Once the black power movement ran its course, John Lindsay left office under a cloud, and the Big Apple teetered towards bankruptcy, the whole community control movement became discredited. Within the city itself, it was a fatal mistake to establish the first three demonstration districts only in minority communities. Had the pilot projects been divided evenly among white middle-class communities and ghetto districts, critics might have understood how the whole city could benefit from decentralization. As it happened, however, community control became eternally joined with black power in the public consciousness.

Second, parents were left out of the community control experiment. The initiative came from black activists, the law allowed any citizen to vote, and ultimately the teachers' union, local politicians, and prominent neighborhood professionals came to dominate the community school boards. Though many boards and even individual schools set up parent advisory councils, these bodies enjoyed no real power and were rarely well attended.

Finally, the decentralized districts in New York remained too large and impersonal. Ranging in size from 11,000 to 36,000 students, each of the 32 New York districts exceeded in size most school districts across the country. These so-called community districts, moreover, rarely coincided with natural geographic or ethnic communities. Politicians gerrymandered some district boundaries, but in many other cases natural communities were simply too small to make up a single district and had to be combined with others. One of the community school districts included the entire borough of Staten Island, comprising a heavily black, urbanized area at the north end of the island and a more suburban, white ethnic area in the south, many of whose residents had fled from black neighborhoods elsewhere in the city. Clearly, community control became a meaningless concept in such a diverse district.[11]

David Rogers found that in these diverse districts, and in others where political squabbles between the elected board and the superintendent paralyzed policymaking, individual school principals were left to their own devices, and many of them thrived on the experience. Free of interference from above, the more creative principals consulted with their teachers and parents and experimented with innovative curriculum plans. Rogers concluded, somewhat reluctantly, "Ultimately, it might well be desirable to push decentralization down to the local school level."[12]

No other urban school system granted as much power as New York did to smaller, local school districts, though a few big cities such as Detroit, Cleveland, and Washington, D.C., did decentralize to some extent. Detroit, which divided its school system into eight subdistricts with elected subdistrict councils, actually declared the experiment a failure and recentralized its school system in 1982.[13] Many educators, however, heeded the implied lesson of the New York experiment by trying to increase parent participation at the level of the individual school. In doing so, they were following the dictum popularized by philosopher E. F. Schumacher, "Small is beautiful."

Reasoning that parents would be more likely to identify with the neighborhood schoolhouse than the largely mythical natural communities of big cities, school authorities in some states encouraged the formation of parent advisory councils with limited authority to examine school budgets, interview principal candidates, and initiate a planning process for school improvement. Specialized federal education programs, such as Title I compensatory education and bilingual maintenance, often required that parent councils be organized before funds would be distributed. Avoiding the loaded terms *community control* and *decentralization*, which had fallen into disfavor after the turmoil in New York, educators began calling for school-based management or school-site management or local school development.[14]

The states of Florida, South Carolina, and California adopted the most comprehensive programs for moving educational planning and administration down to the individual school level. California, as the largest state in the union, probably enjoyed the most influence on educators elsewhere.

The California state legislature passed a school improvement program in 1978 authorizing grants of $140 per pupil to school districts that chose to participate. In order to qualify for the grants, school districts had to organize school-site councils composed of equal numbers of parents and school employees. These bodies were not merely advisory. They enjoyed final authority to decide how the new school grants would be spent. For example, one school might choose to buy more books for the library, another might hire a special education teacher, yet another might invest the money for a rainy day. The school-site councils in California, however, were not authorized to make any personnel decisions, so they could not hire and fire teachers or principals.[15]

The Catholic School Model

Chicago educators looking for successful models of decentralized school management didn't need to look as far afield as the East or West coasts. They could find a prime example right under their noses in the parochial schools run by the Catholic Archdiocese of Chicago.

Catholics in Chicago made a firm commitment to a separate system of religious schools in the nineteenth century and by 1930, 93 percent of the city's Catholic parishes conducted a parochial school. Even in the suburbs, 89 percent of the parishes had a school. This extensive system of Catholic elementary schools reached its peak in the 1960s when it enrolled over three hundred thousand students, roughly two-thirds of all the Catholic school-age children in the area. The burgeoning enrollment made the schools of the Chicago Archdiocese the third-largest school system in the country, behind only the public schools of New York and Chicago.[16]

Though the numbers of Catholic schoolchildren have fallen drastically since the Second Vatican Council, Chicago's parochial schools still comprise the seventh-largest school system in the nation. In the 1987-88 school year, private schools enrolled about 23 percent of the city's elementary and secondary students; 87 percent of these (98,792 students) attended Catholic schools.[17]

Calling these Catholic schools a *system*, however, is a serious misnomer. The schools were and are, in the literal sense, parochial, that is, paid for and operated by a local Catholic parish. The pastors hired the teaching sisters, negotiated their salaries, provided them with a convent, and built and maintained the school buildings; the sisters decided what to teach and what textbooks to use. Theoretically, the bishop enjoyed complete authority over Catholic education, but, in fact, he exercised very little control. As the historian of Catholic education in Chicago has put it, "More uniformity in textbooks, curriculum, and methods of instruction existed among the schools of a single religious order, even when spread over the entire country, than among the schools of different parishes within Chicago."[18]

Cardinal George Mundelein, a vigorous centralizer, attempted to change this early in the twentieth century. Mundelein created a board of supervisors for parish schools (a rudimentary Catholic board of education), sent priests to Catholic University in Washington for studies in educational administration, and appointed a professionally trained superintendent of Catholic schools. Chicago's Catholic cardinal, however, discovered that he could not carry centralization of the schools very far. One of his professionally trained priest-superintendents turned out to be a tactless efficiency expert who bothered the sisters with long statistical reports and trod on the toes of powerful pastors. Mundelein eventually removed this individual and instead of replacing him with another professional, he appointed a gregarious Irish priest, Father Daniel Cunningham, who had been the cardinal's occasional golfing partner. Belatedly,

Mundelein understood that the post of superintendent in a decentralized system required a politician with the gift of gab, not an expert with a slide rule. Cunningham remained in office for over 20 years, and his successor, Monsignor William McManus, though professionally educated, retained Cunningham's light touch.[19]

For the rest of the twentieth century, Catholic schools in Chicago have remained decentralized, despite a few features of centralized direction. The local parish still funds the school (though in recent years poorer parishes have received some archdiocesan subsidies), the school principal is still the educational leader (though the Catholic school board issues guidelines and lists of suggested textbooks), and parents and parishioners retain ultimate authority through their control of the collection basket. Since the Second Vatican Council, local parents' groups have begun to exercise more influence over parish schools, often even hiring the principal.

The Catholic school model was not limited in its applicability to any particular time period, ethnic group, or social class. Pastors in the inner city, such as the nationally famous Rev. George Clements of Holy Angels parish, have successfully applied it in black communities. Indeed, Holy Angels School, though it is located in one of Chicago's poorest neighborhoods and charges a substantial tuition, still draws the largest enrollment of any black Catholic school in the country due to its proven record of educational achievement. Altogether, in 1987-88, the Chicago Archdiocese sponsored 135 schools in minority neighborhoods. Over 80 percent of the 42,000 students in these schools were black, Latino, or Asian, and more than 40 percent were not Catholic.[20]

In the early 1980s, University of Chicago sociologist James S. Coleman rocked the educational establishment with a study comparing public schools to Catholic and other private schools. Coleman and his associates found clear evidence of higher student achievement in Catholic schools, even when they applied statistical controls for family background and economic status.

In fact, the Coleman study concluded, provocatively, "Altogether, the evidence is strong that the Catholic schools function much closer to the American ideal of the 'common school', educating children from different backgrounds alike, than do the public schools." The greater discipline and higher academic demands of Catholic schools seemed to make the difference for inner-city children who may have been poor but who harbored high aspirations.[21]

In Chicago, many observers noted that the Catholic Archdiocese conducts successful schools with a much smaller bureaucracy than the public schools and at a fraction of the per-pupil cost. Joe Cappo, a columnist for *Crain's Chicago Business*, remarked half-jokingly that the state should throw Chicago's public schools into receivership and appoint the Catholic Archdiocese as receiver. After pointing out that the public schools employed about 4,500 administrators, Cappo remarked, "The Catholic school central office has a total of 32 professionals plus about 10 clerical workers. This is not a typo."[22]

False Starts in Chicago

An educational study in 1975 concluded that "of all the large cities...Chicago appears to rank lowest in decentralization." Superintendent Benjamin Willis had established district superintendents' education councils in 1965 to defuse civil rights agitation by providing an illusion of consultation. His successor, James Redmond, reorganized the central bureaucracy and created three area associate superintendents to take charge of the north, south, and west sides. He also mandated local school councils at each school in December 1970. The efforts at administrative reorganization simply amounted to shuffling boxes on an organization chart, and the local school councils enjoyed no power.

Chicago civil rights leaders never mounted a strong push for meaningful community control in the sixties, because the long struggle to remove Ben Willis absorbed nearly all their energies and organizational abilities. Mayor Daley responded to occasional protests against specific abuses in the system by removing an offending principal and creating more illusory advisory bodies. In short, the struggle against Ben Willis exhausted civil rights leaders in the 1960s, Superintendent Redmond lulled them to sleep with reorganizations, and Mayor Daley co-opted them.[23]

More than a decade later, a black state legislator from Chicago's west side, Representative Douglas Huff, finally raised a call for community control and decentralization of the city's schools. A flamboyant and somewhat erratic individual, Huff was largely unschooled himself. Yet he felt deeply that the poor kids in his district deserved a better chance than they were getting in the public schools, and he remembered the community control controversy from his days as an activist in the sixties. The legislative leadership didn't take Huff's initiative too seriously, but they saw no harm in voting him a token appropriation for a study.

Huff hired Michael Bakalis, then a professor at Northwestern, to direct the Chicago Community Schools Study Commission. Bakalis conducted hearings throughout the city, then wrote a report recommending that the Chicago school system be decentralized into 20 autonomous school districts. Huff released the report in March 1983, and Bakalis hired the Jasculca/Terman public relations firm to publicize it. The legislature ignored the study, but from 1983 one legislator or another introduced a decentralization bill in each session of the General Assembly, only to see it die in committee. Newspaper editorialists still considered decentralization a black issue, just as it had been in the 1960s, and dismissed it with the glib comment, "Politics and education don't mix well, as Chicago history clearly shows."[24]

Designs for Change pushed the next decentralization initiative in the legislature, this one patterned after the California school improvement program. The 1985 dropout study, "The Bottom Line," included a brief recommendation for school-site management on the California model. Representative Al Ronan, a Democratic stalwart from Chicago's northwest side, approached Don Moore and said he'd like to sponsor a bill authorizing school improvement councils. Representative Carol Moseley Braun, Mayor Washington's floor leader in the lower house, had been thinking along the same lines after a high school principal in her district refused permission to hold a parents' meeting on school property. Designs for Change hired an experienced lobbyist who worked with Ronan and Braun and recruited Senator William Marovitz as a cosponsor of the Urban School Improvement Act. The bill passed out of committee, but the teachers' union lobbyists then weighed in and the legislature amended the bill so that it was barely recognizable. Instead of local school councils, the revised bill called for school councils based in the 20 school subdistricts of the city. All provisions for funding the process were deleted. The legislative hatchet work was so sloppy, however, that some of the bill's original language survived, and the provisions for local school councils were incorporated in the omnibus school reform bill moving toward passage at the same time.[25]

The resulting school improvement program, mandated in part by the Urban School Improvement Act and in part by the omnibus bill, was poorly drafted and very confusing. It provided that "each school building...shall have a local school improvement council composed of teachers, community residents, and parents of students." It further required that each local school improvement council (LSIC) elect one representative to a subdistrict advisory council. At least 70 percent of all subdistrict council members had to be parents of students currently enrolled. Finally, the legislation allowed all citizens of a school's attendance district to attend an annual meeting in the spring of the year to vote on the principal's discretionary budget for the school. The citizens could disapprove a budget and send it back to the principal for revision and resubmission at a second meeting. The principal had to explain his revisions, or lack of same, at the second meeting, but he or she was not obliged to heed the citizens' suggestions and no vote would be taken at the second meeting.[26]

The General Assembly passed this curious piece of legislation, not out of any passion for decentralization, but as part of a political compromise. White suburban and downstate legislators had introduced a bill requiring an elective Chicago Board of Education. Since the mayor of Chicago currently enjoyed the power to appoint school board members, black legislators and most other Democratic leaders from the city wanted to protect Harold Washington's authority and derail the elective school board bill. In the end-of-session horsetrading, the weak provisions for local school councils and budget approval meetings survived as token responses to the movement for greater citizen participation.

In responding to the local school improvement program, Manford Byrd committed his first major mistake as superintendent. Instead of greeting the movement for citizen participation with at least a token gesture of concern, as the legislators did, he ignored it. Designs for Change, which had been training parents to take advantage of an opportunity like this, pressed Byrd and the school administration to draw up regulations and procedures for implementing the Urban School Improvement Act, but they ran into a stone wall. The state board of education refused to intervene, for nothing in the legislation explicitly mandated them to do so. The local school improvement councils, therefore, never performed their main function of drawing up education improvement plans.[27]

The Chicago Board of Education did implement the citizens' budget approval hearings, though only halfheartedly. On Tuesday and Wednesday, March 4 and 5, 1986, a sprinkling of parents, reporters, and curious onlookers filed into the 549 school buildings in the city to hear principals give budget presentations. A school board spokesman emphasized beforehand, however, that 90 percent of the budget at every school was carved in stone by union wage agreements, state mandates, and federal court orders. The bemused citizens, therefore, listened politely, argued over a few points, then approved the budgets in 89.7 percent of the schools. Even some principals admitted that the procedure was ridiculous. One commented, "We can decide if the band needs oboes or saxophones and if we need calculators or computers. It's a farce, it's a sham...."[28]

The turnout for these citizens' meetings was the subject of much debate and analysis. The *Chicago Tribune* conducted a phone survey of 29 schools on the night of March 4 and reported that attendance ranged from a low of 3 to a high of 46. Their coverage emphasized the sparseness of the turnout. The *Sun-Times*, on the other hand, quoted Fred Hess from the Chicago Panel on Public School Policy and Finance, a civic watchdog group, who estimated that the relatively low attendance at each school still totaled almost 12,000 citizens citywide. "We had more people involved in budget discussions at one time than have ever been involved in the history of the country," Hess avowed. The size of the turnout, therefore, depended on the analyst's point of view.[29]

None of this mattered, however, for the school administrators refused to make any changes at all in their budgets. As Carol Moseley Braun has remarked, "The bureaucracy stood in the schoolhouse door." The second round of meetings was conducted dutifully on April 2 and 3 at the 66 schools where citizens had voted down the original budget, but not an iota was changed in response to the public criticisms. Under the law, there was nothing the citizens could do about it. Fred Hess remarked, in a wry understatement, "This was not exactly a good-faith effort."[30]

Though no one realized it at the time, these citizens' budget meetings marked an important threshold. Had Byrd made a few concessions and rearranged a few budget lines in some high-profile schools, he might well have deflected the growing public disenchantment with his administration. Instead he repeated the same charade in the spring of 1987, holding budget hearings at each school but not changing any of the details when citizens objected. Byrd confided to a legislative oversight committee, which was assessing the effectiveness of the 1985 omnibus school bill, that the annual budget hearings had failed to achieve their main purpose of giving citizens a voice in budgetary matters. He blandly refused, however, to recommend that the law be repealed because the budget hearings "are extremely useful as a forum for sharing information and answering questions."[31] It would be hard to find a clearer example of professional arrogance.

The Urban School Improvement Act fiasco led to some important consequences. First of all, it familiarized key legislators with the concept of school-based management. Carol Moseley Braun and William Marovitz, for example, would later sponsor the 1988 School Reform Act based on the C.U.R.E. plan. Furthermore, it convinced Don Moore, Mike Bakalis, and other reformers that only a radical measure granting real power to parents' councils would work. In 1986 and 1987, after assessing the failure of the local school improvement plan, Designs for Change decided not to press further for its implementation and to shift attention to developing the C.U.R.E. proposal instead.

They were not alone in their assessment. At the end of 1986, the national education magazine, *Phi Delta Kappan*, published an article by James W. Guthrie, the author of a leading textbook in educational administration. Guthrie stated flatly, "The time is ripe to implement school-based management. In fact, without such a step, the education reform movement seems likely to lose its momentum."[32] Most Chicagoans, including Manford Byrd, didn't know it yet, but, in year five of the education reform movement (counting from the publication of "A Nation at Risk" in April 1983), the city's schools were poised for a plunge into school-based management.

Notes

1. Samuel P. Hays has provided an insightful framework for understanding these long-term political trends in his seminal article, "The Changing Political Structure of the City in Industrial America," *Journal of Urban History* 1 (November 1974): 6-38. Joseph M. Cronin, *The Control of Urban Schools: Perspective on the Power of Educational Reformers* (New York: The Free Press, 1973), traces these political trends through the history of education in the United States.

2. Diane Ravitch, *The Great School Wars: New York City, 1805-1973* (New York: Basic Books, 1974), xiv.

3. Diane Ravitch, Ibid., provides the fullest historical account of the New York community control controversy. See pp. 292-311 for the story of IS 201. Briefer accounts are presented by Mario Fantini and Marilyn Gittell, *Decentralization: Achieving Reform* (New York: Prager Publishers, 1973), and by David Rogers and Norman H. Chung, *110 Livingston Street Revisited: Decentralization in Action* (New York: New York University Press, 1983). The *New York Times* included a brief historical overview in its series "Decentralization: New York's Schools a Decade Later," 24 June 1980, 1.

4. Mayor's Advisory Panel on Decentralization of New York City Schools, *Reconnection for Learning: A Community School System for New York City,* (1967)—usually referred to as the Bundy Report.

5. Ravitch, *Great School Wars,* 352-77.

6. Ibid., 381-87.

7. Ibid., 388-98; *New York Times,* 26 June 1980, 1.

8. The series appeared on the front page of the *New York Times* every day from 24 June to 28 June 1980, inclusive. The quote from Kenneth Clark appeared on 24 June.

9. Rogers and Chung, *110 Livingston Street Revisited,* xvi.

10. Ibid., 214.

11. Ibid., 174-94.

12. Ibid., 212-13.

13. The educational quarterly, *Education and Urban Society,* published a special issue in August 1975 devoted to "Perspectives on the Decentralization of Urban School Districts." At the height of the reform movement in Chicago, Renee Montoya of Designs for Change prepared a graceful, concise four-page memo outlining previous decentralization plans for the information of Illinois state legislators: Renee Montoya to Senators del Valle, Kustra, and Marovitz, and Representatives Braun and Ronan, 13 May 1988, C.U.R.E.-SON/SOC papers.

14. There are no good histories or case studies of this recent educational movement. C. L. Marburger, *One School at a Time* (Columbia, Md.: National Committee for Citizens in Education, 1985) is probably the best introduction for a general audience. John Greenhalgh, *Schoolsite Budgeting: Decentralized School Management* (Lanham, Md.: University Press of America, 1984) is a technical treatise for administrators.

15. Don Davies, "Citizen Participation in Decision Making in the Schools," in *Communities and Their Schools,* ed. Don Davies (New York: McGraw Hill, 1981), 83-119; *New York Times,* 28 June 1980, 1. Paul

Berman and Tom Gjelten, *Improving School Improvement: An Independent Evaluation of the California School Improvement Program*, Vol. 2, *Findings* (Berkeley, Calif.: Berman, Weiler Associates), 1983.

16. James W. Sanders, *The Education of an Urban Minority: Catholics in Chicago, 1833-1965* (New York: Oxford University Press, 1977), 4-11.

17. Ed Marciniak, "Chicago's Private Elementary and Secondary Schools: Enrollment Trends," (Loyola University of Chicago, Institute of Urban Life, 1990), 5-9.

18. Sanders, *Education of an Urban Minority*, 145.

19. Edward R. Kantowicz, *Corporation Sole: Cardinal Mundelein and Chicago Catholicism* (Notre Dame, Ind.: University of Notre Dame Press, 1983), 12, 14-15, 85-87.

20. Marciniak, "Chicago's Private Schools," 12.

21. James S. Coleman, Thomas Hoffer, and Sally Kilgore, *High School Achievement: Public, Catholic, and Private Schools Compared* (New York: Basic Books, 1982). See, especially, chapters 6 and 7. The quotation is on p. 177.

22. Joe Cappo, "Public Schools Need Catholic Knuckle Rap," *Crain's Chicago Business,* 7 September 1987, 6; Cappo repeated the basic point, with variations, in his columns of 21 September 1987 and 29 February 1988.

23. James G. Cibulka, "School Decentralization in Chicago," *Education and Urban Society* 7 (August 1975): 412-38.

24. Michael Bakalis, interview by authors, 13 July 1990; *Chicago Tribune,* 10 March 1983, sec. 2, p. 3; 23 March 1985, 10.

25. Don Moore, interview by authors, 1 August 1990; Carol Moseley Braun, interview by authors, 5 February 1991.

26. PA 84-126, sec. 34-18a and 18b.

27. Moore interview.

28. *Chicago Tribune,* 7 March 1986, sec. 2, p. 2.

29. *Chicago Tribune,* 5 March 1986, sec. 2, p. 1; 7 March 1986, sec. 2, p. 2; *Chicago Sun-Times,* 5 March 1986, 6; 7 March 1986, 16.

30. *Chicago Tribune,* 6 April 1986, sec. 3, p. 1; *Chicago Sun-Times,* 4 April 1986, 23; Braun interview.

31. *Chicago Tribune,* 31 March 1987, sec. 2, p. 2.

32. James W. Guthrie, "School-Based Management: The Next Needed Education Reform," *Phi Delta Kappan,* (December 1986): 305-9.

The Crisis

The two-year calm enveloping Chicago school politics ended with a crash in the fall of 1987. The Chicago Teachers Union and the 20 other unions representing public school employees walked out on strike September 8 and stayed out for a record-breaking 19 days. For the first time in the city's history, the entire month of September passed without a single day of teaching in a public school classroom.

The strike came as no surprise to anyone despite the deceptive calm of the previous two years. The teachers had already struck eight times in 16 years (1969, 1971, 1973, 1975, 1980, 1983, 1984, and 1985) for a combined total of 66 days. Governor Thompson had swiftly settled the last strike in 1985 by advancing emergency state aid, and in 1987 he proposed a massive increase in the state income tax to provide two hundred million dollars more for education funding. The governor warned, however, that if the General Assembly adjourned without passing his tax package there would "very likely" be a teachers' strike in Chicago.[1]

The Democrats who controlled the state legislature felt betrayed by Thompson's turnabout on taxes. In his reelection campaign the previous year, the Republican incumbent had repeatedly denied any need for new revenues, but once safely embarked on a fourth term, he swiftly proposed a $1.6 billion increase. Democratic leaders Michael Madigan in the house and Phil Rock in the senate blocked the governor's tax increase. As a result, Thompson slashed over one hundred million dollars from the proposed education budget, threatening the existence of the year-old Math and Science Academy in Aurora and conjuring up the specter of a school strike in Chicago.[2]

Yet a strike was not inevitable. When the board of education met in July to consider the next year's budget, Fred Hess, director of the Chicago Panel on Public School Policy and Finance, testified that the school system could afford to offer the teachers a 3.5 percent pay raise for the coming year. The Chicago Panel (also known as CHIPS) had been organized by a number of civic groups in the wake of the school board's 1979 financial crisis to provide impartial budget analysis, and over the years it had proven itself a reliable watchdog agency with credible numbers. Yet the board of education ignored the panel's testimony in July 1987 and voted instead to reduce the school year by three days, resulting effectively in a 1.7 percent pay cut for the teachers. This decision made the strike a near certainty.[3]

School reformers have likened the 1987 teachers' strike and its aftermath to the fall of the Berlin Wall and the sweeping away of Communist regimes in Eastern Europe two years later. Michael Bakalis, the founder of C.U.R.E., has remarked retrospectively that the reforms emerging from the school strike resembled *perestroika* in the Soviet Union and Eastern Europe. In both cases, an entrenched bureaucracy was overthrown in favor of local democracy. Even at the time the comparison was obvious; in the midst of the 1987 strike, Donald S. Perkins, chairman of the Jewel grocery chain wrote:

> The Chicago public school system has not worked for the same reason the Soviet economy has not worked. The initiative and creativity of potentially responsible managers at the local level are stifled by a bureaucracy whose interest in the perpetuation of the system typically outranks its interest in the needs of the people being served.[4]

Some observers believe that Superintendent Byrd and the board of education provoked the 1987 strike in an attempt to break the teachers' union. They may have believed that the wave of strikes over the past two decades had so eroded support for the teachers that they could break their union the way President Reagan had broken the air traffic controllers' union. Certainly the board showed a marked intransigence. Superintendent Byrd, Board President Frank Gardner, and influential board member Clark Burrus all told reporters on September 3 they were ready to accept a long strike rather than give in on the proposed pay cuts.[5]

The education bureaucrats miscalculated. Rather than breaking the union, they precipitated a crisis that threatened to sweep them away. Mike Bakalis testified to a legislative committee that "a kid who was a senior in high school, from the day that kid was born the Chicago public schools have been on strike every other year of his life."[6] After the 1987 strike, the public decided they had finally had enough.

The 1987 Teachers' Strike

When the teachers' contract expired at the end of August, the Chicago Teachers' Union (CTU) countered the school board's proposed pay cut with a demand for a 10 percent raise in the first year of a new contract followed by a 5 percent raise the second year. CTU President Jacqueline Vaughn made it clear that she would not settle until she had attained three goals: a multiyear contract, a pay raise, and some reduction in class size. In a strike vote on Friday, September 4, union members chose to walk out by a margin of 4,437 to 438. This 10-to-1 majority is not quite so impressive as it looks, however, for nearly 24,000 teacher-unionists did not vote. As in most previous strikes, the union rank and file simply went along with their militant leaders.[7]

The walkout began on Tuesday, September 8, which had been scheduled as a teacher preparation day. Negotiations between the school board and the union representatives broke off just before midnight that night, so no students showed up for school on Wednesday the 9th. Both metropolitan newspapers expressed their usual outrage at the biennial fall strike. The *Tribune* editors blamed the teachers' union for making "unrealistic salary demands." The *Sun-Times* simply screeched, in a front-page editorial, "Chicago's dismal rite of fall must end....For God's sake, wake up!" Both sides, however, dug in for a long confrontation. No significant talks were held during the first week of the strike. Both the governor and the mayor indicated they lacked financial resources to hasten a settlement. Governor Thompson took off for a two-week trade mission to Europe, and Mayor Washington continued his hands-off policy towards the schools.[8]

The school strike posed a terrible dilemma for Chicago's newly ascendant black politicians. For the first time in the city's history, all the major players in the schools drama—the superintendent, the board president, and the CTU president—were black. This made it difficult for the black mayor and his followers to take sides. Both the central bureaucracy at its Pershing Road headquarters and the teaching staff in the classroom employed significant numbers of middle-class, black professionals who were enjoying good-paying jobs for the first time in their lives. Harold Washington could not afford to alienate this emerging black bourgeoisie that had always been his most reliable voting constituency. On the other hand, the great majority of the strike's victims, the students who were left idle outside the classroom, were either black or Latino.

Washington and the main-line black organizations, such as Jesse Jackson's Operation PUSH, Leon Finney's Woodlawn Organization (TWO), and Nancy Jefferson's Midwest Community Council, remained relatively quiet and uninvolved for the first 10 days or so of the strike. Yet some black leaders close to the mayor had already begun to mobilize damage control. In late August, as the strike loomed, Benjamin Kendrick, the director of Marcy-Newberry social service center on the near west side, met with Washington's commissioner of human services, Judith Walker, to plan Freedom Schools as alternative learning programs during the strike. When the teachers walked out, Kendrick and others opened about three or four hundred Freedom Schools in community centers, church basements, park fieldhouses, and even in private homes. Walker's city department furnished free lunches to students at most of these locations.[9]

At the same time, grassroots black and Latino leaders were mobilizing parents to pressure the warring board and union for a settlement. Sokoni Karanja, a scholarly activist who had organized a series of service centers on the South Side called Centers for New Horizons, and Tomas Sanabria, the Puerto Rican leader of Network for Youth Services, took the lead in forging a poor peoples' coalition of outrage. Coretta McFerren, with a charismatic presence and a commanding voice, emerged as the leading spokesperson for this coalition, which was as yet unnamed.[10]

About a thousand poor parents turned out for a demonstration at the board's Pershing Road headquarters on the first Friday of the strike, September 11. A slightly larger crowd, estimated at 1,500, returned the following Friday, September 18, and Coretta McFerren warned that parents and children might soon camp outside the board offices if the strike continued much longer. That same day, a largely white parents' group from the north side rallied in the Daley Center plaza downtown.[11]

This provided sufficient pressure for Mayor Washington to break his silence. On Wednesday, September 16, he urged the board and the union to resume round-the-clock negotiations. Then on Saturday, after the dramatic demonstrations the day before, the mayor appeared personally at board headquarters, pleading for an end to the stalemate. Previous mayors had always called the contending parties into his or her city hall office and knocked heads together until a settlement was reached, no matter how costly. Washington had pledged not to force a budget-breaking contract and he kept his vow. Without any financial leverage, however, he could only beg for an agreement, not order one.[12]

The teachers reduced their salary demands only slightly during this first flurry of bargaining talks, so the strike dragged on into a third and then a fourth week. The school board began furnishing some alternative services of its own as the reality of an extended walkout sank in. On Tuesday, September 22,

Manford Byrd announced that 20 schools throughout the city would offer free hot lunches to grade school students from poor families. On ordinary school days 276,000 students received free lunches at school and for many this was the only nourishing hot meal they ate during the day. For them, a school strike meant not only an educational crisis but a nutritional crisis as well. The lunch program started slowly, serving only 582 meals on the 22nd, but more and more children showed up during the week so that the schools served about 1,500 meals on Friday the 25th. In addition, Judith Walker's human services department provided at least 11,000 lunches at numerous other sites.[13]

On Friday, September 25, the school board also opened six counselling centers for high school seniors who needed to take college entrance exams and begin preparing college applications. The following week, health workers offered immunizations and physical examinations to students at three school sites. The *Tribune* noted drily, "Schools [are] open for almost anything, except classes." The teachers' union denounced all these activities as strike-breaking efforts. Yet, when the strike reached its 16th day, on Tuesday, September 29, breaking the previous record for the longest teachers' strike in Chicago, there was still no end in sight.[14]

As September turned into October, however, parent and community pressure finally forced a settlement. Sokoni Karanja and Coretta McFerren's black parents' group on the south side had coalesced with Sanabria's Latinos and a group of white parents, mainly from the magnet schools on the north side, and had begun calling themselves the Peoples' Coalition for Educational Reform. The coalition turned out the largest demonstration yet at the downtown State of Illinois Building on Friday, October 2. Working on a parallel course, Leon Finney from TWO stepped forward as the main spokesman for the older black protest organizations, demanding that the school board offer the teachers a raise and settle the strike. With the implicit support of the marching parents behind him, Finney threatened that if a settlement wasn't reached by the following Monday his coalition of community groups would take over and open the schools.[15]

Leon Finney, Nancy Jefferson, and other leaders who demanded an end to the strike were acting as surrogates for Harold Washington, for the mayor had not been as uninvolved as he seemed. Behind the scenes, Washington and his staff kept in touch with both sides in the dispute and encouraged the community groups to apply pressure. During the final week of the strike the mayor began intensive talks with Robert Healey, who had been Jackie Vaughn's predecessor at the teachers' union before he ascended to the presidency of the Chicago Federation of Labor. As head of all organized labor in Chicago, Healey had to consider the interests of the many craft unions that went out on strike along with the teachers, as well as the image of labor in general. So he urged Vaughn to show some flexibility. Finally, on Thursday, October 1, Harold Washington and two aides, Ernest Barefield and Jackie Grimshaw, spent the entire night at the mayor's Hyde Park apartment talking to Vaughn, Healey, and Board President Frank Gardner on the phone. Harold grabbed a few hours sleep about 3 A.M., but Grimshaw and Barefield worked the phones all night, then went down to the board of education offices the next day and stayed until the strike was settled.[16]

On Saturday, October 3, the school board and the union reached a tentative agreement. The board offered the teachers a two-year contract with a 4 percent raise in each year. Fifteen of the 19 strike days would be made up by extending the school year to the end of June. The four missing strike days, however, reduced the value of the first year's 4 percent raise to a net increase of only 1.8 percent. In order to appease Jackie Vaughn's demand for reduction in class size, the board offered some token reductions in the 36 most overcrowded schools. The cost of the settlement package would have to be financed mainly by layoffs.[17]

The CTU's house of delegates approved the strike settlement on Sunday, October 4 by a 563-to-95 vote. The strike officially ended when teachers returned to their classrooms on Monday the 5th, but students did not report to school until Tuesday the 6th. Two weeks later, on Friday, October 16, the rank-and-file teachers ratified the contract by a narrow 3-to-2 margin (13,320 to 9,058).[18]

Despite the strike's termination, the Peoples' Coalition did not ease up its pressure. Tomas Sanabria, recalling the Latino march to Clemente High School, had planned to forge a human chain across the Loop with parents linking arms between the State of Illinois Building and the Federal Office Building, while organizers carried a coffin symbolizing the death of education in Chicago. Sanabria exhorted the coalition to go ahead with the march so they could ride the crest of the wave before it lost momentum. They marched on Thursday, October 8, calling for thorough reform of the system and protesting the board's plan to pay for the strike by laying off teachers with low seniority. They only made it half-way across the Loop, from Clark and Randolph to Clark and Monroe, but the "funeral procession," whose coffin represented "all the reports calling for changes and reforms in the Chicago public schools that have been buried," kicked off the post-strike movement to restructure the school system.[19]

Responsibility for Chicago's longest teachers' strike could be debated endlessly. Republicans blamed the Democratic legislators, and Speaker Mike Madigan in particular, for blocking the governor's proposed tax increase that would have ensured adequate education funding. Democrats, however, felt justifiably double-crossed by Governor Thompson who campaigned against taxes in 1986 then hypocritically proposed a large tax increase in 1987. They believed Thompson's bad faith justified killing the raise in income taxes. The teachers certainly demanded a larger pay raise than could realistically be expected, but in previous years, someone had always found the money, so they may be excused for believing it could happen again. Finally, the school board and the superintendent misjudged the tolerance of the public for their tough, hold-the-line policy on pay increases.

However murky the causes of the strike, its results were clear: a deep sense of frustration on the part of the public and a firm resolve by the press and politicians that the city's schools should not return to business as usual.

In the very first week of the strike, Senate President Phil Rock suggested "that schoolchildren may be better served by the kind of system former state schools superintendent Michael Bakalis is proposing." On the first Sunday after the walkout began, the education writers for the *Sun-Times* concluded that the strike was "likely to anger state lawmakers so much that they may finally act on a proposal that has been percolating in Springfield for 10 years: decentralizing the giant Chicago public school system." As the strike dragged on, voices became more shrill. Casey Banas, who had covered every teachers' strike for the *Tribune*, proposed that all 11 members of the board of education be fired, the superintendent dismissed, the teachers locked out, and the schools remain closed all year if necessary to bring about a thorough restructuring. When the strike finally ended, Linda Lenz, Banas's counterpart at the *Sun-Times*, concluded:

> A record four-week strike didn't produce much for Chicago public school teachers this year. But it likely will pay major dividends for the system in the future. It electrified community leaders, whose attention had strayed from the schools, and it thrust education to the top of the mayor's agenda.[20]

Mayor Washington Scales the Summit

Harold Washington had seemed rather slow of foot during the teachers' strike, probably intentionally so. With no financial rabbits to pull out of his hat, he stayed off stage. Activists and community leaders did not want to embarrass the city's first black mayor, so they took a long time building up pressure, but finally, angry parents took matters in their own hands and the mayor helped force a solution behind the scenes.

In the aftermath of the strike, Mayor Washington sensed political opportunity as well as political danger. At the same time that he announced the strike settlement, he also promised to lead a campaign for sweeping reform of the public schools. In fact, Washington required both the board of education and the teachers' union to sign an agreement that they would actively pursue school reform as part of the settlement. On Sunday, October 4 he granted a long, exclusive interview to the *Tribune*'s Casey Banas in his Hyde Park apartment overlooking the lake. Washington confided to Banas that "the public school system has no effective political power base because almost none of the 'movers and shakers' in local and state government attended public schools." Therefore he intended to build a power base for them by convoking a parent/community council (PCC). Rather than let groups like the Peoples' Coalition disband or else start sniping at him, Washington intended to harness their energy into a restructuring of the system. When Banas asked the mayor what he had learned during the strike, he answered, "We have learned in order to run a system, you've got to have the constant oversight of the parents, the citizens, the concerned people."[21]

A few days later, the mayor's office announced a summit conference of business, civic, and community leaders to be held on the campus of the University of Illinois at Chicago the following Sunday, October 11, at 3:00 in the afternoon. Before making the announcement, the mayor had met with the entire Chicago delegation of the state legislature, including Senate President Rock and House Speaker Madigan. He asked them to derail any hasty school legislation in Springfield and thus give his summit conference time to produce a well-thought-out reform plan. The Democratic lawmakers agreed to give him until March.[22]

The education rally was a political masterstroke by Harold Washington, capitalizing on a moment of anger and outrage in the city, but some of the groundwork for it had been laid before the teachers' strike. The mayor had actually assembled an education summit more than a year previously, in an attempt to build a credible education record for his 1987 reelection campaign and set the tone for his second term.

In the summer of 1986, with the Council Wars stalemate finally broken and the reelection campaign looming, Washington asked his chief policy advisor, Harold Baron, to reexamine all the campaign promises and issues of the 1983 election. Baron had prepared Harold's issues papers, not only in the 1983 campaign but also in the abortive first try for the mayoralty in 1977. He has been involved with education issues since the 1960s, when he was research director of the Urban League. Recalling that period in his life, Baron said: "Every morning I would wake up and I knew exactly what I had to do: Get Ben Willis out of Chicago." Now, twenty years later, Baron's staff discovered that education was still a disaster area in the city, so they prepared a long laundry list of possible remedial actions. Washington took one look at the list and told them to come up with something simpler and more focused for him to campaign on. Baron finally recommended that the mayor gather together top business and civic leaders and forge a partnership between business and the public schools.[23]

The Boston Compact served as a model. In the early 1980s, with the economy of the Boston area booming in the so-called Massachusetts miracle, black public school students were being left behind, uneducated and unemployable. So business leaders in the Massachusetts capital formed a learn-earn partnership with the school system. They guaranteed a job for any graduate of a public high school if school officials improved test scores and raised the quality of education. Baron traveled to Boston with a group of educators from Chicago in September 1986 and reported that over 2,800 public school graduates had found permanent employment since the compact's inception four years previously.[24]

In Chicago, mayoral task forces continued to gather information during the winter of 1986-87, but Washington remained reluctant to take a high-profile position on education. He had decided at the beginning of his administration that the public schools were a political deathtrap for any mayor, since he had no legal authority over them and did not control their budgets. He reactivated the informal nominating commission for school board appointments that Jane Byrne had allowed to lapse and tried to make strong appointments, but he did not interfere with day-to-day business of the school board and did not make promises about education he could not possibly keep. Yet during the reelection campaign, he encountered barely suppressed rage at the state of the schools and finally decided to take some risks to improve education. As always, Harold Washington proved most decisive when energized by the dynamics of a campaign.[25]

Hal Baron invited the CEOs of six or seven corporations to join civic leaders and top school officials on the mayor's education summit. Barry Sullivan, chairman of First National Bank, offered the use of a large conference room for the sessions. Baron established a firm rule that only heads of organizations could participate and vote, i.e., no deputies, and Mayor Washington set a good example by attending every single session of the summit, not merely in a ceremonial role. Harold loved the give and take of debate and threw himself into the proceedings with gusto. He asked the Reverend Kenneth Smith, the president of Chicago Theological Seminary and a former school board president under Jane Byrne, to serve as cochair of the summit. Rev. Smith, a soft-spoken and pastoral gentleman, was the perfect moderator for the often rancorous summit debates. Yet he had a firm commitment to improving the schools and a clear sense of priorities. While serving on the school board, he once told Mayor Byrne, "I listen only to God, my wife, and the church that pays my salary, in that order." Jane Byrne didn't quite understand what he was saying, but Harold Washington did. When he appointed Rev. Smith as cochair of the summit, Mayor Washington told him that he "wanted education to be the hallmark of his second term."[26]

After preliminary discussions at the summit, the mayor announced that direct negotiations between a team of business leaders and the top educators in the Chicago public school system would begin in June. Peter Willmott, the chairman and CEO of Carson's department stores, led the business negotiators who faced off with Superintendent Manford Byrd and Board President Frank Gardner. A second negotiating team from the Chicago city colleges met with representatives of organizations that dealt with school dropouts to work out plans for alternative education and adult literacy programs. The board of education's learn-earn discussions were considered the main event, but as always, the eternal dropout problem refused to go away.[27]

This first education summit failed during the summer of 1987. The businessmen were leery about granting outright job guarantees, for the city's economy was not so robust as that of Massachusetts and the public schools were even more notoriously poor. They did, however, try to negotiate a phased-in program, pledging to hire one thousand public school graduates each year over the next five years, if the school system would raise standardized test scores up to national norms during the same five-year period. Manford Byrd's counterproposal astounded the businessmen. He asked them to hire six thousand students per year and join him in lobbying the legislature for an additional one hundred million dollars in funding. While he agreed to accept national norms on standardized tests as a goal, he asked the businessmen to hire the designated number of public school graduates anyway even if the schools did not reach the target goals. By the time of the teachers' strike, in September of 1987, the first education summit had dissolved in frustration.[28]

Though organizers expected about five hundred people at the second summit, at the University of Illinois at Chicago on October 11, 1987, nearly one thousand packed the lecture hall. The mayor's staff had invited key politicians, school officials, and activists, but many others just showed up. The *Tribune*'s Banas reported:

It was the most remarkable gathering to focus on the Chicago public schools in at least 25 years. The mayor, aldermen, state legislators, board of education members, the school superintendent, teachers, parents and other concerned citizens were in the same room together for the first time in a town-meeting atmosphere.[29]

The throng gathered on October 11 at the university listened to the mayor deliver a keynote address. "It's going to be a long tough road," he said. "You're going to get tired seeing your mayor talking about education in this city. Can you stand it?" The crowd bellowed out a resounding "Yes," then broke out into smaller groups for further discussion. When they regrouped for a final plenary session, a large number of individuals rose to deliver passionate speeches. Warren Bacon, a black business leader who was the grand old man of Chicago's school wars, having served on the board of education during the civil rights struggles of the 1960s, denounced all policies of incrementalism or step-by-step reform. He called instead for a radical restructuring of school governance. Bernie Noven, a teacher at a north side magnet school, also denounced the system, which took a lot of guts for a school employee. At the end of the session, the mayor announced that he would choose a 50-member parent/community council from among those attending and they would convoke community meetings throughout the city to keep the momentum of reform going.[30]

Having learned from the failed summit of 1986-87, Harold Washington transformed the post-strike summit. The mayor's staff passed out nomination forms to anyone who wanted to serve on the new parent/community council that would be added to the summit. Janice Metzger, a parent from the near northwest side Wicker Park neighborhood, remembers that she almost didn't apply because her cynical friends told her she would need cosigners with clout. She threw her name in anyway and was not only chosen for the council but as one of the cochairs. Hal Baron's staff chose 50 members of the parent/community council, making sure that they represented the ethnic and racial makeup of the school system and came from all geographical areas of the city. What impressed Metzger is that Baron consciously included some "troublemakers" on the council. Mayor Washington signed off on the list without any elaborate background checks, and then met with the chairman, James Deanes, and the three cochairs: Bobbi Cobb, Carlos Heredia, and Jan Metzger. He instructed them to hold community hearings throughout the city and to elect 10 of their members to meet periodically with the businessmen, civic leaders, and school officials on an expanded summit.[31]

The parent protests during the strike, the rally at the university, and the appointment of a parent/community council to work in tandem with business and educational leaders on the summit breathed new life into the process of school reform.

The Bennett Blast

Before the invigorated summit could get itself organized, the city's schools suffered more body blows as the miserable fall of 1987 wound down. The state released the second annual school report cards at the end of October, revealing the usual bad news. Chicago high school students who took the widely used American College Test exams averaged a dismal score of 13.9, compared to a 19.6 score achieved by students in other Illinois school districts. Over half of Chicago's high schools, 33 out of 64, ranked in the very bottom percentile of ACT scores nationwide.[32] Then, in the wake of these depressing revelations, the nation's highest ranking education official came to town and delivered a shot heard 'round the country.

U.S. Secretary of Education William Bennett was a blunt, plain-spoken individual who had already earned himself a reputation as a loose cannon on the deck of the Reagan ship of state. Shortly after his appointment to succeed Terrell Bell, he blasted college students for spending their government grants on stereo systems rather than college texts. He was constantly on the lookout for forums where he could advance the Reagan agenda of reduced education spending and lesser government regulation. So when he scheduled a midwestern trip early in November 1987, his staff arranged for him to attend a meeting of Chicago United, the leading business-civic organization in the city. Warren Bacon, the executive director of Chicago United, was out of the country, but Patrick Keleher, the group's director of public policy, had planned to deliver a slide talk on proposed school reforms to a gathering of business leaders on Friday, November 6. Keleher invited Bennett to sit in.[33]

Bennett had seen the state report cards detailing Chicago's educational failures, so he confided to school officials at a reception the night before the Chicago United meeting that he would likely speak out frankly. George Muñoz, who had stepped down as school board president but still sat on the board, told him to go ahead and tell the truth. The next night, Bennett did not play a major role at the Chicago United meeting, but he did address a few pointed remarks to the assembled business leaders at the end of the session. Among other things, he told them that Chicago needed "the educational equivalent of a Mike Ditka." He then stepped outside the hotel meeting room and delivered a blast to the press.[34]

"Chicago's public schools are the worst in the nation...." Bennett stated bluntly. "You've got close to educational meltdown here." When one reporter quoted some equally dismal statistics from another big-city school system, Bennett dismissed the comparison:

> If it's not the last, I don't know who is. There can't be very many more cities that are worse. Chicago is pretty much it....Supposing you're at the bottom with two others. Should that make you feel better? No, it shouldn't make you feel better.

Another reporter asked what changes the secretary proposed to reform the system. Bennett shot back, "Explode the blob. Slash the educational bureaucracy." He then spoke in favor of experiments in school-based management, such as Keleher was proposing at the Chicago United meeting. Finally revealing his

Reaganite agenda, Bennett concluded that the nation's public schools should establish a tuition voucher system that would allow parents complete freedom of choice in schooling.[35]

Mayor Washington reacted angrily to Bennett's blast. The acrimonious politics of Council Wars early in the mayor's term had prompted national reporters to tag Chicago "Beirut on the Lake," but the city's reputation had recovered of late and the New York bond-rating agencies had recently restored the city's "A" rating. The last thing Chicago needed was a new label, "Worst Schools in the Nation," so Harold slammed back at the education secretary:

> Mr. Bennett has a lot of gall to be criticizing Chicago public schools or any other school system...in light of the fact that he's employed by Ronald Reagan, who has literally dismantled public education in this country... Hell, they helped create the problem.[36]

However painful it may have been to the mayor, the Bennett blast punctuated the citizen outrage unleashed by the teachers' strike. It deepened the sense of educational crisis in Chicago.

The Death of Harold

Shattered by the longest school strike in its history and blasted by an emissary from the nation's capital, the city of Chicago hit rock bottom during Thanksgiving week of 1987. On November 25, the day before the holiday, Mayor Harold Washington slumped over his desk, the victim of a massive heart attack; he was 65 years old. Washington collapsed about 11 A.M. while talking with his press secretary Alton Miller. Just a few minutes before, Rev. Kenneth Smith had buttonholed the mayor in the corridor and reported on an executive committee meeting of the education summit. Harold invited Rev. Smith to come over to his apartment during the Thanksgiving holiday for a fuller discussion. After he collapsed, the mayor was rushed to nearby Northwestern Hospital and was pronounced dead at 1:30

P.M. Everyone knew Washington was a big man, in several senses, but most were surprised when the coroner announced that he weighed 285 pounds, a full 100 pounds over fighting weight for a man of his height.[37]

Harold Washington's death bore an eerie resemblance to the demise of Richard J. Daley, 11 years before. Each of these legendary mayors turned over spadefuls of dirt to inaugurate a new building project on the morning of his death, then died of coronary arrest back at city hall.

The mayor's body lay in state at city hall on Thanksgiving Day while tens of thousands of citizens, both black and white, filed by the casket late into the night. For a man who had ignited such controversy while alive, Harold inspired a lot of tears when he died. Even his worst political enemies admitted that his love for Chicago was genuine and his zest for political battle infectious. Since the day after Thanksgiving was a holiday for many, a great crowd followed the mayor's body to Oakwoods Cemetery on the south side or else watched his funeral on television.

Before the last eulogy was intoned, however, the city's politicians had begun to plot and conspire. During the time of mourning for Washington, the 49th Ward alderman, David Orr, who held the ceremonial post of deputy mayor, presided over the city administration as interim mayor. The Illinois Constitution, however, authorized the city council to choose one of their number to serve out the unexpired term as acting mayor. Black leaders met with Jesse Jackson at O'Hare airport when he hastily returned from a fact-finding mission in the Middle East. On November 30 they transformed a memorial service for Harold Washington into an election rally for the alderman they hoped would become his successor, Timothy Evans from the south side's Fourth Ward.

White politicians, however, were pursuing other angles. Edward Vrdolyak, Harold's old nemesis, had recently switched his party allegiance to the Republicans and thus was out of the running to succeed the mayor. But the "other Eddie," 14th

Ward alderman Edward Burke, led a behind-the-scenes caucus, attempting to build a coalition for a white candidate, but it soon became evident that this was impossible, and perhaps dangerous. "The successor would almost have to be black," Alderman Roman Pucinski warned. "There would be a strong reaction if the city council tried to change the complexion of the mayor's office." The conspirators finally settled on Sixth Ward Alderman Eugene Sawyer.

On the evening of Tuesday, December 1, after a five-day mourning period for Harold Washington had elapsed, the city council convened in special session to choose his successor. Black and Latino leaders mobilized thousands of citizens to pack the galleries and ring the old grey city hall building. Though George Bush, Michael Dukakis, and the other presidential hopefuls were staging one of their early debates that evening, Chicagoans tuned in to the televised proceedings from the council chambers instead. The Nielsen ratings revealed that over 480,000 viewers stayed tuned past midnight. Alderman Orr presided as the Evans supporters, who knew they had insufficient votes to elect their candidate, tried one parliamentary maneuver after another to stall a decision. Alderman Sawyer remained closeted in his office and wavered several times before he was convinced to place his name in nomination. A roll-call vote completed at 4:01 in the morning finally elected Sawyer over Evans by a 29-to-19 margin. A mild-mannered individual who spoke so softly he was swiftly dubbed Mayor Mumbles, Sawyer was no political innocent, but a long-time machine stalwart whose middle-class black ward turned out some of the highest Democratic vote totals in the city.

Twenty-three of Sawyer's supporters were white, only six black. In a piece of political theatre that was surrealistic even by Chicago's standards, the city's second black mayor was chosen by the white remnants of the Daley machine, while more militant black citizens surrounded the building, denouncing the choice.[38]

Many of the school reformers, both black and white, believed that Harold Washington's sudden death actually made their task easier. Harold had breathed new life into the summit with his convocation of the parent/community council, but many saw this primarily as a public relations exercise.

Mike Smith from SON/SOC and Coretta McFerren of the Peoples' Coalition have made this point most bluntly. Smith, who was not a member of the summit, has surmised that Washington would never have allowed significant reform legislation to reduce the power of the school bureaucracy. The status quo at Pershing Road fed the black middle class with both traditional patronage and pinstripe patronage (i.e., contracts), and Washington could not have afforded a direct attack on this. McFerren, who did sit at the summit as one of the delegates from the parent/community council, concluded,"It was a joke. They chose our chair and our cochairs for us. When we came to a meeting everything was arranged....It was never supposed to work."[39]

Insiders who were close to Mayor Washington contribute at least indirect support for this interpretation. Jackie Grimshaw, the mayor's legislative liaison, insists that Harold's concern for education was deep and sincere and that the education summit was not mere window dressing. Yet she adds that Washington was very cautious and would have resisted the "artificial sense of urgency" that built up after the strike. He probably would have opted for a less thoroughgoing plan than the one adopted. Carol Moseley Braun, the mayor's floor leader in the state house of representatives, believes that Washington's main educational concerns were increased funding, the preservation of one district for Chicago, and the retention of his power to appoint the board of education. As long as he could protect these three fundamental positions, he would have been largely neutral on the question of further reforms.[40]

Implicit in all these lines of reasoning is the assumption that Harold Washington was a strong leader who would not brook any attack on his own authority or on his hand-picked board of education. Conversely, Acting Mayor Sawyer, without Washington's charisma and clout in the black community, was unable to control the summit and the reform process. Thus Washington's death created a power vacuum that eased the way for school reform.

This interpretation is probably too simple. Washington was a complex and subtle politician whose cautious strategies were easy to misread. Certainly his convocation of the parent/community council was a standard piece of political footwork. When a crisis strikes, any politician might be tempted to appoint a commission to study it and hope it will go away before the commission reports back. Yet the parent/community council was no ordinary study commission, but a volatile conclave of angry parents and community activists. Though he might try to control it by appointing its chairpersons and directing its agenda, Washington was too shrewd a politician not to sense the risks he was running. The conscious inclusion of activists and "troublemakers" indicates that the PCC was expected to do more than simply finesse the issue.

It is useful to compare Washington's actions in the wake of the school strike with another crisis he faced earlier in his administration: the gang crime furor following the murder of Ben Wilson in 1984. Mayor Washington avoided hasty action after Wilson's death and tried to build a citywide consensus for antigang programs. He convened a mayoral task force on gang violence, which held community hearings throughout the city. This allowed the public to blow off steam and to make their views known and it also introduced some of the community activists on the task force to the movers and shakers of the business and political community. This is precisely the same strategy Harold mapped out after the school strike: a mayoral summit composed of business leaders and grassroots activists, a series of community hearings, and hopes for a consensus plan of reform at the end of the process.

In 1985, Mayor Washington adopted the traditional youth worker model for antigang activities, avoiding more radical proposals that would employ gang members themselves to deal with the problem. Had he lived through the school reform process in 1987-88 he probably would have been looking for some similarly cautious plan. Earl Durham of Designs for Change, who had known Harold personally since school days, tried to get him to commit to the C.U.R.E. proposal shortly before he died, but Washington refused to say either yes or no. He was keeping his options open. Jackie Grimshaw and Carol Braun are surely correct: Mayor Washington would not be stampeded on this issue.

No one will ever know for sure just what Harold Washington had in mind. Like the question of what President John Kennedy would have done in Vietnam had he not been assassinated, historians will debate this matter endlessly.[41]

Yet a few things seem reasonably clear. First of all, Washington wanted the summit conference to produce a genuine reform plan for the Chicago public schools. His aides emphasize Harold's deep love of children and his decision during the second term to take a more active stance for improvement of the public schools. When we asked Senator Arthur Berman, the chairman of the Senate Education Committee, whether Harold Washington was committed to producing substantive action on school reform, he answered without hesitation, "Definitely." Some observers even believe the mayor was ready to ease out Manford Byrd from the post of superintendent. Second, Washington did not want to be rushed; he didn't want Springfield legislators imposing a hasty solution on the city. Nevertheless, as Senate President Rock has concluded, "I think Harold understood it would take legislation. As a former member himself, I don't think he ever doubted that the General Assembly would have to act." Finally, whatever plan Mayor Washington ultimately would have backed, if the reform process got out of his control, he was too clever a politician to be left behind. He would not have let the train leave the station without him.

Perhaps it's best to close this discussion of Harold Washington's role in school reform by returning to the medical meta-phor implicit in the acronym C.U.R.E. Harold is best under-stood, both at the time of Ben Wilson's murder and in the aftermath of the school strike, as a general practitioner faced with a puzzling illness. He wasn't sure of his diagnosis and didn't know what treatment to prescribe, but he knew which specialists to call and was open-minded enough to weigh their recommendations carefully while avoiding any radical, irrevers-ible surgical procedures. Furthermore, Harold exhibited a superb bedside manner. Unlike the specialists who were urging swift action, he wanted to involve the patient's whole family and make sure they understood both the diagnosis and the prognosis. Had Dr. Washington lived, he would have been part of the healing process for the Chicago public schools, even if the exact details of the cure might not have been the same.

Notes

1. *Chicago Tribune,* 4 June 1987, sec. 2., p. 3.

2. *Chicago Tribune,* 3 August 1987, sec. 2, p. 3; Charles N. Wheeler III, "Spring 1987: Portrait in Political Expediency," *Illinois Issues* 13 (August-September 1987): 8-10; Michael D. Klemens, "A Long, Long Time from February to July," *Illinois Issues* 14 (February 1988): 6-7.

3. *Chicago Tribune,* 3 August 1987, sec. 2, p. 3; G. Alfred Hess, Jr., interview by authors, 23 October 1990.

4. Michael Bakalis, interview by authors, 13 July 1990; Donald S. Perkins, "Chicago's School System Must be Restructured," *Chicago Tribune,* 16 September 1987, 15.

5. Hess interview; Diana Lauber, interview by authors, 15 October 1990; *Chicago Tribune,* 4 September 1987, 1.

6. Bakalis interview.

7. *Chicago Tribune,* 1 September 1987, sec. 2, p. 1; 4 September 1987, 1; 5 September 1987, 1.

8. *Chicago Tribune,* 9 September 1987, 18; *Chicago Sun-Times,* 11 September 1987, 1.

9. Coretta McFerren, interview by authors, 11 September 1990.

10. McFerren interview; Tomas Sanabria, interview by authors, 5 October 1990; Sokoni Karanja, interview by authors, 16 October 1990.

11. *Chicago Tribune,* 13 September 1987, sec. 2, p. 1; 19 September 1987, 5; *Chicago Sun-Times,* 19 September 1987, 5.

12. *Chicago Tribune,* 18 September 1987, sec. 2, p. 1; 20 September 1987, 1.

13. *Chicago Tribune,* 21 September 1987, 2; 23 September 1987, sec. 2, p. 1; 25 September 1987, sec. 2, p. 1; 26 September 1987, 6.

14. *Chicago Tribune,* 26 September 1987, 6; 27 September 1987, sec. 2, p. 3; 29 September 1987, 1; *Chicago Sun-Times,* 29 September 1987, 1.

15. *Chicago Tribune,* 2 October 1987, 1; 3 October 1987, 1; *Chicago Sun-Times,* 2 October 1987, 3; 3 October 1987, 1.

16. Jacqueline Grimshaw, interview by authors, 29 November 1990.

17. *Chicago Tribune,* 4 October 1987, 1; *Chicago Sun-Times,* 4 October 1987, 4.

18. *Chicago Tribune,* 5 October 1987, 1; 17 October 1987, 1; *Chicago Sun-Times,* 5 October 1987, 1; 17 October 1987, 3.

19. *Chicago Sun-Times,* 9 October 1987, 7; Sanabria interview.

20. *Chicago Sun-Times,* 11 September 1987, 7; 5 October 1987, 5; *Chicago Tribune,* 13 September 1987, sec. 4, p. 1; 20 September 1987, sec. 4, p. 1.

21. Grimshaw interview; Harold Baron, interview by authors, 4 December 1990; *Chicago Tribune,* 4 October 1987, 14; 5 October 1987, 1.

22. Baron interview; Philip Rock, interview by authors, 27 August 1991; Arthur Berman, interview by authors, 30 September 1991.

23. Baron interview.

24. *Chicago Tribune,* 18 December 1986, 22; *Crain's Chicago Business,* 29 September 1986, 15; Patrick Keleher, interview by authors, 22 October 1990; Hess interview.

25. Baron interview.

26. Rev. Kenneth Smith, interview by authors, 29 November 1990; Baron interview.

27. *Chicago Tribune,* 29 May 1987, sec. 2, p. 3; *Crain's Chicago Business,* 16 March 1987, 21; 15 June 1987, 44.

28. *Crain's Chicago Business,* 21 September 1987, 3; *Chicago Tribune,* 11 November 1987, sec. 2, p. 12; Baron interview.

29. *Chicago Tribune,* 12 October 1987, 1.

30. Ibid.; *Chicago Sun-Times,* 12 October 1987, 6.

31. Janice Metzger, interview by authors, 26 November 1990; Baron interview.

32. *Chicago Tribune,* 29 October 1987, 1; *Chicago Sun-Times,* 1 November 1987, 5.

33. Keleher interview.

34. Keleher interview; George Muñoz, interview by authors, 20 September 1990.

35. *Chicago Tribune,* 7 November 1987, 1; *Chicago Sun-Times,* 7 November 1987, 1.

36. *Chicago Sun-Times,* 7 November 1987, 1.

37. Alton Miller, *Harold Washington: The Mayor, The Man* (Chicago: Bonus Books, 1989), 1-18, is the best firsthand account of Mayor Washington's death. See also Melvin G. Holli and Paul M. Green, *Bashing Chicago Traditions: Harold Washington's Last Campaign* (Grand Rapids: William B. Eerdmans, 1989), 181-95.

38. *Chicago Tribune,* 2 December 1987, 1; *Chicago Sun-Times,* 3 December 1987, 1; Holli and Green, *Bashing Chicago Traditions,* 193-95.

39. Mike Smith, interview by authors, 19 September 1990; Coretta McFerren, interview by authors, 11 September 1990.

40. Grimshaw interview; Carol Moseley Braun, interview by authors, 5 February 1991.

41. We discussed this matter in interviews with Michael Bakalis (13 July 1990), Earl Durham (6 August 1990), Coretta McFerren (11 September 1990), Kelvin Strong (12 September 1990), Mike Smith (19 September 1990), Roberto Rivera (20 September 1990), Mary Dempsey (5 October 1990), Tom Coffey and Norton Kay (23 October 1990), Fred Hess (23 October 1990), Janice Metzger (26 November 1990), Jackie Grimshaw (29 November 1990), Kenneth Smith (29 November 1990), Hal Baron (4 December 1990), Carol Moseley Braun (5 February 1991), Philip Rock (27 August 1991), and Arthur Berman (30 September 1991). These individuals expressed different points of view on the question. The interpretation presented in the text is the authors' responsibility and should not be attributed to any of the people interviewed.

11

The Search for Alliances

Recognizing a rare window of opportunity in the aftermath of the teachers' strike, numerous groups and individuals reached out to each other to forge alliances during the winter of 1987-88. Chicagoans United to Reform Education (C.U.R.E.), who had been meeting for about a year when the teachers' strike hit, greatly expanded their base by recruiting three new community organizations with predominantly black and Latino membership. In addition, Al Raby, one of Mayor Washington's closest personal friends and political advisors, secured funding for C.U.R.E. to hire political consultants who could help their coalition coalesce.

In the meantime, two other groups that had previously forged a tentative alliance, the Chicago Panel on Public School Policy and Finance and the United Neighborhood Organization, fell out with each other. For different reasons, both organizations found themselves temporarily isolated from the growing school reform movement.

Finally, a most improbable alliance began to come together at the mayor's summit. Mayor Washington had gathered together representatives from all walks of life. CEOs of leading Chicago corporations sat side by side with parents of school children and activists from community organizations. Of course, just sharing seats at the same table did not overcome the deep diversity of interests. Yet, slowly and tentatively, as the summit members studied and debated throughout the winter, school reformers built bridges across the chasms of race and class.

As the reformers readied themselves for political battle in Springfield, an improbable multiracial, cross-class coalition came together and held firm throughout the following year.

C.U.R.E. Expands Its Base

In the summer of 1987, even before the September strike, C.U.R.E. was well placed strategically to lobby Springfield, with a detailed reform plan already formulated and the beginnings of a multiracial coalition in place. Yet, they needed to resolve a thorny issue that was hampering their coalition building and, most urgently, they needed to expand their base.

C.U.R.E. members had agonized over whether the central board of education in a reformed system should be appointed by the mayor or elected by the people. An elected board was more consistent with the democratic theory of school-based management, but Chicago had the only appointed board of education in the state and the city's mayors jealously guarded this prerogative. Ever since a black mayor had taken office, the black community considered his appointment powers sacrosanct and any attempt to reduce them a direct attack. Don Moore, from Designs for Change, reported to a C.U.R.E. meeting in August 1987:

> We find it to be so compelling an issue for black parents and community activists who identify with the mayor that it often makes it impossible to discuss any other aspect of the plan in a rational way. Further, we have found that the opponents of C.U.R.E. do not hesitate to focus on the crudest and most racially divisive counterarguments against C.U.R.E. Advocacy of an elected board gives them a potent emotional issue to exploit.[1]

Moore proposed a solution to this dilemma that was adopted by C.U.R.E. and ultimately written into the reform bill. Parent and community representatives on the local school councils would elect a school board nominating commission. This commission in turn would nominate slates of three candidates for each vacancy on the school board and the mayor would make the final choice from these slates.

With this potentially divisive issue settled, C.U.R.E. addressed the urgent matter of expanding its membership. Though it had tried to attract a wide range of groups and interests, the organization remained too "male and pale." They still needed to recruit black and Latino organizations, "each of whom brings some important new quality to the coalition. Some will bring numbers of supporters, some expertise, some access to a particular constituency or set of decision-makers."[2]

The first organization to join up at the time of the teachers' strike, the Near North Development Corporation, was no newcomer to C.U.R.E. activities. Kelvin Strong, the director of Near North Development, attended the initial C.U.R.E. conference at Loyola in April 1987 and he or a delegate had sat in on several additional meetings over the summer.

Near North Development Corporation labored in a decaying strip of brownstones and small apartment buildings wedged between the Gold Coast and the towering high rises of the Cabrini-Green public housing development. Most white Chicagoans were unaware that the 36 blocks between North Avenue and Division Street, Sedgwick and Larrabee avenues even existed, unless they wandered too far off the Old Town entertainment strip. Near North Development was organized around 1970 to arrest the decay that threatened this all-black neighborhood. The organization built 268 units of subsidized housing for families, the elderly, and the handicapped. Then they turned their attention to other issues affecting the quality of life in the neighborhood, particularly education and crime. They could hardly avoid education. Near North's headquarters in an old Protestant social service center on Cleveland Avenue backed up against the playground of Manierre Public School.

In the mid-1980s, Near North had adopted a very adversarial stance towards the staff at Manierre, but after a change in principals, they slowly began to form a relationship of trust. Every August the organization sponsored a leadership retreat at which parents planned school support activities for the upcoming year. Annually during Black History Month the parents conducted a student read-a-thon, organizing all the details themselves without requiring the teachers to spend any extra time on the project. Kelvin Strong had formed a close friendship with Don Moore and Joan Jeter Slay of Designs for Change, and that organization provided valuable training for Near North's staff and Manierre's parents.[3]

In August 1987 at Near North Development's annual retreat, Regina Glover Stewart, a mother who had given up on Chicago public schools, decided to give them one more chance. She had lived in the near north neighborhood nearly all her life. As a young wife expecting her first child, she stood on her balcony in the Green Homes project and watched children trooping into the ancient hulk of Schiller Public School that dated back to the Chicago Fire. Before her child was even born she joined the community agitation to tear down Schiller School and replace it with a new building named after the black abolitionist, Sojourner Truth. Her son was one of the first to enroll at Sojourner Truth, and Regina remained active in PTA and other school activities for the next 20 years.

By 1987, however, she had reached the end of her rope with public education. As another teachers' strike loomed, she decided to take her kids out of the maelstrom and enroll them instead at nearby St. Joseph Grade School. Someone invited her, however, to attend Near North Development's retreat, and Joan Slay, whom she had known years before, convinced her that C.U.R.E.'s reform plan held out hope for a totally new kind of public school system. Regina walked over to St. Joseph's and got her tuition deposit back. She would give the public schools one more chance. On September 15, in the midst of the strike, Kelvin Strong appointed her education coordinator for Near North Development.

During her first week on the job, Regina Stewart packed parents from Manierre on buses and demonstrated with them at Pershing Road. Then Kelvin Strong took her to her first

C.U.R.E. meeting. She was quiet, nearly speechless at first, but she soon grew comfortable with the vigorous give-and-take and Kelvin let her represent his organization at most of the subsequent sessions. The term *grassroots organizing* is often used glibly without much reflection, but Regina Stewart's approach to C.U.R.E. illustrates very specifically what it means. After each C.U.R.E. meeting, she would spend at least six hours on the phone calling up Manierre parents and explaining the issues discussed at the meeting. She fielded a lot of suspicious questions: "What does this mean for black people? How will it work?" She would reply, "You tell me. Let's work it out." She convened numerous workshops with the local parents and they engaged in a lot of role-playing. The C.U.R.E. proposals were not abstract ideas to her, but tested realities.[4]

This was the most important contribution that Near North Development brought to C.U.R.E. They already practiced school-based management at Manierre School and had demonstrated what poor, black parents could do when they were properly trained and were treated as equal partners by educators. They furnished firsthand experience that the school reformers could benefit from. Now, as Kelvin Strong phrased it, C.U.R.E. "provided an opportunity to take on the whole damn system."[5]

Near North Development's participation in C.U.R.E. also held important symbolic significance. Though most of the organization's activities were concentrated in the low-rise area just east and north of Cabrini-Green, its proximity to that public housing project lent it an air of gritty notoriety. Though not the largest project in Chicago, Cabrini-Green was the best known. First developed in 1941 as barrackslike rowhouses in the so-called Little Hell Italian district of the north side, Frances Cabrini Homes (named after a saintly Catholic nun who worked in Chicago early in the century) soon became all-black after World War II. Between 1958 and 1962, 15 high rise-buildings in the Cabrini extension and eight more at William Green Homes (named for the long-time American Federation of Labor president) expanded the project to nearly three thousand housing units.[6]

Though its crime and drug problems were probably no more severe than in other housing projects, Cabrini-Green's proximity to the Gold Coast and to the Old Town night life district earned it far more publicity. Mayor Jane Byrne shone the spotlight even more brightly on it in 1981 when she and her husband moved into a Cabrini-Green apartment for a brief time in a nationally heralded publicity stunt.[7] Therefore, when C.U.R.E. recruited an all-black neighborhood organization from the Cabrini-Green area, important minority credentials were added to the coalition.

The Peoples' Coalition for Educational Reform, which sprang up during the teachers' strike, also joined C.U.R.E. shortly after the strike ended. Though it is accurate to say that the Peoples' Coalition arose as a response to the strike, this statement fails to recognize a good deal of previous agitation by the coalition's leaders. School reform was not born on the 15th day of the strike. Tomas Sanabria, Sokoni Karanja, and Coretta McFerren, who led the Peoples' Coalition, had been challenging the system for a long time.

Tomas Sanabria, a lifelong resident of the Logan Square neighborhood, dedicated himself to uplifting his Puerto Rican community after his brother, a Vietnam veteran, died of a drug overdose on Chicago's mean streets. Trained as an art therapist, Tomas helped angry youth at Roberto Clemente High School transform their rage into creative energy. He worked closely with the Network for Youth Services in planning the march on Clemente and took over the post of NYS coordinator on the very day of the march, March 26, 1984. NYS was flat broke when Sanabria took the helm so he worked about six months without pay before securing new funding. NYS operated an alternative high school after the 1985 school reform laws authorized state grants for that purpose. So when Ben Kendrick was planning the Freedom Schools at the time of the 1987 strike, Sanabria was one of many people he called for advice and assistance. Tomas mobilized the member agencies of NYS to provide out-of-school help for students, and he threw himself into the demonstrations that the incipient Peoples' Coalition staged during the strike.[8]

Sokoni Karanja had traveled the world before coming to Chicago in 1971. By his own admission, he was a degree gatherer during the 1960s, picking up several master's degrees and a Ph.D. in urban planning and economics from Brandeis University. On an extended stay in Tanzania, he acquired the habit of African dress, and more important, he imbibed the self-reliance philosophy of Julius Nyerere. When he came to Chicago, he applied this developing nation philosophy to the low-income communities on the south side.

A soft-spoken, scholarly man, Dr. Karanja didn't earn headlines like other black leaders, but he gained the respect of foundations that helped finance his string of social service centers called the Centers for New Horizons. The 11 centers, stretching from 22nd to 67th streets east of the Dan Ryan expressway, try to foster stronger family structures in an area with one of the heaviest concentrations of public housing in the nation. Like Sanabria's organization, Centers for New Horizons had operated an alternative school for a time, and they had long focused their efforts on early childhood head start programs, agitating for improvements to public school kindergartens.[9]

Coretta McFerren came to school reform as a "consumer" of education. She and her husband put eight adopted children through the public schools and their five grandchildren lived with them in the same house, with Coretta as the matriarchal grandmother. Coretta was raised to believe that there are two ways of liberation for African-Americans, God and education, so she mapped out a systematic program of preschool instruction for her grandchildren. Yet when the children entered the public schools in South Chicago (the former steel mill district), Coretta found them unlearning much of what they had already learned at home. When she protested to the principal and the teachers, she and her family were swiftly branded as troublemakers.[10]

The events leading to formation of the Peoples' Coalition began with a series of conferences convoked by the Leadership

Council for Metropolitan Open Communities, a citywide agency that promoted racial integration. The council sponsored three high-level meetings with Mayor Washington, Cardinal Bernardin, and other civic leaders, in 1986 to explore the issues of poverty and racism 20 years after Martin Luther King's historic open housing marches in Chicago. Anne Hallett, the director of the Wieboldt Foundation that partially funded the conferences, Sokoni Karanja, Ben Kendrick, Kale Williams, and Al Raby played leading roles in organizing these assemblies.[11]

As a result of these meetings, Karanja and Raby, who was one of Mayor Washington's closest confidants, set up a poverty task force to examine the issues of education and hunger in the black community. Coretta McFerren joined the education subcommittee that Dr. Karanja headed. This group formed the nucleus of the Peoples' Coalition for Educational Reform. Though it arose initially out of the black community, the Peoples' Coalition reached out to Tomas Sanabria and the Latinos and to Bernie Noven and his white parents' groups on the north side to form a true rainbow coalition. For one of the first times since Dr. King's death, whites and blacks marched together during the strike.[12]

C.U.R.E. had not yet recruited a Latino organization so they invited Tomas Sanabria to attend a meeting immediately after the strike. Tomas asked Coretta McFerren and Sokoni Karanja to accompany him and they all decided to join the effort. The organizational lineup becomes a little tangled at this point. Karanja joined C.U.R.E. in a dual capacity, as director of the Centers for New Horizons and as a member of the Peoples' Coalition. Sanabria, who laughingly calls himself the token Hispanic in the group, was unable to sign up NYS as an official member of C.U.R.E., since his organization was suffering some internal divisions. The educational coordinator of NYS, Enrique Fernandez, wanted to focus on specifically Hispanic issues, primarily at Clemente High School, whereas Sanabria sensed the importance of the citywide reform movement. So Tomas initially joined C.U.R.E. as a member of the

Peoples' Coalition, not the Network for Youth Services. At an organizational retreat held just after the first of the year, Sanabria was elected chairperson of the Peoples' Coalition, Ben Kendrick vice-chairperson, and Sokoni Karanja treasurer. The public voice of the coalition, however, was the coordinator, Coretta McFerren. She and one of her daughters, Gwen Burns, made their home in South Chicago the group's headquarters.

By October 1987, therefore, C.U.R.E. had filled out its multiethnic coalition with the addition of three largely minority organizations. The full coalition now included the Loyola School of Education, Save Our Neighborhoods/Save Our City, Designs for Change, the Near North Development Corporation, Centers for New Horizons, and the Peoples' Coalition for Educational Reform. Later Tomas Sanabria managed to secure Network for Youth Services' formal membership, and several smaller organizations signed on as well. C.U.R.E. included black, white, and Latino activists from nearly all ends of the city. No other school reform organization built such a broad base of support.

Since the death of Harold Washington, a split has developed in Chicago's black community between those who wish to recapture city hall in his name through a process of "movement politics" and those who follow the lead of Eugene Sawyer by accommodating the white power structure. The black school reformers do not fit neatly into either camp; certainly their campaign for school reform could hardly be called accommodating. Yet after the passage of the reform law, these black members of the reform coalition have been either ignored or denounced by the black movement politicians. These politicians brand school reform as the product of a white conspiracy, or at best, a white-Hispanic coalition.[13]

This interpretation exasperates the many black members of C.U.R.E. Near North Development and Centers for New Horizons were all-black organizations and both Designs for Change and the Peoples' Coalition had significant black representation. Kelvin Strong remarks forcefully that when people tell him no blacks were involved he can't imagine what they're talking about since the last time he looked in the mirror he was still black. Sokoni Karanja adds, "Most of the people in the first protest wave were African-Americans. But...it was a different group from the usual protestants."[14]

If any ethnic group was underrepresented at this stage, it was the Latinos. This is surprising considering their important role in inaugurating the reform movement. However, the Latino community returned to prominence later in the reform process with the emergence of UNO as a major player.

The Haymarket Group

C.U.R.E. took another decisive step in October 1987 when they engaged the services of political consultants, the Haymarket Group, to help them draft a reform bill and secure its passage. Haymarket was an unusual consulting firm composed of lawyers, media specialists, and community organizers. Founded earlier in the year by Tom Coffey, formerly the director of intergovernmental affairs for Mayor Washington, and Norton Kay, who had served Democratic Governor Dan Walker as press secretary a decade before, the fledgling group of consultants had gathered an interesting assortment of individuals, including Al Raby when he resigned as director of the city's Human Rights Commission.

Albert A. Raby grew up in Woodlawn on Chicago's south side. When his father died, he helped his mother support four other children by shining shoes and hawking newspapers out on the street. As early as fourth grade, Al began ditching school and he soon dropped out. Though he returned to the classroom for awhile, when he was put back from eighth grade to seventh, he dropped out again. While serving time in the army he missed a promotion to an office job because he could not spell. This humiliation motivated him to resume his education after leaving the army. He finally completed grade school at age 24, then swept through high school and college and became a public school teacher.

As convener of the Coordinating Council of Community Organizations in the turbulent 1960s, Raby led the drive to oust Ben Willis and integrate the public schools, and he brought Martin Luther King, Jr., to Chicago. A decade and a half later, he managed the chaotic, but successful, campaign to elect Harold Washington the city's first black mayor. No one in the black community enjoyed more credibility than Al Raby; no one felt more deeply and personally the pain of inadequate and insensitive public schooling.[15]

When Raby joined Haymarket, Richard Dennis, a millionaire commodities broker who often bankrolled liberal causes, told Raby, "Give me an agenda and I'll fund it." Dennis had first earned notoriety in 1986 when he donated $570,000 to Adlai Stevenson III's bid to oust James Thompson as governor. This huge contribution turned Dennis into a campaign issue himself. Dennis also liberally supported Harold Washington's reelection campaign, and in 1987, when he approached Raby, he was underwriting most of Arizona Governor Bruce Babbit's ill-fated run for the presidency.

Michael Bakalis had already tried to tap Dennis for funding and Earl Durham, a lifelong friend of Raby's, urged Al to place school reform at the top of his Dennis-funded agenda. Thanks to this combination of influences, Al Raby secured financial support from the liberal broker. All of C.U.R.E.'s member groups enjoyed 501(c) (3) tax status, which made contributions to them tax deductible, but drastically limited the amount of lobbying they could engage in. So a separate organization, called the Institute for School Reform, was incorporated with 501(c) (4) status that permitted unlimited lobbying. Richard Dennis funneled $250,000 through this organization to underwrite the expenses of the Haymarket Group's services to C.U.R.E. None of his contributions were tax deductible.[16]

On Sunday, October 4, the day after the school strike was settled, Don Moore, Renee Montoya, and Earl Durham from Designs for Change met with Al Raby, Tom Coffey, and Mary Dempsey to work out the details of Haymarket's involvement with C.U.R.E. Mary Dempsey provided bill drafting assistance, Tom Coffey mapped out an overall legislative strategy for the drive on Springfield, and Norton Kay handled the press. Coffey emphasizes, in retrospect, that Haymarket furnished far more than mere technical or legal assistance. "What we do is not a science, it's an art," Coffey insists. "Haymarket's business is to understand the realities of Chicago politics and assist others to operate within those realities."

Certainly, Haymarket did provide plenty of technical assistance, so C.U.R.E. was the only school reform group with a fully drafted bill ready to go when the state legislature convened in 1988. Haymarket also furnished the meeting space for the weekly C.U.R.E. meetings at which the participants laboriously drafted the bill, line by line. Above all, Coffey concludes, what Haymarket did for C.U.R.E. was "to inject some political discipline into the process."[17]

All participants in the C.U.R.E. meetings agree that Al Raby's participation proved crucial. Regina Glover Stewart recalls the awe she felt when she walked into her first meeting and saw Raby sitting there. She had admired the civil rights leader for years, and as a teenager had rehearsed a little speech to deliver if she ever met him. Now, however, she was tongue-tied, but overflowing with joy that she had finally met the man who brought Martin Luther King, Jr., to Chicago.[18]

Even Raby couldn't keep Stewart and the other C.U.R.E. members speechless for long. They wrangled long and hard over every point in the reform bill, but Raby did exercise a calming and uniting influence in the group, helping them not to draw permanent lines in the sand. A journalist once wrote, "An interesting thing about Al Raby: no one seems to recall exactly what he said on any of the multitude of occasions when an organization was caught in a crisis or some significant event was about to occur—just that he was there and his presence or words made a difference." The memories of the C.U.R.E. members jibe exactly with this statement. They can't recall any dramatic incidents but they all emphasize his peace-keeping role. A newspaper editorial at the time of his death aptly summed up Raby's contributions to Chicago politics: "He was a coalition builder in a town better known for its divisions."[19]

Raby's involvement with C.U.R.E. throws additional light on the Harold Washington question. It's unlikely that Raby would have committed himself to the reform process, and secured funding for it, if he thought the mayor would ultimately oppose it. For all his activist background, Raby did not believe in tilting at windmills, he believed in getting things done. He must have felt that at the appropriate moment he could win Mayor Washington's approval. As it turned out, however, Washington died in November 1987 and Raby followed him to the grave almost exactly one year later, just before the final version of the school reform bill passed.

Until his death, however, Raby's presence and the assistance of the entire Haymarket team provided C.U.R.E. with a decisive edge enjoyed by no other school reform group.

CHIPS and UNO: Odd Men Out

The Chicago Panel on Public School Policy and Finance (also known as the Chicago Panel or CHIPS) and the United Neighborhood Organization (UNO), two loosely allied organizations with a long history of involvement in public school politics, found themselves temporarily out of touch with the school reform movement at the time of the teachers' strike. Together they had backed an unsuccessful pilot program in school-based management, and each was experiencing other problems in the search for alliances.

The Chicago Panel had been organized by a number of civic organizations, such as the League of Women Voters and the Citizens Schools Committee, after the school board's financial crisis at the beginning of the decade. The financial crisis had taken these civic groups by surprise; they did not foresee it, they did not understand it, they did not possess the expertise to analyze school budgets. Therefore, in 1982 they hired Anne Hallett, a self-taught school finance expert, who as a housewife in the state of Washington had recently organized a statewide initiative to rewrite the school finance laws. Hallett modeled the Chicago Panel on a New York organization called the Educational Priorities Panel, and she swiftly commissioned a series of research reports analyzing Chicago's bloated school budgets. Her first researcher, G. Alfred Hess, Jr., a former Methodist minister with a Ph.D. from Northwestern, succeeded her as director of the Chicago Panel in August 1983.[20]

Hess expanded the panel's focus beyond school finance to encompass broader issues of educational policy. He and Diana Lauber coauthored a dropout study, published in 1985, which employed a larger database than either the Aspira or the Designs for Change dropout reports.[21] After assessing the results of the 1985 school reform laws and witnessing the farcical school budget hearings held in the individual schools, Hess concluded that only a system of school-based management would suffice to improve education in Chicago. Don Moore and Designs for Change had reached similar conclusions about the same time (summer of 1986) and a not-so-healthy rivalry developed between Moore and Hess.

Hess's assessment of the legislative prospects for school-based management differed from Moore's. He believed that an experimental pilot project to test the concept was more realistic; whereas Moore and the C.U.R.E. team felt that a pilot project would prove futile, since the school bureaucracy would throw all its resources against it and ensure that it failed.

It appeared, at first, that Hess had made the right call. Manford Byrd's tactless sabotage of the school budget hearings angered powerful House Speaker Michael Madigan, and armed with a report from the Chicago Panel, Madigan blasted the school system at a press conference in June 1986. Later in the year, his staff contacted Hess and asked him to draft amendments that would strengthen the local school improvement councils. Hess countered with a proposal for his three-year local school autonomy pilot program. School management councils would be established at two schools in each of the city's 23 subdistricts. The experimental councils, comprising equal numbers of parents and school staff, would enjoy broad powers over curriculum and budget allocation. Barbara Flynn Currie, a Democratic representative from Hyde Park, sponsored HB 935, and with Speaker Madigan's backing it sailed through the house.[22]

At this point, UNO became involved with the bill. The United Neighborhood Organization, founded by Mary Gonzales and Gregory Galluzzo but led in its citywide policy initiatives by Danny Solis, had long agitated against the public school system. The constituent organizations of UNO in South Chicago, Back of the Yards, Pilsen, and Little Village had pressured the school authorities and the legislature for many years to alleviate overcrowding in Latino schools. This finally paid off in 1985 when the legislature passed a $24 million appropriation for new school construction and a shrewd lobbying campaign by UNO convinced Governor Thompson to sign the measure.

In the spring of 1987, UNO was trying to fashion a more comprehensive education policy. They interviewed several hundred educators and business executives and began looking for a legislative strategy. Mary Gonzales and Danny Solis talked with Mike Smith and Bob Gannett from C.U.R.E., but decided that C.U.R.E.'s comprehensive reform plans were unrealistic for the time being. They also held meetings with Fred Hess from the Chicago Panel and decided that his pilot program looked more promising.[23]

UNO adopted HB 935 as its education policy at a citywide convention in the Conrad Hilton Hotel in May 1987. Mayor Washington, Senator Paul Simon, George Muñoz, and other dignitaries made appearances. In typical Alinsky fashion, UNO put Harold Washington on the spot and asked him to endorse HB 935. What precisely Harold said is not clear. UNO meetings consciously create a pressure-cooker atmosphere to force politicians into promises they might not otherwise make. Yet Harold was usually deft enough to avoid embarrassing commitments. In any case, Fred Hess interpreted whatever Harold said as a promise to back his pilot project.[24]

After the bill cleared the house on May 22, however, it ran into a stone wall in the senate. Both the Chicago Panel and UNO were neophytes at the Springfield legislative game. They had neglected to line up a senate sponsor, assuming that House Speaker Madigan's authority would carry the bill all the way. However, Arthur Berman, the powerful education chairman in the senate, throttled the bill when it arrived at his committee. He called together in his office representatives from the Chicago Board of Education, the Chicago Teachers Union, the school engineers' union, the city government, and the Chicago Panel, and all of the interest groups ganged up on HB 935. Designs for Change also lobbied vigorously against the pilot project, as did Jackie Grimshaw and the city government's lobbying team. Meanwhile back in Chicago, UNO did not choose to fight. No school buses filled with Mexican parents arrived in Springfield that month. Fred Hess went down to defeat alone.[25]

Both Solis and Hess are philosophical about all this today. Danny says that he gained some valuable experience in this brief legislative foray. He got to know "who's who in the zoo down in Springfield" and he learned that next time he tried to pass a law he needed more allies. Hess acknowledges that UNO rarely made permanent alliances with anyone. "Danny was kind of a loose cannon looking out for places to have influence," and UNO had neither permanent friends nor permanent enemies. C.U.R.E. had come to the same conclusion. Because of UNO's "minute-by-minute assessment of 'self interest'," the C.U.R.E. members were glad they had not invited that organization to join them. Hess and the Chicago Panel did ally with UNO, however, and got burned.[26]

At the time, Hess felt extremely bitter over what he had interpreted as the mayor's betrayal, and he lost his composure during the meetings in Senator Berman's office. He openly denounced the mayor as "not serious about education reform."

As a result, Hal Baron fired him from his staff position with the mayor's education summit in June 1987.[27]

When the teachers' strike hit and Mayor Washington expanded the education summit, the Chicago Panel found itself temporarily isolated from the action. Tee Galley, however, the president of the panel, was selected to be a member of the parent/community council and also elected as one of the 10 parent delegates to the wider summit. Fred Hess sat right behind her as staff assistant when she took her place at the plenary sessions, but he sensed that the mayor's staff still resented his presence. The Chicago Panel continued to plot a separate course throughout the early months of 1988, reintroducing the pilot program bill and pushing it as a moderate alternative to the C.U.R.E. bill, but eventually they did participate in the drafting of the final, more radical reform bill that passed the legislature.

UNO was in an even more precarious position at the time of the strike, for they had previously cut an informal deal with the teachers' union. The teachers enjoyed a common interest with the Latino community in reducing overcrowding. Latino parents demanded new schools and smaller class sizes and the teachers agreed, for both measures would result in more teaching positions. So at the time of the strike, UNO provided the only significant public support for the teachers' position. They mounted several demonstrations supporting the teachers' demands for higher pay and smaller classes, and refused to join the Peoples' Coalition.

When the strike ended and public outrage mounted, UNO found itself badly compromised and seemingly weakened. In fact, the decision to support the teachers had been controversial within the organization and narrowly carried a vote of the federation's leadership. Mary Gonzales and Danny Solis also harbored deeper philosophical disagreements over the role of UNO in public education. Gonzales believed that a church-based organization should avoid heavy involvement with the pubic schools, but Solis noted that the great majority of his

Latino constituents could not afford Catholic education and thus had no choice but to patronize the public schools. This disagreement was papered over for a time, but it later split Gonzales from the organization she had founded.[28]

UNO continued to pursue a separate course for awhile, working out a model schoolhouse plan with the help of influential magnet school principal Lourdes Monteagudo and the support of the teachers' union. UNO didn't remain odd man out for very long, however. Danny Solis won a place on the education summit and watched closely as the business community began to coalesce with the more radical parent representatives. Renee Montoya from Designs for Change met Solis confidentially for breakfast once or twice a month to keep him informed of C.U.R.E.'s progress. Eventually, he displayed some of his famous footwork and joined the school reform coalition. In the final push for legislation in Springfield, UNO played a major role.[29]

Corporate Execs and Parent Reps

The most intriguing, and improbable, alliance of all was the coalition that developed between CEOs of Chicago's major corporations and the members of the parent/community council. Over the winter of 1987-88 the city's top businessmen found a community of interest with the black, white, and Latino parents as both grew increasingly frustrated at the lack of progress on the summit.

Chicago's business leaders were very slow to push for school reform, as Mike Bakalis had discovered in 1986 when he circulated his initial recruiting letter for C.U.R.E. Though corporate leaders had advanced a high-profile program of vocational education early in the century, trade union opposition had killed it and the ensuing controversy over corporate involvement convinced most business leaders to withdraw entirely from public school politics.[30] This decision might have been anticipated since most of the top executives lived in the suburbs or sent their children to private schools.

Two events in the 1980s, however, angered business leaders sufficiently that they dipped their toes back into the public school whirlpool. In 1981 Chicago United, the leading business-civic organization, issued a massive management study of the Chicago public schools. Chicago United had been founded at the time of the race riots following Martin Luther King, Jr.'s assassination and was the only business group in Chicago formally dedicated to interracial harmony. Half of its 80 member-corporations were majority white and half were minority owned. CEOs, called *principals* in the organization, or their designated representatives, called *deacons*, discussed and formulated policies on local socio-economic issues. The 1981 schools report, laid out literally hundreds of recommendations to improve efficiency and cut costs in public schooling.[31]

The bureaucracy of the Chicago Board of Education formally accepted the Chicago United recommendations and reported that they had implemented 65 to 75 percent of them. When Patrick Keleher, a former Illinois Bell executive, assumed the post of public policy director for Chicago United in 1987, he commissioned a follow-up study and discovered that the school board had adopted only the most trivial recommendations and had not significantly improved the efficiency of their administration. Since Chicago United performed the original study *pro bono* and had determined that it was worth over three million dollars in consultants' fees, Keleher and Chicago United president Warren Bacon felt betrayed.[32]

The other disillusioning experience for Chicago's business leaders took place during the first education summit in the summer of 1987. Peter Wilmott's team of businessmen, negotiating the learn-earn proposal with Manford Byrd, were utterly flabbergasted when the superintendent asked them to guarantee jobs for high school graduates even though he was not prepared to guarantee improvements in test scores. It is impossible to overestimate the impact of this fiasco on the business community. Byrd's arrogance put them in an uncharacteristically radical mood at the time of the teachers' strike. As far as they were concerned, the public school administration had lost all credibility.[33]

A dozen business leaders, including the CEOs of IC Industries, Amoco, and the Harris Bank, sat on the education summit. Yet businessmen had fashioned another vehicle for dealing with education as well. In response to a 1986 study of business relations with the Harold Washington administration, eight business federations, such as the Chicago Association of Commerce and Industry and the Commercial Club, had formed a loose umbrella organization called the Chicago Partnership. After the school strike, the partners designated Chicago United to speak as their representative in dealing with the education crisis. So when Patrick Keleher or Warren Bacon spoke out, they were not just speaking for the 80 member-corporations of Chicago United but for 4,500 corporations throughout Illinois.[34]

On the night in November when Education Secretary William Bennett came to town and unleashed his blast at Chicago's public schools, Chicago United released the first draft of their proposed solution to the education crisis. It was not a detailed plan but a series of bullet points: radical downsizing of the school bureaucracy, empowerment of parents and professionals at the local school level, professionalization of teachers, performance contracts for principals, and a powerful oversight committee to monitor the results of reform.[35]

Chicago United's plan agreed in general with the legislative solution C.U.R.E. was formulating. This was not altogether coincidental, since Designs for Change, a leading member of C.U.R.E., held a consulting contract with Chicago United. The business organization proved reluctant, however, to forge any closer links with C.U.R.E. Shortly after the strike, Pat Keleher and David Paulus from First National Bank met with Mike Bakalis, Renee Montoya, and Mike Smith for lunch at the University Club on Michigan Avenue. As Paulus outlined the business community's general stance on school reform, Mike Smith jumped in impulsively, pointing out to Paulus that his ideas were nearly identical to the C.U.R.E. plan. Paulus looked puzzled, and turned to Keleher. "If that's true, Pat, where's the problem between us and C.U.R.E.," he queried. Keleher answered enigmatically, "It's the monochromatic problem." Paulus didn't pick up the reference, so Keleher explained, "Monochromatic. Black and white." The old bugaboo about Mike Smith's organization, SON/SOC, had surfaced once again. Since Chicago United represented the leading minority-owned businesses in the city, they felt reluctant to ally themselves formally with the white ethnics from the northwest and southwest sides. So despite the convergence of ideas, the business community remained aloof from C.U.R.E. for the time being.[36]

Without anyone planning it, however, the businessmen began to move closer to an alliance with the parent representatives on the education summit. At the first few meetings that the 10 parent/community council delegates attended with the full summit, the atmosphere was decidedly chilly. Coretta McFerren remembers that Ken West, the CEO of Harris Bank, thought she was plain crazy. The parents, for their part, did not trust the representatives of big business. At first, the minority parents even refused to talk directly with the CEOs, but sent Janice Metzger, the only white cochair, on back-and-forth missions to explore their positions. Yet as the weeks wore on with endless sessions in the city council chambers, the businessmen began to share the parents' frustrations. Already predisposed against the board of education bureaucrats from their earlier experiences, the businessmen on the summit began to view the board and the union as hopeless obstructionists and the parent/community council delegates as possible allies.[37]

Business leaders could no longer remain isolated from the problems of the public schools, for they found it increasingly difficult to recruit a trained work force from them. Every personnel director had a horror story about interviewing 80 applicants for a receptionist's position before finding one with adequate language skills. The situation promised to get worse as service jobs increasingly replaced manufacturing jobs in the city's economic mix. If corporate leaders worried about finding employees, parents feared their sons and daughters would graduate (or drop out) from the public schools unemployable. Self-interest, then, threw wealthy executives and the poor or middle-class parents together. Kelvin Strong from C.U.R.E. has nicely summed up the economic interest that all shared: "These children will be paying my social security some day. I want my social security. I paid for my parents and I want my children to pay mine."[38]

As every politician knows, however, a common enemy makes an even stronger binding force than common interests. Manford Byrd proved to be just such an enemy, unwittingly paving the way for the business-parent alliance. Byrd made a strategic error in both 1986 and 1987 when he stonewalled the parents' objections at the local school budget hearings, thus destroying whatever good will he had enjoyed after the tumultuous Ruth Love administration. Then, in the summer of 1987, he outraged the businessmen with his arrogant posture in the learn-earn negotiations. Finally, his go-for-broke strategy during the teachers' strike alienated just about everyone in Chicago. Byrd's actions inadvertently pushed the businessmen into the arms of the angry parents, in an odd but highly effective alliance.

The pact was sealed in early February 1988 at a breakfast meeting in the offices of Chicago United on the 57th floor of the First National Bank building. Thereafter, the parent representatives met regularly with the business leaders at the Chicago United offices after the official summit meetings adjourned. Other dissidents from the summit, such as UNO, C.U.R.E., and the Chicago Panel, gradually began to join them, and in late spring they formalized their reform coalition, christening it the Alliance for Better Chicago Schools (ABCs).

Though this is getting ahead of the story, chronologically speaking, it's important to point out that ABCs was the alliance that finally pushed through the reform bill. The parents alone lacked resources to mount a successful legislative campaign, and businessmen lacked the credibility and the manpower. But together with the intellectual resources of the Chicago Panel and C.U.R.E. and the political savvy of the Haymarket Group, the bankrolls of the businessmen and the outrage of the parents made a powerful combination. The winning alliance that gathered its forces in the winter of 1987-88 bridged the sharp ethnic and racial divisions of the city and reached across class lines, from ghetto streets to corporate boardrooms.

Notes

1. Don Moore to C.U.R.E. members, 27 August 1987, C.U.R.E.-SON/SOC papers.

2. Ibid.

3. Kelvin Strong, interview by authors, 12 September 1990.

4. Regina Glover Stewart, interview by authors, 18 September 1990.

5. Strong interview.

6. For background on Cabrini-Green, see Devereux Bowly, Jr., *The Poorhouse: Subsidized Housing in Chicago, 1895-1976* (Carbondale: Southern Illinois University Press, 1978); and William Mullen, "The Road to Hell," *Chicago Tribune Magazine,* 31 March 1985, 12-19, 27-30.

7. *New York Times,* 23 March 1981, 12; 1 April 1981, 16; *Chicago Tribune,* 22 March 1981, 1; 24 March sec. 2, p. 2; 1 April 1981, 1.

8. Tomas Sanabria, interview by authors, 5 October 1990.

9. Sokoni Karanja, interview by authors, 16 October 1990.

10. Coretta McFerren, interview by authors, 11 September 1990.

11. *Chicago Tribune,* 1 June 1986, sec. 16, p. 1; 13 November 1986, sec. 2, p. 3.

12. Anne Hallett, interview by authors, 17 October 1990; McFerren, Karanja, Sanabria interviews.

13. See, for example, Alex Poinsett, "School Reform, Black Leaders: Their Impact on Each Other," *Catalyst* 1 (May 1990): 7-11, 43.

14. Strong, Karanja interviews.

15. Robert McClory, "The Activist," *Chicago Tribune Magazine,* 17 April 1983, 26-34, 39; obituary in *Chicago Tribune,* 24 November 1988, sec. 4, p. 15.

16. Al Raby died on 23 November 1988. This account of his involvement with C.U.R.E. was pieced together from interviews with Michael Bakalis (13 July 1990), Donald Moore (1 August 1990), Tom Coffey and Norton Kay (23 October 1990), and Mary Dempsey (5 October 1990).

17. Coffey and Kay, Dempsey interviews.

18. Stewart interview.

19. McClory, "The Activist," 27; *Chicago Tribune*, 27 November 1988, sec. 4, p. 2.

20. Hallett interview; G. Alfred Hess, Jr., interview by authors, 23 October 1990; Diana Lauber, interview by authors, 15 October 1990.

21. G. Alfred Hess, Jr., Diana Lauber, "Dropouts from the Chicago Public Schools" (Chicago Panel on Public School Policy and Finance, 1985).

22. For the legislative history of HB 935, see *Final Legislative Synopsis and Digest*, 85th General Assembly, 1987 sess., 2: 1251-53.

23. Mary Gonzales, interview by authors, 12 October 1990; Danny Solis, interview by authors, 17 October 1990.

24. Hess interview; Jacqueline Grimshaw, interview by authors, 29 November 1990.

25. Hess interview; Lauber interview; Grimshaw interview; "Why We Oppose HB 935" (Designs for Change memo), C.U.R.E.-SON/SOC papers.

26. Solis interview; Hess interview; C.U.R.E. minutes, 14 July 1987, C.U.R.E.-SON/SOC papers.

27. Hess interview; Grimshaw interview; Hal Baron, interview by authors, 4 December 1990.

28. Gonzales, Solis interviews.

29. Renee Montoya, taped memoir, November 1990.

30. Julia Wrigley, *Class Politics and Public Schools, Chicago, 1900-1950* (New Brunswick, N.J.: Rutgers University Press, 1982), 61-89.

31. Chicago United, Special Task Force on Education, *Chicago School System* (March 1981).

32. Patrick Keleher, interview by authors, 22 October 1990; David Paulus, interview by authors, 16 November 1990.

33. Keleher, Don Moore, Fred Hess, David Paulus, Hal Baron and others made this point emphatically in interviews.

34. Keleher interview. The 1986 report of the Chicago Project, commissioned by the Chicago Central Area Committee and authored by University of Chicago historian Pastora San Juan Cafferty, assessed the

state of business-government relations in Chicago during the 10 years since the death of Richard J. Daley. It concluded that the leading players were not working together because "they didn't understand, respect, or trust each other." See *Chicago Tribune*, 31 October 1986, 22; 2 November 1986, sec. 7, p. 1.

35. *Chicago Tribune*, 10 November 1987, 1; *Crain's Chicago Business,* 9 November 1987, 72.

36. Mike Smith, interview by authors, 19 September 1990; Keleher interview; Paulus interview.

37. McFerren, Keleher interviews; Janice Metzger, interview by authors, 26 November 1990.

38. Strong interview.

(12)

A Race With Time

"It hit 1988, and it was January, and we knew...we had to get ready, get that finished package together, and hold a press conference to announce it, then make a bee-line to Springfield. That's what our job was."[1]

Regina Glover Stewart was speaking of C.U.R.E., but her statement applied equally well to the parent/community council of the education summit. In the winter of 1987-88, both groups were racing with time, and with each other, to write a school reform bill that could pass the legislature by the end of the session on June 30.

C.U.R.E. enjoyed a head start and many other advantages. They had been meeting for over a year and had already fashioned an overall plan, which needed only to be hammered into legislative form. They were well funded and were backed by expert advice. The parent/community council, on the other hand, had just organized in October 1987 and its members were only beginning to build up trust among themselves. Furthermore, they formed part of a larger, and more cumbersome, process. Even after they fashioned a plan, they had to report it to the full summit conference and mesh it with the plans of others. Not surprisingly, the process bogged down.

Tom Coffey from the Haymarket Group outlined a winning strategy for C.U.R.E. First of all, you cannot win or lose in politics without a candidate, in this case a bill, so they concentrated their efforts on writing a bill while the summit was dragging on in endless debates. Then they moved to obtain stellar sponsors in the legislature, to put forward expert witnesses, and to shape the debate so that education became the defining theme of the legislative session.[2] The summit lacked such clear direction, since Harold Washington's successor as mayor did not seize leadership in the education crisis. In the end, the summit negotiations failed to produce a bill in timely fashion for the legislature.

Mornings at Haymarket

The Haymarket Group rents a suite of offices in the century-old, former county courthouse north of the Chicago River on Hubbard Street (recently this building has been doubling as the headquarters of a fictional newspaper on Jamie Lee Curtis's TV series, "Anything But Love"). Haymarket's conference hall still resembles an antique courtroom, with rounded Romanesque windows, dark wood paneling, and 20-foot-high ceilings. From October 1987 to January 1988, C.U.R.E. held court there nearly every week, usually on Monday or Tuesday mornings, weighing and judging hundreds of provisions for a school reform bill. The C.U.R.E. members ventured out in the early morning darkness of a Chicago winter, braving the icy blasts off Lake Michigan, and assembled about 8 A.M., when the building's furnace had barely lifted the chill off the cavernous old courtroom. Each meeting consumed nearly the whole morning, as well as a lot of coffee and cake that Haymarket catered in. The participants argued ferociously over every line in the bill; sometimes, a single meeting resulted in only three or four lines of text.[3]

Attendance at these drafting sessions varied between 10 and 20 people from the six sponsoring organizations, but a hardcore of 14 participants showed up nearly every week.[4] Six of these regulars were white, six were black, and two Latino, mirroring almost exactly the racial makeup of the city. Nine of the participants were male and only five female, but no one would dare call such strong women as Joan Jeter Slay and Coretta McFerren shrinking violets or mere tokens.

Social scientists have theorized that when minority group members join dominant group individuals in social action movements, the dominant group members assume disproportionate influence and co-opt the minority group members. However valid this theory may be for other times and places, it emphatically did not apply to the sessions of C.U.R.E. Debate was candid and agreement not always easily reached. No one felt co-opted or left out. Joan Jeter Slay became positively enraged when someone suggested to her that if blacks and whites negotiate in the same room, the whites will win. "We're stronger than that now," she asserted. Regina Stewart agreed:

> I'm a black woman. I gave birth to black children. I live in a black community. I live black, I pray black, I buy black....I sat in that room and I had just as much to say about what went into that bill as anybody else at that table.[5]

Some important disagreements within C.U.R.E. did break down along racial lines, but the final decisions were a product of interracial bargaining and compromise, not majority group dominance.

The debate over redistribution of State Chapter I funds provides a good example of how C.U.R.E. negotiated a compromise across racial boundaries. Since 1968 the state legislature has provided extra money to big-city school districts in recognition of the special problems low-income, disadvantaged schoolchildren face. This additional money is usually referred to as the State Chapter I program (sometimes called, alternatively, State Title I).[6] Since 1982, the school districts receiving Chapter I money have been mandated to distribute 60 percent of the additional funds to local schools in proportion to their numbers of disadvantaged students, whereas the rest of the money is distributed equally among the schools. A disadvantaged student is defined as one who receives a government subsidized school lunch. Thus the clear intent of the law is that most of the Chapter I money should follow the disadvantaged children who generate it.

Over the years, however, the Chicago Board of Education has used the Chapter I money to help pay administrative costs at Pershing Road. Even when it did distribute the money to needy schools, it often used it for standard services that would have been provided anyway out of general revenue. In other words, Chapter I money supplanted general revenue and did not result in any compensatory education programs for disadvantaged children. The amounts of money involved were not trivial. The state identified 186,478 Chicago schoolchildren as disadvantaged in 1987-88, earmarking $238,699,998 as compensatory Chapter I money. If the full 60 percent of additional funds were distributed to needy schools, it would amount to $143,219,999 for additional programs.

Black parents and politicians had long protested the diversion of Chapter I money away from needy children, and the black members of C.U.R.E. insisted that the reform bill remedy the problem. The SON/SOC representatives from the white northwest side did not disagree with this, but they feared the white schools that had previously gotten more Chapter I money than they deserved would suffer if the money were removed all at once. They therefore argued for a hold harmless clause specifying that no individual school would lose money from the redistribution. The board of education would have to come up with the extra money by slashing its own administrative costs, not reducing instructional funding to any school.

Sokoni Karanja finally convinced the group this was a reasonable compromise that would not harm either black or white schools but would place additional pressure on the school board to streamline its administration. So C.U.R.E. recommended that "funds generated by the low-income pupils at a particular school shall be available to that school"; that "State Title I funds shall not be used to supplant other general aid funds"; but that "no school shall lose resources because of the changed requirements for allocating State Title I funds."[7] Compromise turned an explosively divisive issue into a win-win situation.

Another thorny disagreement cropped up over the composition of the local school councils. Blacks and Latinos wanted parents of schoolchildren to dominate the school governing councils. Yet the SON/SOC members insisted that taxpayers without children in the public schools deserved equal representation with parents and teachers. Otherwise they would suffer from taxation without representation.

C.U.R.E. acceded to the SON/SOC position after much debate, proposing 19-member local school councils with six parents, six teachers, and six community members (the school principal would serve ex officio). They were unable to win this position in the legislature, however, for various parent groups such as P.U.R.E (Parents United to Reform Education), Concerned Parents' Network/Believe in the Public Schools, and the parent/community council of the mayor's summit insisted on a parent majority. Unfortunately, this proved to be an Achilles' heel of the reform law much later when it was judged unconstitutional. The SON/SOC position proved prescient, for the Illinois Supreme Court ruled that a built-in parent majority, voted in only by other parents not the general electorate, violates the one person-one vote doctrine.

More important than the details of these racial cleavages within C.U.R.E. was the process of compromise that finally produced agreement. Though the white and black members did not initially trust each other, though they each harbored strong opinions and represented entrenched special interests, they finally agreed to put kids first and keep arguing until they found common ground. Many of the participants in the Haymarket drafting sessions have not seen each other since 1988, but when interviewed, they were remarkably consistent in their accounts of those sessions. Clearly they built an esprit de corps, a sense of trust and loyalty, during those long mornings at Haymarket. All the members of C.U.R.E. agree that they were the most remarkable multiracial meetings they had ever attended.

Renee Montoya summed it up best. Usually when advocacy groups get together, each representative just waits a turn to speak, rehearsing his own bargaining position in his mind, and doesn't really listen to what the others are saying. Over the course of four months at Haymarket, however, the diverse members of C.U.R.E. began to listen carefully to both the words and the hearts of the others. They began to realize that C.U.R.E. formed a microcosm of Chicago. If they could compromise and reach agreement, they could sell their agreement citywide.

The "Kids First" Bill

C.U.R.E. completed most of its legislative draft at a meeting on December 20, 1987, just before Christmas, then they refined it at four meetings in January. Norton Kay and his aide, Tom Gradel, worked closely with Don Moore and Renee Montoya to prepare a press conference, and on February 3 they unveiled their proposal, calling it the "Kids First" bill.

The heart of the C.U.R.E. plan was the school governing council composed of equal numbers of parents, teachers, and community representatives. The councils would enjoy the power to hire the school's principal directly by majority vote. The principals would lose tenure and would work instead on three-year performance contracts. Anyone with state certification as a principal could be hired. This was an important provision, for the Chicago Board of Education artificially narrowed the talent pool by stipulating many burdensome additional requirements. C.U.R.E. proposed to open up the process and try to recruit new blood into the principals' ranks.

Principals would be granted power to hire teachers according to merit and without regard to seniority, and they would enjoy supervisory authority over building engineers and other support staff in the school. In short, the principal would act as CEO of the local school, accountable to the school governing council, its board of directors.

The C.U.R.E. bill proposed that the current members of the board of education all be replaced, following the precedent set at the time of the schools' financial crisis in 1980. The mayor would appoint a new 11-member board from slates presented by a nominating commission. A transition-oversight commission would be appointed for a three-year term to monitor the implementation of all the various reforms and to conduct a management study and devise a spending cap on the central board's administrative expenses. Finally, the bill mandated that, after a five-year transition to the reformed system, parents be allowed to send their children to any school in the city, subject to space availability.

After completing the draft bill, C.U.R.E. began organizing support and gaining publicity for it. Ambitious plans to hire a full-time campaign manager, five full-time area coordinators, and 10 part-time organizers foundered for lack of funds. Eventually, they hired one full-time staff person to coordinate the publicity and lobbying campaign and recruited about one hundred volunteers to drum up community support for the bill. Designs for Change produced an attractive logo, portraying one black, one brown, and one white child, each reading a book and enthusiastically raising his or her hand. They also collaborated with Haymarket's consultants to produce buttons, bumper stickers, and a glossy, bilingual brochure, titled "Kids First—Los Niños Primero."[8]

In the meantime, Mary Dempsey, the chief bill drafter for C.U.R.E., made contact with the Legislative Reference Bureau (LRB) in Springfield and began working with the bureau's education expert, Terry Helmich. Dempsey laughingly calls the LRB "the last of the great tyrants," but its services proved essential to hammer the bill into proper legislative form. Dempsey and Don Moore flew down to Springfield in mid-March, in a blinding snowstorm, to file the bill. The snow fell so thickly they had to return by train. From then on, Renee Montoya and Mary Dempsey represented the C.U.R.E. coalition in Springfield. Montoya estimates that she spent at least two weeks a month in the state capital for the rest of the year, and Haymarket billed Richard Dennis for 22 round-trip plane fares to Springfield.

Back in the Chicago neighborhoods, the various members of C.U.R.E. started lining up the sponsorship of local lawmakers. Don Moore and others approached Miguel del Valle, who had won election to the senate in the aftermath of the dropout controversy primarily to deal with education issues. Del Valle was waiting for the education summit to produce a consensus reform plan. The chairman of his district education committee, Janice Metzger, was a cochair of the summit and she urged him not to dive into the legislative arena prematurely. But del Valle told her, "I didn't come all this way to sit on the sidelines." Though just a freshman legislator, he knew that the best way to win a seat at the table when final decisions were made was to sponsor a bill, and he had begun to suspect that the summit might never produce a reform plan of its own. So he agreed to throw the C.U.R.E bill into the senate hopper.[9] The black members of C.U.R.E. recruited Carol Moseley Braun, Mayor Washington's former floor leader, as the main house sponsor. Two white Democrats from the north side, Al Ronan in the house and William Marovitz in the senate, signed on as cosponsors.

SON/SOC was the only member of the C.U.R.E. coalition with ties to the Republican party. During and after the Council Wars imbroglio, the long-moribund Chicago Republicans encouraged white ethnic Democrats to defect from their "black dominated" party. Alderman Ed Vrdolyak and Sheriff James O'Grady were the most noteworthy converts, but the Republicans were looking for more recruits and they openly cultivated the SON/SOC community organizations. SON/SOC was able to sign up Senator Robert Kustra from Park Ridge, just over the city limits, as the lone Republican sponsor of the C.U.R.E. bill. This attempt at bipartisanship ultimately failed, for Kustra later jumped ship and the reform bill passed without any Republican votes, but at this stage, in spring 1988, C.U.R.E. was still pursuing a bipartisan strategy of coalition building.

SB 2144, sponsored by del Valle, Kustra, and Marovitz, and HB 3707, sponsored by Braun and Ronan, were officially registered for first reading in their respective houses on April 8. Tom Coffey and Norton Kay flew to Springfield on April 13 for a press conference with the legislators to announce the

C.U.R.E. legislation, right on schedule, just as Coffey had out-lined it back in October.[10]

Parents Take Control

While C.U.R.E. was completing its legislative draft, the parent/community council (PCC) faced a January 23 deadline to report its own plan to the education summit. Three other groups sitting at the summit, the Chicago Teachers Union, the Chicago Board of Education, and Chicago United, representing the business community, were also mandated to present reports by then.

Harold Washington's death had hit the parent representatives hard and many feared the whole summit process would immediately unravel. But James Deanes, a community leader from the far west side Austin neighborhood, rallied the council members and transformed their grief into motivation. He dedicated the work of the PCC to the late mayor, and every subsequent report issued by the council and the summit began with this quote from Harold: "For the sake of our young people, it is time to take anger and turn it into positive energy for reforming the school system."

The same night that the city council chose Mayor Washington's successor, the parent/community council conducted its first community forum at Hyde Park High School on the south side. About 250 people pulled themselves away from the televised maneuverings of the politicos to express their continuing outrage at the state of the public schools. Nine other forums, in all parts of the city, followed in short order over the course of a week; then the PCC held more formal hearings for various education advocacy groups on the weekend of December 12 and 13.[11]

The choice of Eugene Sawyer as acting mayor, however, did not bode well for the progress of school reform. Everyone agreed that Gene Sawyer was a genuinely nice man—this is not a statement made very often about Chicago mayors.[12] Yet he utterly lacked charisma and had no political experience outside his comfortable middle-class ward. Clearly out of his depth as mayor, Sawyer relied heavily on Erwin France, a politically connected management consultant who had worked for every Chicago mayor dating back to Richard J. Daley. France received a consulting contract from Sawyer that paid him $125 per hour and immediately became the mayor's *eminence grise*.[13]

Rev. Kenneth Smith scheduled a meeting with Sawyer on the Saturday after his selection. After cooling his heels for a full hour outside the mayor's office, Smith finally got to see Sawyer and France for about six minutes. He offered to stay on as cochair of the summit and Sawyer agreed, but Smith found it curious that the acting mayor gave so little time to the most electric issue facing the city. Smith admits that he left the fifth floor of city hall "feeling a little bothered."[14]

Hal Baron's experience with the new administration was similar, but he found himself even more vulnerable because he was white. Baron also offered to stay on as staff manager of the summit—he too could only grab a few minutes with Erwin France—and though he was asked to continue working with the summit, he was relieved of his other policy duties. A few months later, Sharon Gist Gilliam, Sawyer's chief of staff, admitted to Baron that they only kept him on so that the mayor could distance himself from the summit when it failed.[15]

The PCC harbored no thoughts of failure, but they did expect manipulation or even betrayal from the Sawyer administration. Deanes and his three cochairs jealously guarded their prerogatives as the legitimate voice of parents in the city, but they did try to work with Baron and his staff as best they could. A more militant rebel faction, however, sprang up in the PCC and questioned nearly every decision the mayor's staff made. They particularly resented the hiring of Northwest Regional Education Laboratory as consultants to the PCC. One of a series of educational research labs funded by the federal government, the Portland, Oregon, firm was recommended to Hal Baron by Nelvia Brady of the Chicago Community Trust, which was partially funding the summit. They brought in experts from across the country to lecture the parents on school-based management and planned to write the actual draft of the PCC plan.

Coretta McFerren, who was not only the coordinator of the Peoples' Coalition and a member of C.U.R.E. but a parent representative on the PCC as well, stirred up the rebel faction against the Northwest Labs. She was strongly supported by Russell Green, a black lawyer from the far north side lakefront neighborhood of Rogers Park. They pointed out the obvious, that the Portland consultants knew nothing about Chicago politics, and they expressed sharp resentment at the attempt by white outsiders to control their deliberations.

The whole controversy came to a head when the Northwest Labs presented their analysis of the community forums. The consultants had quantified and coded all the public speeches at these forums, concluding that student achievement was a very low priority for Chicago parents. This outraged nearly all the members of the PCC. Although members of the general public may not have used exactly the right buzz words the consultants were looking for, they were clearly angry that students were not learning. The PCC, therefore, voted to toss out the Northwest Regional Labs consultants. Baron agreed, but since they had a signed contract he retained them as his personal consultants.[16]

Members of the PCC, therefore, decided to write their own school reform plan. Coretta McFerren and her rebel faction took over the offices of Voices for Illinois Children, an advocacy group headed by one of her fellow rebels, Malcolm Bush, as soon as the premises closed each day. They worked nearly nonstop at nights, on weekends, and over the Christmas holidays to hammer out a draft reform plan. They feared that the composition of the central board would prove to be the thorniest issue, so they deferred that matter until the end and tackled the composition of local school councils and other questions first. As the January deadline approached, the full council packed up for a weekend retreat in Des Plaines where they reached decisions on all the contested issues and finally overcame the suspicions between the militant and the moderate factions. In Jan Metzger's judgment, this was the first time they really gelled as a group.[1]

The school reform plan that the PCC approved on January 19 and 20, and submitted to the mayor's summit on January 22, called for local school governing boards of between 10 and 20 members, depending on the size of the school. The plan mandated that at least 60 percent of the council members must be parents of children enrolled at the school. Hal Baron pointed out that this automatic parent majority might pose some constitutional problems, but the PCC remained adamant. The composition of the central board didn't prove as difficult to settle as the council had originally feared. No one wanted to break up the Chicago district into several autonomous districts, for this would simply weaken Chicago's bargaining power in Springfield. They reached an easy consensus, therefore, to retain one central board of education. However, the proposed plan enlarged the board to 23 members, with 20 elected from the local school councils in each district of the city and only three appointed by the mayor. To monitor school reform, they proposed an all-parent oversight commission with the first members drawn exclusively from the PCC.[2]

The parent/community council was the only one of the four summit groups to finish their report on time. The board of education did not even receive its consultants' report until January 21, so they asked for a few weeks' extension to hammer it into final shape. Neither the teachers' union nor the business community met the January 23 deadline either. The strategic decision by Mayor Washington and Hal Baron to let the PCC drive the summit proved correct; only they felt sufficient urgency to move the process along. The PCC members, however, still had a chip on their shoulders concerning the Sawyer administration. Rather than hand over their completed document to the acting mayor, they presented the official copy to Mary Ella Smith, Harold Washington's long-time companion and fiancee.[3]

The Summit and the Rump Summit

When Harold Washington appointed the parent/community council he indicated that 10 of its members should sit on the full education summit, but he didn't outline an exact procedure for choosing the 10. So the chair and the cochairs decided that the four of them would sit ex officio and the PCC would elect six others. Coretta McFerren and her rebel faction dominated the PCC delegation, and McFerren ostentatiously refused to sit with the PCC cochairs at the full summit meetings. Though her strong personality earned her a major role in PCC deliberations, her membership in C.U.R.E. led to considerable suspicion of her motives. Quite frankly, the cochairs of the PCC considered her a C.U.R.E. mole.[4]

When they sent off their delegation to the full summit discussions in February, the PCC instructed them to vote as a bloc. Tee Galley, the president of the Chicago Panel on Public School Policy and Finance (CHIPS), who was also a parent delegate, refused to abide by this rule, so the PCC voted her out and replaced her with another parent. Mayor Sawyer, however, kept Galley on the full summit to represent CHIPS. The overthrow of Galley sent a clear message to Coretta McFerren who became more cooperative with the other parent delegates.

The PCC directed its suspicions at other members of the summit as well. They refused to let Hal Baron's consultants from the Northwest Labs dominate the process of consolidating the four reports into one. Instead, they insisted that the full summit break out into five working committees to write the final draft themselves. The five committees met throughout February and were still arguing as the original March 1 deadline for completion slipped by. Their labors finally produced the five major sections of the summit report: "Improve Student Performance," "Professionalization of Teaching," "Strengthen Leadership," "Achieve Greater Role for Parents and Staff," and "Streamline Central Governance." The summit's executive committee took these five sections with them for the so-called Amoco weekend, a two-day working session at the Amoco building on the weekend of March 19 and 20. The next day, March 21, the full summit approved their draft.[5]

The draft report of the education summit contained both more and less than the C.U.R.E. bill. It presented a much more comprehensive blueprint for school reform than C.U.R.E. did, but it also manifested a few glaring omissions.[6]

The section titled "Improve Student Performance" set out a series of performance goals, such as increased test scores and reduced dropout rates, for the school system to reach within five years. This statement of goals was a direct carryover from the first learn-earn summit that Manford Byrd had torpedoed and it was eventually translated with only a few changes into the final law. The section on "Professionalization of Teaching" clearly reflected the position of the teachers' union in its calls for increased salaries, a professional career ladder, a longer school day and/or school year, and reduced class sizes. The "Strengthen Leadership" section provided for principal training and principal accountability but it also laid out the full authority of the principal over all staff at the local school. The next section outlined plans for a "local school body" at each school composed of 11 members: six parents, two teachers, two community members, and the principal. Though revised from the original PCC proposal, this plan for the local school councils retained a clear parent majority, unlike the C.U.R.E. plan that called for equal representation of parents, teachers, and community members. The summit model was adopted in the final law and then later declared unconstitutional by the courts. The final section, "Streamline Central Governance," clearly remained unfinished in the March draft. It provided for a central board of 11 to 15 members, appointed by the mayor, but it indicated that further negotiations were necessary to fashion a grassroots nominating process.

The summit reform plan was breathtaking in its scope, including nearly every reform idea that had surfaced since the appearance of "A Nation at Risk" five years previously. Indeed, whole sections appeared to be a fantasy wish list for teachers and reformers. Yet three omissions stood out in the March draft: there was no provision for redistributing State Chapter I funds to disadvantaged schools, no attempt was made to slash the central bureaucracy and cap administrative expenses, and there was no mandate for an oversight commission to monitor the progress of reform.

The summit proposal received a frosty greeting. One of its own members, Bruce Berndt from the Principals' Association, objected strongly to the loss of tenure by the principals. The *Chicago Tribune*'s editorial pointed out the obvious: "The urgent need for more revenue is glossed over." This concern took center stage when a member of the technical review panel that Hal Baron assembled to examine the plan reported that the summit recommendations would add "at least $210 million to $290 million in additional spending."[23]

It became painfully obvious that the summit proposal was dead on arrival when the education committees of the Illinois House and Senate held joint hearings at the State of Illinois Building in Chicago on March 30 and 31. Mayor Sawyer testified the first day. Though he delivered a folksy preamble thanking the summit "as a grandparent, a former teacher and as a ward committeeman, who has to answer to the residents in his ward"; he undercut the impact of the report by disagreeing with one of its key features, the power of the local school councils to hire and fire principals. His address also made clear that he did not want to diminish the power and authority of the general superintendent in any way.[24]

The legislators deemed the summit plan too costly; it would never win acceptance unless it proposed deep cuts in the central bureaucracy. Representative Ellis Levin stated flatly, "The proposal as it is constituted now, isn't going to fly, it's going to take a dive." More diplomatically and constructively, Senator Arthur Berman, the chairman of the Senate Education Committee, counselled the summit members to "set priorities on their recommendations and consider phasing in programs." The day after the hearings, the *Tribune* headlined its editorial, "Education Summit must do better."[25]

The summit members went back to the drawing boards, but in the meantime a smaller group within the summit began holding outside meetings. As early as February, the business executives had grown restive at the slow pace of deliberations and had started meeting informally with some of the parent representatives at Chicago United's offices in the First National Bank building. Coretta McFerren and her rebel faction joined the group as did some PCC members who had not won election to the full summit and felt left out. Don Moore, representing Designs for Change and C.U.R.E., and Danny Solis from UNO also took part. Moore called this group the "progressive caucus" of the education summit. Others, less complimentary, referred to it as the "rump summit." Ken Smith knew the meetings were going on, but he didn't see anything he could do to prevent them. Jan Metzger attended the rump summit at first, but finally dropped out when she realized she was jeopardizing her credibility as a cochair of the PCC.[26]

Without all the participants realizing it, the rump summit became a vehicle for advancing the C.U.R.E. plan. They insisted on a redistribution of Chapter I funds as a matter of basic equity and pushed for a radical downsizing of the central bureaucracy. The full summit finally added a strong section on funding equity that required Chapter I funds to be "allocated to local schools in proportion to their numbers of eligible low-income students" and stipulated "they must not be used to replace or supplant these other funds."[27] Yet the final draft still did not address the question of downsizing the bureaucracy.

The business executives on the rump summit injected another issue into the debate that caused no end of controversy throughout the year-long battle for school reform. Chicago United's first proposal, unveiled the night of the Bennett blast in November 1987, had included a provision for an oversight commission, modeled on the school finance authority established during the board of education's financial crisis a decade earlier. C.U.R.E.'s plan also called for a transition-oversight commission. Even the parent/community council's original proposal envisioned a parent oversight commission to monitor reform. No one trusted the board of education and the superintendent's bureaucrats to implement reform in good faith. As David Paulus, the vice-president for government and community affairs at First National Bank, phrased it, this would be like Communist *apparatchiks* in Eastern Europe trying to effect *perestroika*. You simply couldn't expect the group needing reform to reform itself.[28]

Late in March, Paulus, Peter Willmott, and George Muñoz, who had been advising Chicago United quietly behind the scenes, and a number of other executives met with Vernon Loucks, the chairman of Baxter Travenol in north suburban Deerfield. In the course of their discussion, they decided to focus most of their lobbying on a strong oversight commission. As Muñoz urged them, "The business community needs something simple to focus on."[29]

When Willmott brought the business proposal for an oversight commission, which would function practically as a receiver for the Chicago public schools, back to the full summit, all hell broke loose. James Deanes of the PCC likened the oversight commission to a plantation overseer under slavery. From that point on, the oversight commission became a lightning rod for black leaders and a major divisive force in the reform coalition. The final summit report simply referred the question to a legislative implementation subcommittee for further study.[30]

By the time the education summit issued its final 74-page report on May 19, both the summit and the report had become largely irrelevant. The lawmakers had grown increasingly restless and started lining up with various reform organizations to sponsor their own bills.[31] C.U.R.E. had carefully refrained from buttonholing sponsors in February and early March so as not to undercut the efforts of the summit, but when the preliminary summit report met with opposition and the rump summit started to assert itself, C.U.R.E. swiftly lined up del Valle, Braun, and their other sponsors.

Just before the summit adjourned, Hal Baron resigned. Erwin France had eliminated his budget and undercut his authority; France even refused to assign a bill-writer to the summit. Then in late April, France took away Baron's city hall office. Baron assumed he could remain indefinitely and draw a paycheck, for Sawyer and France would be unlikely to force a public confrontation, but he could take a hint. He resigned on Monday, May 2. Rev. Kenneth Smith, the moderator of the summit, stayed on until the final report was published, but he refused to attend the formal thank-you ceremony for summit members at the old public library cultural center. This was a powerful symbolic action for such a courtly gentleman as Rev. Smith.[32]

The education summit, and particularly its leading edge, the parent/community council, performed a valuable service by channeling and focusing public outrage in the wake of the 1987 teachers' strike. Kenneth Smith, Hal Baron, James Deanes, and the other leaders of the summit wrapped themselves in the mantle of Harold Washington and pushed for the most comprehensive reform they could conceive. They kept the momentum of the teachers' strike alive and ensured that some reform bill would pass in 1988. Many of their specific proposals, such as the statement of performance goals and the 11-member local school councils, with a parent majority, were embedded in the final law.

Yet the summit proved too ambitious. Its grand plans were far too expensive for the fiscal atmosphere of the 1980s, and the endless debates put the summit out of sync with the time-tables of the legislature. It is true that almost anything is possible in Springfield before June 30, and Senator Berman had carefully introduced several shell bills in the legislature that could be amended into vehicles for the summit's recommendations. Yet the summit proposals were not conveyed to the legislature until the end of May, and by that time the lawmakers had lined up with more specific, more focused proposals such as the C.U.R.E. bill.

Above all, the summit failed due to lack of leadership by the city government, specifically Acting Mayor Sawyer. Harold Washington had attended every meeting of the summit while he was alive, but Sawyer showed up only a couple of times, and only in a ceremonial capacity. Rev. Smith has concluded, in retrospect, that he should have insisted on more time one-on-one with Sawyer and more active participation by the mayor in plenary sessions. If these attempts to force the issue failed, he should have resigned. As it turned out, Rev. Smith admits, "I think that the legislation we have today can be credited chiefly to that other group [the rump summit, C.U.R.E., ABCs]."[33]

Notes

1. Regina Glover Stewart, interview by authors, 18 September 1990.

2. Tom Coffey, interview by authors, 23 October 1990.

3. Tom Coffey provided us with timesheets from the C.U.R.E. meetings as well as many other documents relating to Haymarket's work for C.U.R.E. (hereafter cited as C.U.R.E.-Haymarket papers). The time-sheets indicate that C.U.R.E. held 14 drafting sessions between October 9 and January 20. Full meetings assembled less frequently thereafter.

4. One of the authors, Charles L. Kyle, was a participant in the Haymarket meetings. We interviewed 12 of the other members: Michael Bakalis (13 July 1990), Don Moore (1 August 1990), Joan Jeter Slay (2 August 1990), Earl Durham (6 August 1990), Bob Gannett (19 July 1990), Mike Smith (19 September 1990), Cathy Greenwood (26 November 1990), Kelvin Strong (12 September 1990), Regina Glover Stewart (18 September 1990), Sokoni Karanja (16 October 1990), Coretta McFerren (11 September 1990), and Tomas Sanabria (5 October 1990). Renee Montoya sent us a tape-recorded memoir in November 1990. In addition, Mary Dempsey, Tom Coffey, and Al Raby usually attended the meetings as consultants. We interviewed Dempsey (5 October 1990) and Coffey (23 October 1990), Raby died in 1988. The following account is based on these interviews.

5. Gary T. Marx and Michael Useem, "Majority Involvement in Minority Movements: Civil Rights, Abolition, Untouchability," *Journal of Social Issues* 27 (1971): 81-104; Slay and Stewart interviews.

6. The Chapter 1 provisions are outlined in chapter 122, article 18.8.5 (i) (1) of the School Code of Illinois. We have based our discussion of this matter on a lengthy memorandum, "Outline of State Title I," January 1988, probably prepared by Renee Montoya, in C.U.R.E.-Haymarket papers.

7. This quote, and all subsequent references to the C.U.R.E. bill, is from the "C.U.R.E. Legislative Plan," February 1988, C.U.R.E.-Haymarket papers.

8. Much of C.U.R.E.'s organizational detail is contained in two long memos: Don Moore to Al Raby, "C.U.R.E. Campaign Strategy," 6 December 1987; Don Moore to Al Raby, "Update on the Progress of the C.U.R.E. Campaign," 1 February 1988, C.U.R.E.-Haymarket papers.

9. Miguel del Valle, interview by authors, 29 January 1991.

10. *Final Legislative Synopsis and Digest,* 85th General Assembly, 1988 sess., 1: 737-38, 1750-51; *Chicago Tribune*, 14 April 1988, sec. 2, p. 2; *Chicago Sun-Times*, 14 April 1988, 28.

11. *Chicago Tribune*, 30 November 1987, sec 2, p. 4; 2 December 1987, sec. 2, p.3; 11 December 1987, 1; Janice Metzger, interview by authors, 26 November 1990.

12. Apologies to Arnold R. Hirsch from whom we stole this idea. Hirsch wrote the following about Martin H. Kennelly: "He was a nice man. It is not the sort of thing one usually says about Chicago's mayors...." See Hirsch's article about Kennelly in *The Mayors: The Chicago Political Tradition,* eds. Paul M. Green and Melvin G. Holli (Carbondale: Southern Illinois University Press, 1987), 126. Aside from Kennelly and Sawyer, we can't think of any other Chicago mayor to whom the adjective nice is applicable.

13. *Chicago Tribune*, 4 December 1987, 2; 11 February 1988, 1; *Chicago Sun-Times*, 25 March 1988, 1.

14. Kenneth Smith, interview by authors, 29 November 1990.

15. Harold Baron, interview by authors, 4 December 1990.

16. Baron, Metzger, McFerren interviews.

17. Metzger interview.

18. "Parent/Community Council—Complete Proposal Draft," 19 January 1988, C.U.R.E-SON/SOC papers; *Chicago Tribune*, 10 January 1988, sec. 2, p. 1; 12 January 1988, sec. 2, p. 8; 21 January 1988, sec. 2, p. 1.

19. *Chicago Tribune*, 24 January 1988, sec. 2, p. 3.

20. Metzger, McFerren interviews.

21. Baron, Metzger, Kenneth Smith interviews; *Chicago Sun-Times*, 21 March 1988, 1.

22. The following exposition is drawn from two summit drafts: "Agreements of the Mayor's Education Summit, A Preliminary Paper," 29 March 1988; and the final glossy report, "An Agenda for the Reform of Chicago Public Schools," 19 May 1988.

23. *Chicago Tribune*, 27 March 1988, sec. 4, p. 2; 28 March 1988, sec. 2, p. 1.

24. "Mayor Sawyer's Statement before the Joint Legislative Committee on Education," 30 March 1988, C.U.R.E.-Haymarket papers.

25. *Chicago Tribune*, 31 March 1988, 1; 1 April 1988, 12; *Chicago Sun-Times*, 31 March 1988, 8.

26. Kenneth Smith, Metzger, McFerren, Moore interviews; Danny Solis, interview by authors, 17 October 1990.

27. Mayor's Education Summit, "Agenda for Reform," 17.

28. David Paulus, interview by authors, 16 November 1990.

29. Paulus interview; Patrick Keleher, interview by authors, 22 October 1990.

30. Mayor's Education Summit, "Agenda for Reform," 33; *Chicago Tribune*, 7 April 1988, sec. 2, p. 8; 29 April 1988, sec. 2, p. 1.

31. *Chicago Tribune*, 20 May 1988, 1.

32. Baron, Kenneth Smith interviews; *Chicago Tribune*, 4 May 1988, sec. 2, p. 2.

33. Kenneth Smith interview.

⓵⓷ "Don't Come Home Without It"

Out of the wreckage of the mayor's summit, a larger coalition emerged. Finding support in unexpected places, a grand alliance of parents, community organizations, and businessmen waged a year-long battle in Springfield under the banner of ABCs, the Alliance for Better Chicago Schools. Community organizations chartered yellow school buses to haul wave after wave of parents to Springfield, while CEOs of Chicago's largest corporations flew down to the capital in their corporate jets. More rhetorical blasts from outsiders kept the legislative pot boiling, and in a number of Chicago wards the voters showed strong support for decentralization of the schools. To the surprise of many, the Chicago Teachers Union also became an ally in the reform cause. Encouraged by all these positive signs, the ABCs coalition warned the lawmakers continually, "Don't Come Home Without It."

The Referendum

While the education summit was still debating, the state of Illinois held its 1988 presidential primary on March 15, and the voters chose candidates for many state and local offices as well. Native sons Jesse Jackson and Paul Simon divided up most of the Democratic votes, temporarily slowing the front-runner for the presidential nomination, Michael Dukakis. Meanwhile, George Bush buried Robert Dole on the Republican side. Far down the ballot, in only one corner of Chicago, an advisory referendum on school reform received very little publicity in the news media but caught the attention of state politicians, who read closely the grammar and syntax of votes.[1]

Bob Gannett and Mike Smith from SON/SOC had recently obtained legislation facilitating such advisory referenda. They were primarily interested in another issue altogether: home equity insurance in neighborhoods threatened by racial change. If the voters in a designated district approved home equity, they could tax themselves to form an insurance pool that would guarantee their property values. Organizers hoped such an economic guarantee would stop the headlong white flight that usually greeted the appearance of a black homeowner in the city's bungalow belt. To make this scheme possible, SON/SOC won a major change in the election code, authorizing referenda in districts smaller than a municipality. While pursuing the home equity plan on both the northwest and southwest sides, Gannett and Smith pointed out that this small-scale referendum mechanism was available for any public policy issue, including school reform.[2]

Mike Bakalis, Don Moore, and others opposed the referendum as a diversion of scarce time and manpower, and they feared that school reform might be fatally damaged if the voters turned it down. They finally allowed SON/SOC to pursue the idea, but none of the other groups in C.U.R.E. followed suit in their own neighborhoods.[3]

In late October 1987, Gannett and Smith delegated one of their organizers, Pat Bower, to work nearly full time gathering signatures from 10 percent of the voters in their target district on the northwest side. Bower recruited about one hundred individuals who collected at least 70 signatures each. It was during this door-to-door canvass that he found Cathy Greenwood, a housewife and mother who had never even heard of SON/SOC previously. Greenwood agreed to gather her quota of 70 signatures, then threw herself into the school reform movement and wound up as secretary of C.U.R.E. Thanks to her efforts and the efforts of those like her, the petition drive reached the minimum number just in time.[4]

The referendum asked voters to check *Yes* or *No* to the following question: "Shall there be instituted in the Chicago public school system a decentralized system of management whereby each local school shall be managed by an elected council consisting of parents, community residents and teachers, whose authority shall include, but not be limited to, the hiring of the school's principal and teachers, control of the school's operating budget and the design and implementation of comprehensive school improvement plans?" This question appeared on the ballot in parts of six wards, the 30th, 33rd, 35th, 36th, 38th, and the 45th, covering an area roughly from Irving Park Road on the north, to Pulaski on the east, to the Milwaukee Road railroad tracks on the south and west. SON/SOC touted this referendum as a last chance for the public schools. If it failed, they planned to ride the tax revolt of the eighties and seek a state law mandating voter approval before any tax increase for education could take effect.[5]

The school reform referendum proved successful. Nearly 19,000 voters found the question at the bottom of the ballot in the 136 precincts where it appeared. A total of 15,617 (82.8 percent) voted Yes. Haymarket's Norton Kay organized a news conference, with Earl Durham from C.U.R.E. and Barbara Phillips, a northwest-side mother, as spokespersons. Though they garnered meager press coverage, they made certain that legislators received copies of the vote totals.[6]

The Save Our Neighborhoods/Save Our City coalition sometimes seemed like an albatross around the neck of C.U.R.E. With their assertive white ethnic agenda, they engendered suspicion among minority parents. Yet the referendum that they pulled off single-handedly proved an important asset. It represented the only vote ever taken on the issue before passage of the law, and it demonstrated decisively that even voters without children in the public schools favored school reform. As business executive David Paulus remarked in another context, "Never underestimate the value of surprise in Springfield." By demonstrating support for local school councils in an unlikely quarter, SON/SOC jolted the reform movement forward another step. Don Moore admitted later that C.U.R.E. should have organized referenda in other parts of the city.[7]

The Coalition Grows Larger

With the political primaries out of the way and the legislative clock ticking in Springfield, both politicians and school reformers grew restless at the lack of progress by the education summit. Besides the C.U.R.E. bill, a flood of other school reform plans were thrown into the legislative hopper in March and April of 1988.

Senator Arthur Berman, the chairman of the education committee in the upper house, prudently introduced several shell bills dealing with education so he would be ready for any eventuality. A shell bill, or vehicle bill, is a sketchy first draft introduced to hold a spot on the legislative calendar. When the final draft becomes available, the sponsor of the bill grafts it onto the shell bill in the form of an amendment, which reads something like this: "Delete everything after the enacting clause and add the following." Berman designated one of his shell bills (SB 1837) specifically "for implementation of reform measures resulting from the Chicago Mayor's Education Summit" and as a vehicle for the major platform of the rump summit, the creation of a Chicago Education Authority that "shall facilitate, oversee and assure that the Chicago Board of Education implements reform measures."[8]

Other education bills crowded the calendar in 1988. The Chicago Panel on Public School Policy and Finance (CHIPS) reintroduced their pilot project bill, calling for school-based management at two schools in each district of the city (HB 935 and SB 2222). Barbara Flynn Currie sponsored the measure in the house again, and this time CHIPS secured a senate sponsor as well, Richard Newhouse, a black senator from the south side. Howard Carroll, a north side Democrat, introduced the usual bill calling for the breakup of the Chicago school district into 20 smaller districts (SB 0699). This scheme had turned up in one form or another ever since decentralization entered the political arena in the early 1980s. Rep. Robert Terzich from the far southwest side introduced a more radical, and more blatantly political, decentralization plan that he had hatched along with Congressman William Lipinski and Alderman William Krystiniak. Terzich's HB 4012 would divide the Chicago school district into 50 new districts, each one coterminous with a city ward. This measure came straight out of the nineteenth century and must have made the remaining ward bosses of the Democratic machine chuckle.

A parents' coalition from Hyde Park and the north side lakefront, cumbersomely titled the Concerned Parents' Network/Believe in the Public Schools, secured support from north side legislators John Cullerton and Dawn Clark Netsch for their reform bill (HB 3446 and SB 2045). This parents' alternative, as they liked to call it, closely resembled the C.U.R.E. bill. However, the local school councils would have a clear parent majority, and the legislation also called for reduction in class size, which everyone agreed was desirable but which would prove very costly.

Nothing much happened with any of these bills in April or early May, but behind the scenes a broad coalition began building consensus behind the C.U.R.E. bill. The education summit had not yet drafted its own legislation by May 20, the deadline for bills to clear one house of the legislature. It would still be possible to graft the summit's results on a shell bill at the last moment, but no one felt certain the summit would ever produce any final results.

Chicago United, the business community's lead organization for school reform, originally expressed support for Berman's shell bill, SB 1837, since it made specific provision for their pet measure, an oversight authority. UNO, the strongest Latino voice on the mayor's summit, and a number of smaller community organizations also lined up behind it, though they vowed to push for reduced class sizes and increased school funding as well. Yet as the summit floundered, Don Moore negotiated carefully with the business representatives on the rump summit and agreed to add a strong oversight authority to the C.U.R.E. bill in exchange for their support. Because Chicago United was soliciting its members to build a war chest, they welcomed the prospect of increased financial backing for reform.[9]

Then Danny Solis of UNO made his move. Renee Montoya from Designs for Change had been meeting Solis privately for breakfast in the early months of 1988. After the various bills were introduced, Montoya tried a final pitch to win Solis's support for the C.U.R.E. bill. She told him bluntly, "You know, Danny, we're gonna win." Solis bristled and asked defensively, "How do you know that?" Montoya looked him straight in the eye and replied, "Because we have more money than you."[10]

A few weeks after her confrontation with Solis, Montoya was working all night in Springfield on some draft amendments to the bill. Before seven in the morning, after only two hours of sleep, she was awakened in her hotel room by the jangling of the phone. A voice on the other end of the line told her, "You've got a deal." Shaking the cobwebs from her head, she stammered, "Who is this?" The voice replied, "This is Danny. I'll meet you in your hotel lobby in a half an hour." They met for breakfast and sealed the deal over coffee.[11] Solis knew that money—the mother's milk of politics *and* community organizing—was key to achieving reform.

UNO announced its support for HB 3707, the Kids First education reform bill, at a press conference in the offices of the Haymarket Group on Monday, May 16. The Clarence Darrow Center, a social service organization serving the LeClaire Courts public housing project, and the Developing Communities Project, a community organization on the far south side, also adhered to the reform coalition at the same press conference. UNO, however, was the key convert. They insisted that the reform coalition hold out for a redistribution of Chapter I funds, something that C.U.R.E. was committed to anyway, and they demanded a symbolic nod to the "Neighborhood Schoolhouse

That Works," the product of UNO's earlier education efforts.

At the press conference, Mike Bakalis pointed out that "UNO becomes the first Summit member to publicly endorse another legislative plan." Veronica Cabrera, the education coordinator for UNO, remarked diplomatically, "We are not deserting the Summit. We are carrying forward its principles. If anything, the Summit has not kept pace with legislative requirements." Carol Moseley Braun, the house sponsor of the C.U.R.E. bill, concluded, "It would be in the best interests of school reform if more organizations could coalesce around one bill. I believe it should be around HB 3707. As it stands today, it is the only comprehensive school reform package before the legislature."[12]

Chicago United and the eight business organizations they represented, C.U.R.E. (by this time swelled to 13 sponsoring groups), and UNO's six constituent Latino organizations formalized their coalition in late May, christening it the ABCs, or Alliance for Better Chicago Schools. They demanded, as an absolute minimum, that school reform must include six elements: local school decision making, authority to principals, teacher accountability, equity of resources, cuts in central administration, and an oversight commission with powers to ensure reforms are carried out. They issued a four-page checklist spelling out the details of these six demands and began rating the various school reform bills floating around Springfield. ABCs did not formally endorse any particular bill, but their brochure did include the following statement:

> The single bill now under consideration that passes these tests is HB 3707 as amended, sponsored by Representatives Braun and Ronan. This same bill has been championed by Senators del Valle and Marovitz as SB 2144. But we are not concerned about bill numbers. We will support any bill that passes these critical tests.[13]

ABCs was a larger, looser, more flexible version of C.U.R.E. It championed essentially the same reform plan and included a very broad cross-section of the city. The addition of

business money from Chicago United and community organizing manpower from UNO gave it considerably more muscle to
influence the lawmakers. As Danny Solis has concluded, "With
the power of money that the corporate community represented
and with the organized people power that UNO represented, we
injected each other with a sense of enthusiasm."[14]

More Blasts from Bennett, and Others

The emerging reform coalition received some indirect aid
from outside sources. U.S. Education Secretary William
Bennett, who had blasted Chicago's schools as "the worst in the
nation" back in November of 1987, refused to go away or to
shut up. When Jacqueline Vaughn, the president of the Chicago
Teachers' Union, discovered that Bennett was scheduled for a
speech in Chicago to a Republican women's club in March, she
challenged him to visit some Chicago schools in person. On
Wednesday, March 23, Bennett took the dare and accompanied
Vaughn to Bogan High School, one of the few successfully
integrated schools in the city, and Terrell Elementary, an all-
black school with a dynamic principal. Bennett acknowledged
the positive features he saw but affirmed he hadn't changed his
mind about Chicago: "Two schools do not a system make."[15]

When Coretta McFerren heard at the C.U.R.E. meeting
about Bennett's visit, she feared that the teachers' union had
given him a snow job, and she decided to counteract it. She
called Washington, D.C., and somewhat to her own surprise,
managed to get through to Bennett's secretary. She then contacted the regional director of the education department in Chicago, Rosemary Thomson, and arranged a meeting next time
Bennett came to town. The other black members of C.U.R.E.,
however, convinced Coretta that publicly consorting with the
Reagan administration could badly damage their credibility in
the black community. So Cathy Greenwood and the other
SON/SOC representatives took over. They brought a delegation
of white parents from the northwest and southwest sides to
meet with Bennett in the early morning of May 11 at Midway

Airport. This is one of the clearest examples of interracial co-operation (or perhaps more accurately, collusion) in the school reform movement.

Bennett remarked to the press after the Midway meeting, "What I heard about this morning was the atrocities of this city. The parents were very angry and sad." The secretary of education then proceeded to Springfield and delivered the Reagan party line, telling the legislature not to throw money at the schools. Instead they should "shrink the blob," the bloated educational bureaucracy in Chicago.[16]

A week later, a Republican education bill became the first to clear one house of the state legislature. Senator Robert Kustra, an original sponsor of the C.U.R.E. bill, abandoned the reform coalition and signed on as cosponsor of the 20-district decentralization bill instead. Though this was presented as a reform measure, it was actually backed by the Illinois Education Association, the teachers' union that represented all the downstate school districts and had been itching for a chance to compete with the rival Chicago Teachers Union for the allegiance of the big city's teachers. If the Chicago district were broken up, it would leave a wide-open field for the IEA to contest union elections in each of the 20 new districts. SB 2261 passed the senate on May 20 with solid Republican support as well as the backing of 14 Democrats.[17]

Then on May 29, Chicago's leading newspaper, the *Tribune*, published a tough editorial with a radical conclusion. The editors began their blast in words reminiscent of William Bennett:

> What will save Chicago's public schools, the worst in America? Not the Chicago Board of Education. It hasn't the guts or know-how....Not the superintendent of schools. Dr. Manford Byrd is shamefully ignorant about his own school system.... Not the teachers. The Chicago Teachers Union has a militant interest in only two things—getting more money for its members and preventing even the most incompetent of them from ever being fired. Not Chicago's mayor. He doesn't count.

The *Tribune* then proposed that "the quickest, surest way to explode the bureaucratic blob, escape from the self-seeking union and develop schools that succeed for children is to set up a voucher system." If parents were given tuition vouchers redeemable at any school in the state, private or public, competition and free enterprise would force each school to do a better job or else close for lack of students. This proposal was eminently Reaganesque and Republican, but it also held a strong appeal for Chicago's large Catholic population who supported their own schools and complained about double taxation.[18]

Secretary Bennett jumped into the fray one more time with a speech to the Chicago Council of Foreign Affairs on June 7. Tying the education crisis directly to America's loss of economic competitiveness, Bennett too championed a voucher system, specifically citing the *Tribune* editorial for support.[19]

Union Strategy

All these rhetorical blasts heated up the atmosphere in Chicago and Springfield. More important, they reinforced the decision made by the teachers' union executive to adopt a cooperative stance toward school reform. Tuition vouchers, which might sound the death knell of public education altogether, and a breakup of the Chicago district into smaller districts, where the IEA could compete for members, were the two most threatening approaches to the education crisis from the CTU's point of view. The passage of Kustra's senate bill indicated that some kind of action was a certainty at this legislative session. All of a sudden the local school council plan being pushed by the ABCs coalition looked more moderate and less threatening than the alternatives.

The CTU had long proposed substantive educational reforms for the Chicago schools, such as reduced class size, better textbooks, and a revised curriculum.[20] The union had also been exploring ways of restructuring schools so that teachers and parents would share decision-making authority with principals. It should not be surprising that the teachers' union kept up with the latest reform ideas. After all, along with the students, teachers would be the major beneficiaries of any positive changes in the schools. Yet this very fact, that teachers would benefit from school reform, always made their proposals suspect to others. Calls for reduced class size, for example, were often perceived as attempts to create more jobs, if not downright featherbedding. And as David Peterson, the principal lobbyist for the CTU has pointed out, whenever the union talked about school-based management, it was viewed as a "power grab to take power away from principals."

The 19-day teachers' strike in the fall of 1987 turned this suspicion of the union into downright hostility in many quarters. It would be hard to say whether Pershing Road or the CTU was the greater villain in the public mind. This hostility led to sharp policy consequences. Governor Thompson and the Republicans in the legislature made it crystal clear that they would not provide any new money for Chicago schools unless radical changes were made in the governance structure. The passage of the Kustra bill indicated that it was open season on Chicago down in Springfield. David Peterson summed up that bill's impact, "His designs, we always felt, were really not predicated on what might be good for the system but rather, by his own statements, were really designed at trying to break the Chicago Teachers Union and the ancillary trade unions that work for the Board." The union leaders had to fend off volleys aimed at them, rather than putting forth a positive agenda of their own.

Though placed on the defensive, the union leaders pursued a sophisticated and intelligent strategy. They took part in the education summit and in all the legislative negotiations concerning school reform. They were willing to participate in the reform process as long as they could retain basic structural protections for their membership. When the final school reform bill took shape, they used their substantial political muscle to lobby for its passage.

Peterson, the CTU lobbyist, sums up the pitch he gave to labor-oriented legislators:

> Look, here are the issues as we see them. We see components of this education reform bill that we certainly will be willing to work with. Are we happy with all of it? Absolutely not. If it were our legislation, would it be different? Most definitely. But is it a frame we can work with? We can. Where are the problems? Basically, it was the seniority question.

It seems reasonable to conclude that the teachers' union viewed reform of the structure and governance of the schools as a necessary political precondition for other reforms they cared more deeply about, such as increased funding, reduced class size, and a multiyear contract for their members. Shrewdly, they chose to become part of the solution rather than part of the problem.[21]

On to Springfield

The passage of the Kustra decentralization bill effectively ended the bipartisan phase of the lobbying campaign in Springfield. Previously, members of the ABCs coalition tried to work both sides of the aisle. Designs for Change employed their own lobbyist, Larry Suffredin, who worked with the Democrats on behalf of C.U.R.E. The business leaders of Chicago United hired Jim Fletcher, a former chief of staff to Governor James R. Thompson, to lobby the Republicans. Yet in June 1988, the final month of the legislative session, both political parties hardened their positions and made a bipartisan school reform bill impossible.

On the night of June 6, ABCs geared up for battle with a rally at the Bismarck Hotel across the street from Chicago's city hall. The raucous 90-minute kickoff to the final drive in Springfield attracted 2,500 people. Organizers handed out bright yellow buttons reading "Don't Come Home Without It," and the speakers vowed not to return from the capital without a bill that satisfied all of ABCs key criteria.[22]

The school reform coalition mounted one of the most remarkable lobbying campaigns Springfield had ever seen. Harold Washington's decision to require heads of organizations not deputies at the education summit paid unexpected dividends. Corporate CEOs had grown accustomed to dealing with the education issue, so they flew to Springfield personally in their corporate jets. Due to their debates at the summit, they showed the legislators a depth of knowledge unusual for businessmen dealing with a civic issue.

At the same time, scores of yellow school buses hired with funds from the business war chest brought parents from Chicago's barrios and ghettoes to buttonhole the legislators. UNO turned out about 40 percent of the people who filled those buses, Designs for Change recruited another 40 percent, and other community organizations produced the remaining 20 percent. June 1988 was one of the hottest months on record in Illinois, with temperatures regularly hovering above 90 degrees and often exceeding 100 degrees. Yet the parents kept rolling southward in their ovenlike buses. Legislators are used to angry voters showing up at the capitol steps, but they are not accustomed to seeing them come back every day and debate the issues articulately.

Coretta McFerren and her husband literally lived in Springfield for the month of June and she reports that Renee Montoya taught her, her daughter Gwen Burns, and Regina Glover Stewart how to lobby. Regina called their group the rat pack. They learned the legislators' schedules, walked them to the elevators as they came in, met them as they emerged from lunch. They tried not to badger the legislators but to "peaceably be forceful." Above all, they were persistent and consistent. Tom Coffey reminded them of the political maxim: "You don't have any enemies in this process, just people you haven't been able to win over yet."[23]

Coretta has summed up the lobbying campaign in her own unique style:

We saw God perform a miracle in the hearts of those legislators. They didn't want to hear us, they didn't want to see us, many of them ignored us. But as the days went on, I knew that the Scripture which said, "The heart of the king is in the Lord's hands and he turns it wheresoever he will" is absolutely factual. The disdain turned to respect. The disregard turned to attention. And we began to get their ears....We walked the halls, and we prayed, night and day, and we got the bill passed.

Danny Solis from UNO gave it a much more secular twist: "It was an organizer's dream. Anything we needed, we got. We had people, we had money, we had lawyers." Chicago United collected about three hundred thousand dollars from its members for the lobbying campaign. This was small change for the corporations but big money to community organizers. Fueled with cash and enthusiasm, the school reform coalition refused to come home without the bill they wanted.[24]

Notes

1. Both metropolitan newspapers, the *Tribune* and the *Sun-Times,* covered the primaries fully on their front pages of 16 March and 17 March. The referendum, which will be explained in the following pages, was reported in very small type in the *Tribune,* 17 March 1988, 25, and the *Sun-Times,* 17 March 1988, 17.

2. Robert Gannett, interview by authors, 19 July 1990; Mike Smith, interview by authors, 19 September 1990; "The SON/SOC Amendment: Giving a Voice to All Chicagoans," C.U.R.E.-SON/SOC papers. The law authorizing small-scale referenda was PA 84-1467, signed 14 January 1987.

3. Michael Bakalis, interview by authors, 13 July 1990; Don Moore, interview by authors, 1 August 1990.

4. Bob and Mike to Pat, Re: Schools petition drive, 29 October 1987, C.U.R.E.-SON/SOC papers; Cathy Greenwood, interview by authors, 26 November 1990.

5. "Petition for Referendum," C.U.R.E.-SON/SOC papers; the implied threat of a tax revolt appeared in a separate petition to Illinois legislators that SON/SOC gathered about the same time.

6. Fact sheet and press release, C.U.R.E.-SON/SOC papers.

7. David Paulus, interview by authors, 16 November 1990; Moore interview.

8. This, and all the other house and senate bills mentioned subsequently, can be found in the *Final Legislative Synopsis and Digest,* 85th General Assembly, 1988 sess.

9. Moore, Paulus interviews.

10. Renee Montoya, taped memoir, November 1990.

11. Montoya memoir; Danny Solis gave us a less detailed account but confirmed the basic outline of the emerging coalition, in an interview by authors, 17 October 1990.

12. "Key Hispanic and Black Community Organizations Endorse HB #3707," 16 May 1988, C.U.R.E.-Haymarket papers.

13. ABCs brochure, C.U.R.E.-Haymarket papers; *Chicago Tribune,* 1 June 1990, sec. 2, p. 2.

14. Solis interview.

15. *Chicago Tribune,* 23 March 1988, sec. 2, p. 2; 24 March 1988, 1; *Chicago Sun-Times,* 22 March 1988, 3; 23 March 1988, 11; 24 March 1988, 5.

16. *Chicago Tribune,* 12 May 1988, sec. 2, p. 3; *Chicago Sun-Times,* 12 May 1988, 24.

17. *Chicago Tribune,* 21 May 1988, 1; *Journal of the Senate,* 85th General Assembly, 1988 sess., 1: 1422.

18. *Chicago Tribune,* 29 May 1988, sec. 4, p. 2.

19. *Chicago Tribune,* 8 June 1988, sec. 2, p. 9; *Chicago Sun-Times,* 8 June 1988, 4.

20. This section is based primarily on an interview by the authors with David Peterson, area vice-president and legislative director of the Chicago Teachers Union, 2 October 1991.

21. An additional factor that may have contributed to the CTU's cooperative stance on school reform was Jackie Vaughn's reelection to a new two-year term as CTU president at the end of May. Without the need to face her union delegates for another two years, Vaughn may have been freer to maneuver in June. See *Chicago Tribune,* 25 May 1988, sec. 2, p. 1, and *Chicago Sun-Times,* 25 May 1988, 14.

22. *Chicago Sun-Times,* 7 June 1988, 2; Moore interview.

23. McFerren, Stewart, Coffey interviews.

24. McFerren, Solis, Paulus, Keleher interviews.

14

The Legislative Labyrinth

As the school reformers stalked the halls, the Democratic politicians began hammering out the law.

Three major issues dominated the final month of 1988's legislative session: Governor Thompson's proposed income tax increase, the school reform measure, and state financing for a new White Sox baseball stadium. Ordinarily, the three issues would be tied together in some sort of deal, perhaps trading Republican votes for the White Sox stadium and school reform for Democratic votes in favor of the tax increase. Certainly the governor wanted such linkage. He believed his best chance at winning a tax increase was to hold school reform hostage to it.[1]

Democratic Speaker Michael Madigan, however, opposed any tax increase and refused to tie the school reform bill to the governor's proposal.[2] The Republicans in the legislature, for their part, simply rode the downstate "bash Chicago" sentiment and declared Senator Kustra's 20-district decentralization plan nonnegotiable. So Madigan buried the Kustra bill in committee when it arrived in the house and enjoined a task force to write a Democratic school reform bill. The Democratic president of the senate, Phil Rock, authorized Senator Arthur Berman to mark up a version of the bill as well. Finally, Speaker Madigan convened an unprecedented conclave of all the interested parties—legislators, unionists, and school reformers—to negotiate the final compromises and settle on legislative language. The Democrats held a commanding majority in the house of representatives and a narrower edge in the senate, so whatever emerged from the legislature would be a Democratic product.

The legislature, however, went into overtime, past the June 30 deadline, without passing the school reform bill, so negotiations with the governor and Republican leaders again proved necessary. The final bill did not become law until December 1.

Early Versions of the Bill

Senator Arthur Berman, the chairman of the education committee in the senate, was a 20-year veteran in the legislature, elected from the liberal lakefront area encompassing both the Rogers Park neighborhood in Chicago and much of the suburb of Evanston. He had chaired the state's own education commission in the wake of "A Nation at Risk" and had shepherded the 1985 omnibus school reform law through the General Assembly. Berman had also earned a reputation in Springfield as a careful technician, a master of legislative detail. So whenever education matters came before the state senate, President Rock deferred to Berman's knowledge and expertise.

Berman had introduced several shell bills at the beginning of the 1988 legislative session. Now in May, as the education summit stalled, he dusted off one of these legislative vehicles, SB 1839, and called a conference to hammer out the contents of the bill. Berman invited into his office four other Democratic senators who had already introduced education bills that session: Miguel del Valle, Richard Newhouse, Frank Savickas, and Dawn Clark Netsch. It is an invariable rule in Springfield that the best way to ensure a seat at the bargaining table is to introduce a bill on the subject under discussion. These four senators who conferred with Berman over the school reform bill represented a cross-section of the city's major voting groups: Latinos, blacks, ethnic whites, and lakefront whites.[3]

Berman and the other four senators pored over charts matching the main recommendations of the summit with the various interest groups that would be affected by these recommendations. Berman and the other legislative leaders had pledged to Mayor Harold Washington that they would pass a Chicago bill made by Chicagoans, so now they tried to keep this commitment by completing the work of the summit. Berman emphasizes that the substance of SB 1839 "wasn't Berman's ideas, it was Chicagoans' ideas."

The Berman bill retained the 19-member local school councils proposed by C.U.R.E. but required a parent majority on each, as the education summit and various parent groups had insisted. It expanded the size of the new school board to 15 members and authorized a nominating commission to make recommendations to the mayor. Though SB 1839 mandated gradual redistribution of Chapter I funds, it did not include a hold harmless clause. Nor did it address the issue of downsizing the bureaucracy and setting a spending cap. (See appendix 2, p. 350, for a detailed comparison of the major reform bills.) The ABCs found this first version of SB 1839 too narrow and ambiguous and graded it a failure or "needs improvement" on most of their major criteria. Nonetheless, the Berman bill passed the senate on a straight party-line vote, 30 to 25, on June 2.[4]

Due to his technical craftsmanship at this stage of the legislation, Senator Arthur Berman has generally been referred to in the press as the "principal author of the school reform law." He himself proudly claims such authorship: "SB 1839 is my baby. I say that with all lack of modesty."[5]

Nonetheless, the school reform act underwent substantial modifications before it finally became law, and other hands besides Berman's helped shape it. As the next step, a Democratic task force of the house, cochaired by Carol Moseley Braun, Ellis Levin, and Jose Berrios, produced a slightly different draft of the basic school reform plan. The house Democrats retained Berman's 15-member board of education appointed by the mayor from slates submitted by a nominating commission, but they reduced the size of the local school councils to a more manageable membership of 11 (six parents, two community representatives, two school staff, and the principal). This composition of the LSCs remained the norm in all subsequent drafts and in the final law.

The house bill, however, had two gaping holes in it. There was no provision for an oversight authority, as demanded by the business community, and no redistribution of Chapter I funds. The reformers were not the only ones stalking the halls of Springfield. The Chicago Board of Education spent over $50,000 on politically connected lobbyists to influence the school reform bill, in addition to their usual lobbying team headed by Richard Guidice that enjoyed an annual budget of $231,000. They obviously managed to remove the oversight and Chapter I redistribution provisions from this draft of the bill. Carol Moseley Braun has concluded, "There were so many interests and no one person saying Yea or Nay."[6]

The Democratic house plan was introduced as amendment six of a shell bill, HB 4101, on June 15. The Republicans pushed a variant of their "break up the Chicago district" plan as amendment three. The full house voted down the Republican amendment 63 to 49, then passed the Democrats' version on a narrow 57-to-52 vote, indicating that not all house Democrats supported it. The press reports focused mainly on a unique feature of the bill that no other draft of school reform contained. Addressing the fear that parents were too apathetic for school-based management, HB 4101 tried to compel parental interest in their children's education. It required parents to pick up their children's report cards in person at each marking period and defined the failure to do so as criminal child neglect, punishable by fine. ABCs passed over this quirky provision but concluded that the lack of an oversight authority and the failure to redistribute Chapter I funds rendered the bill unacceptable.[7]

Speaker Madigan Takes Charge

At this juncture, when important legislation was at stake, the majority and minority leaders of both houses would normally meet with the governor and work out a final version. Big Jim and the Four Tops did meet on June 16 and they named a bipartisan delegation of 12 legislators to work with the governor's chief of staff, James Reilly, on a compromise bill. But neither side held out high hopes for this process. Republicans continued to tout the breakup of the Chicago district as non-negotiable, and, though Phil Rock was willing to consider a tax increase, Mike Madigan insisted that school reform be revenue neutral, with no new funding and no tax increase. The Speaker's hand was inadvertently strengthened when the Chicago Board of Education performed one of their famous financial flip-flops. The board's financial officer, Barbara Peck, had been trumpeting a $188 million deficit in the upcoming year's budget, but on June 15 the board reported they had found enough extra funds to turn that deficit into a $29 million surplus. A *Tribune* editorial concluded mockingly, "So presto, no deficit. Presto no credibility." This amazing performance by the school board removed any urgency for new money to accompany school reform.[8]

Speaker Madigan then convened his own bargaining session to fashion a consensus school reform bill. Representative John Cullerton, who would play a key role in the subsequent bargaining, recalls how Madigan's conclave came about:

> We [the legislators] weren't making any progress [in reconciling competing versions of the bill], and nothing was happening. So Madigan had this extraordinary meeting where he called all the 'goo-goos' [good government advocates, the tongue-in-check nickname given the school reformers by the politicians] in, the interested parties, and just said, "We're gonna do a deal here. Let's just do the broad outline." So he conducted the conference with all the players represented in the Speaker's office and he basically set forth the outline of the bill, 80 percent of which was basically agreed to by all these people anyway.[9]

The Speaker then left his office and instructed all the parties to negotiate the details of the remaining 20 percent of the bill and write it all up in legislative language. Beginning on June 20 and continuing for the better part of the next two weeks, 40, 50, sometimes 60 people crowded into the Speaker's quarters. Using the Berman bill from the senate (SB 1839) as the basic framework, they recapitulated the experience of C.U.R.E. and the education summit, arguing line by line through the proposed legislation. This procedure was highly unusual. Though lobbyists and advocacy groups frequently influence a particular piece of legislation, they don't often sit down at length and argue every detail of a bill with the legislators. Senate President Rock, who concurred with Speaker Madigan's strategy, believes he has never seen a greater degree of citizen involvement during his 20 years in the legislature.[10]

Don Moore, Joan Slay, and Coretta McFerren represented C.U.R.E. at all the sessions in Madigan's office, backed up by Al Raby and Mary Dempsey from Haymarket. Pat Keleher and Warren Bacon of Chicago United, Danny Solis from UNO, Diana Lauber for Chicago Panel on Public School Policy and Finance (CHIPS), Bernie Noven from PURE, and the lobbyists for the board of education and the teachers' union attended regularly. Many others came in and out. Representatives John Cullerton, Ellis Levin, and Anthony Young, and Senator Arthur Berman attended every session. Cullerton generally chaired the proceedings. All participants agree that Cullerton's sense of humor and light touch with the gavel contributed mightily to the search for consensus.[11]

John J. Cullerton is the scion of a distinguished political family, one that had earned notoriety in Chicago politics long before the Daleys had left Ireland. The first Cullerton arrived in the Windy City in 1835 to help dig the Illinois and Michigan Canal. His son, Edward Cullerton, served a brief term in the state legislature then represented a southwest side ward in the city council for 48 years, from 1871 until his death in 1919, a record never equalled by any other Chicago alderman. Ed Cullerton was one of the "Gray Wolves" of the city council attacked by Lincoln Steffens and other reformers at the turn of the century. One of his descendants, Parker J. "Parkie" Cullerton, was a cog in the Richard J. Daley machine, first as city council finance chairman, then as Cook County assessor.

Another machine stalwart, Thomas Cullerton, still sits in the city council today from the northwest side 30th Ward.

John J. Cullerton, however, represents a more progressive, collateral branch of the family (he is Parkie's first cousin once removed and Thomas's second cousin). He was first elected in 1978 as state representative from a lakefront Lincoln Park district, serving in the house until he was appointed to fill a vacant state senate seat early in 1991. At the time of the school reform battle in 1988, he functioned as Speaker Madigan's unofficial floor leader and one of his most trusted lieutenants.[12]

Before he left the room, Michael Madigan set down a guideline that school reform should be revenue neutral; he was not prepared to push for higher taxes to provide additional school funding. Also, he made it clear to his political lieutenants that they needed to satisfy the black caucus in the legislature. Cullerton recalls:

> Madigan always felt that the key to it was making sure that the black legislators wanted to do the bill. If they didn't want to do the bill, ball game's over. If they stand up there with Jackie Vaughn [teachers' union president] and say "This is a racist bill", Madigan doesn't even call it. He was not going to call the bill unless the blacks were on board.

Madigan had spent years keeping Chicago's poisonous Council Wars out of the legislature, and he didn't want all his hard work to break down now. One of the problems this potential black veto posed, however, was that the black caucus itself remained undecided on key provisions of the bill. The acting mayor of Chicago, Eugene Sawyer, was black, but city politics after Harold Washington's death were so volatile that it looked quite likely a white mayor might soon be elected. So the black legislators were uncertain how much power they wished the city's mayor to gain under the school reform bill.

The debates in "The Room" broke down mainly along predictable special interest lines. Principals did not want to lose tenure, and the school board opposed any restrictions on administrative spending, but they were overruled by a solid phalanx of reformers on both points. All agreed that local school councils (LSCs) with power to hire and fire the principals formed the heart of the reform law and that a reduction in administrative spending was necessary to make the bill revenue neutral. Mary Dempsey from Haymarket wrote the final language detailing the structure and powers of the LSCs, and Diana Lauber from CHIPS wrote the section setting an administrative spending cap. The cap required the Chicago school board to reduce the proportion of its spending on administration to the state average for other school districts. An official at the Illinois State Board of Education estimated that this provision would save about $40 million.

The Chicago Teachers Union proved most skillful at protecting its members' interests, while still compromising sufficiently to avoid obstructionism. The teachers' union supported the main reform proposal for local school councils, conceded a shorter remediation period for unsatisfactory teachers, and waived seniority for new teaching positions, thus allowing principals to choose their own staffs on merit. This was a major concession on the union's part. The CTU, however, dug in their heels over another seniority matter. Each year a number of tenured teachers are laid off due to declining enrollment at their assigned schools. The CTU insisted that these supernumeraries receive first choice of remaining teaching jobs, with the right to "bump" another teacher having less seniority.

Bruce Berndt, the president of the Principals' Association, proved far more intransigent, and unsuccessful, than the CTU delegates. Berndt was new to the job, and may not have taken the reform process as seriously as he should have. At the time of the teachers' strike, Senator Berman had counselled Berndt's predecessor to hire a professional lobbyist to protect the principals' interests during the oncoming school reform wave. The Principals' Association didn't heed this advice, and Berndt was left on his own down in Springfield. Mary Dempsey recalls that when she first introduced herself to him, he told her point blank, "We don't want any of this to happen." Berndt also cast the lone dissenting vote against the final report of the education summit.[13]

During the bargaining sessions in Springfield, the school reformers, particularly members of the business community, tried to gain for the principals full control over all school staff, including janitors, engineers, and food service workers. Businessmen believed such authority necessary for the principal to function as CEO of the school. The principals had long wanted such authority; indeed it was an ancient grievance of the Principals' Association. This issue involved delicate racial politics, for many of the school principals were black (and female). Full control of the school building entailed giving orders to middle-aged, white, male union janitors.

Madigan decided it was important for the principals to win this issue, so he instructed Representative Cullerton to referee private negotiations between the Principals' Association's Berndt and several delegates from the operating engineers' union. Cullerton told the engineers frankly, "You lose. The principals are going to run the schools." As bargaining began in Cullerton's office, the union delegates blandly informed Berndt, "Okay, the principal's in charge of the school. So if the pipes burst at three o'clock in the morning, they're gonna call you."[14] All of a sudden, Berndt realized that "control of the building" would be no simple matter. Negotiations continued for about 10 hours. At one point Cullerton asked his staff to fax him copies of building engineer contracts in downtown Chicago office buildings so they could find standard operating language. Finally, both parties concurred in a complicated set of agreements, which struck most of the school reformers as curiously weak. The principals did not gain full control of the school staff, but merely the authority to carry keys to the building, previously the sole prerogative of the chief engineer.

This incident seemed curious at the time and many school reformers commented on it in subsequent interviews. It seems clearer now. It appears that Bruce Berndt did not join in good faith bargaining, as the CTU did; he probably hoped all along to overturn the law. In 1989, the Principals' Association filed a court challenge to the reform law that resulted in the Supreme Court ruling it unconstitutional.

The structure and powers of an oversight authority continued to cause problems. Only the business executives supported it vigorously and black legislators and community leaders still viewed it as a racist plot to wrest control of the schools from a black school board, superintendent, and union president. A firm decision to redistribute Chapter I funds to disadvantaged schools, however, won over most of the black caucus members. And the conferees recommended an oversight authority with a built-in Chicago majority: four members appointed by the mayor and only three by the governor.

Before this and other decisions were finalized, however, the business executives from Chicago United precipitated a crisis in the Room. After returning from a weekend recess, Warren Bacon from Chicago United, Barry Sullivan, the chairman of First National Bank, and several other executives held a press conference on Monday, June 27, blasting the emerging consensus in Madigan's office as a "watered-down" bill. The business executives never felt comfortable with an exclusively Democratic bill, and they were not used to the excruciatingly slow give-and-take of the bargaining process. Reportedly, they were trying to forge a new alliance between black and other liberal Democrats and the Republican caucus to bypass the Speaker and gain a freer hand in shaping the law. Though such an unlikely alliance had been cobbled together before on other issues, there was little chance of its working this time. The school reform groups had always suspected that the businessmen would eventually walk away from the full roster of reforms and champion a draconian oversight board to throw the schools into receivership. Many believed this press conference presaged the long-feared walkout.

Speaker Madigan had counselled a policy of press silence during the bargaining sessions, so when he heard about the

Chicago United press conference he stalked angrily into his office and a dead hush fell over the room. Glaring directly at the business executives, Madigan growled, "What's going on? Didn't we agree not to talk about what we're doing?" None of the CEOs said a word, but Warren Bacon, the executive director of Chicago United, stood up and defended the press conference. Madigan stared him down and whispered, "Just don't let it happen again"; then he walked out of the room. All the parties returned to the bargaining table as if nothing had happened. The businessmen did not walk out and the quest for compromise continued.[15]

A more serious crisis nearly ended the search for consensus in the Speaker's office. The Chicago Teachers Union continued to insist on seniority protection for supernumerary teachers who lost their jobs due to attrition, but the reformers refused to concede this demand. As the legislative deadlines closed in, the teachers' union lobbied the prolabor Democrats in both the house and the senate against the emerging school reform bill. David Peterson, the union's lobbyist, concludes categorically, "In the final analysis, we had basically defeated the legislation. If they had called it then, I don't believe they would have garnered 19 votes in the house." The school reformers, who had never believed that the CTU was sincere in its backing for reform, thought they had failed, that school reform was dead for this year. However, Representative Cullerton and Senator Berman asked the CTU's Peterson if he would return to the bargaining table if they conceded the seniority protection for supernumeraries. Much to everyone's surprise, Peterson agreed. The reformers had thought that the union was looking for a loophole to torpedo the law; in fact, they were just protecting their members. They were still willing to back the overall reform concept.[16]

At this very late hour in the bargaining process, Erwin France, the mayor's chief aide, joined the conferees to represent the city government's position. Mayor Sawyer had endorsed the first house plan (HB 4101), but was still trying to rally support for a tax increase and additional funding for the schools. This issue never had a chance in Madigan's office, however. Then on the last day of bargaining sessions, a delegation from Jesse Jackson's Operation PUSH flew to Springfield in a last-ditch attempt to derail the oversight authority and save administrative jobs at the board of education. Al Raby met them at the airport, however, and briefed them on the agreements already reached, convincing them not to stand in the way of reform.

The bargaining in Mike Madigan's office finally produced a finished product on Wednesday, June 29, a day before the end of the legislative session. A house-senate conference committee of legislators grafted it back onto Senator Berman's bill, SB 1839, and prepared it for last-minute passage. Members of the ABCs coalition began a vigil Wednesday night on the capitol steps. Dressed in caps and gowns, they slowly rolled up 11,456 diplomas, representing the number of Chicago students who dropped out of school each year. Four years after the march on Clemente High School, the dropout problem still pricked the consciences of reformers and lawmakers.[17]

SB 1839 hit the senate floor about 10:30 P.M. the night of June 30. The senate roster included 31 Democrats and 27 Republicans, so a simple majority required 30 votes. Senator Ethel Alexander, however, had suffered a heart attack earlier in the year and was not present in Springfield; therefore the Democrats needed to hold the loyalty of their remaining 30 caucus members. When the roll was called, 29 Democrats voted yes. Only a single Republican voted no, with the other Republicans answering present. Many in the packed galleries cheered, thinking the law passed. But it did not. Downstate Democratic Senator Sam Vadalabene had suddenly taken sick and left the floor. Rumors spread that the Illinois Education Association had influenced him to abstain, thus killing the bill. Tom Coffey recalls he saw Vadalabene in the doctor's office that night, but no one could say whether he was genuinely ill.[18]

As usual, the legislature went into overtime. To pass a bill after the midnight, June 30 deadline requires a supermajority of

60 percent, if the law is to take effect immediately; passage by simple majority requires that the effective date be postponed a year. This need for a supermajority brought the Republicans back into the bargaining process, for Republican votes would be needed to reach a 60 percent majority in each house.[19]

The governor and the legislative leaders reached a deal for a bipartisan bill, with the Democrats giving up the seniority protection for supernumeraries and mayoral control of the oversight authority. Yet Madigan and Rock faced such strong opposition to these concessions from black and union-influenced legislators in their own caucuses, that they abandoned the agreement, restored the seniority protection and mayoral control provisions, and determined to repass SB 1839 with the delayed implementation date of July 1, 1989. They took no chances with their own troops this time. An ambulance brought Senator Alexander down to Springfield and the state troopers hunted down Senator Jeremiah Joyce who had already left for his vacation. Senator Vadalabene showed up this time too. The bill passed July 2 on a strict party-line vote, 31-24-2 in the senate, and 68-37-11 in the house. The exhausted reformers, who hadn't slept in days, staggered out to a reception on the governor's lawn, then returned to Chicago the next day for the annual July 3 celebration in Grant Park. Somehow, the fireworks seemed pale compared to the pyrotechnics in the capitol.[20]

The Governor's Veto

The battle was not over, however, for another five months. The Illinois Constitution grants the governor a far wider range of veto options than the president of the United States enjoys. The governor can simply veto an entire bill (this is the only veto power the president possesses), or he may exercise the line-item veto, stripping out individual sections or clauses of a bill (Ronald Reagan campaigned unsuccessfully for a constitutional amendment to grant the president similar power). Most curious of all, however, the Illinois Constitution also provides for an amendatory veto, whereby the governor can actually re-write a bill, changing its phraseology and adding whole new sections to it.

This power of the governor to exercise a legislative function had been the cause of continuing controversy, but a number of court challenges upheld it, provided only that "gubernatorial action be consistent with the fundamental purposes and intents of the bill." Needless to say, this clause gave an activist gover-nor such as James R. Thompson ample leeway to make sub-stantial changes in legislation.[21]

The Chicago Board of Education immediately mounted a campaign to overturn or gut the school reform law. Manford Byrd denounced the law as "racist," and the board's bureaucrats churned out a 55-page attack. George Muñoz, who had been quietly advising the business coalition of Chicago United since he stepped down from the school board, estimated that Byrd spent at least $175,000 between July and September to lobby Thompson for a veto.[22]

The ABCs coalition publicly implored the governor to sign the bill without changes, but they expected some sort of veto. Speaker Madigan convened meetings with the main school reform organizations on August 23 and 26 to plan an override. Mary Dempsey and Madigan's deputy, Representative John Cullerton, went jogging on the north lakefront every morning that same week to discuss strategy. The full coalition scheduled a rally for September 8 at Truman College, asking Governor Thompson to "Sign Up for School Reform."[23]

Privately, however, several component groups of the ABCs pursued their own agendas, asking the governor for specific changes they had been unable to secure in Madigan's office. Chicago United rode their usual hobbyhorse, trying to strength-en the powers of the oversight authority. SON/SOC, represent-ing the taxpayers of the northwest and southwest sides who didn't generally send their children to public schools, asked the governor to reinstate the equal representation of community members with parents on the local school councils. They also demanded a full 100 percent hold harmless clause so that their local schools would not lose any money when State Chapter I funds were redistributed (the Madigan bill had allowed only a 90 percent hold harmless provision).[24]

On August 31 the governor announced that he would exercise his amendatory veto on SB 1839. The full veto message, issued on September 26, contained 15 pages of technical changes, including language to insure that the schools adhered to the desegregation consent decree of 1980. Thompson restored the 100 percent hold harmless clause sought by SON/SOC but did not tinker with the composition of the LSCs.[25]

In the most important part of the veto message, however, Thompson stripped out the tenure protection for supernumerary teachers, and he also eliminated the automatic Chicago control of the oversight authority. Instead of four members appointed by the mayor of Chicago and three members appointed by the governor, Thompson's revised oversight authority would consist of three mayoral appointees, three gubernatorial appointees, and added that "one director, who shall chair the Authority's board, shall be appointed jointly by the Governor and the Mayor."

Thompson's preamble to the veto message manifested disappointment at the failure of his tax increase. "I was looking forward to receiving a bill," he wrote, "which would have both energized the educational process in Chicago and funded critical educational needs in the city and elsewhere." He also showed his personal pique when he announced the veto to the press. "I refuse to have any bill, which I don't think lives up to its billing...shoved down my throat...." Yet he made it clear that he welcomed the reform bill as a useful first step in improving the system: "While SB 1839 did not meet my expectations, it does restructure the decision-making process for the schools.... The role of parents is dramatically expanded. These are exciting challenges and opportunities for Chicagoans."[26]

After issuing his veto, the governor adopted a tough take-it-or-leave-it stance and bashed the teachers' union publicly. "You can forget reform if the CTU gets veto power," Thompson told

news reporters in a TV interview. Yet he conveyed more conciliatory sentiments in private, and after the November elections
passed, he began to work openly with the Democratic leaders
to hammer out a compromise.[27]

Several options were available to salvage school reform. If
the lawmakers could summon up a 60 percent majority in each
house, they could override Thompson's veto and enact the
original version of SB 1839. A simple majority of each house
would be necessary to accept Thompson's changes to the bill;
no action at all would kill the legislation. The party leaders
finally played out an alternate scenario. They allowed SB 1839
to die, but then resurrected another of Senator Berman's shell
bills, SB 1840, and grafted onto it the final version of the law
agreed to by both political parties.

SB 1840 resembled its predecessor in most particulars. It
solved the oversight authority mess by granting oversight powers to the already existing Chicago School Finance Authority,
established at the time of the school board's financial crisis in
1980. Since this was a "devil they knew," opponents of the
oversight board grudgingly accepted it. It settled the supernumerary issue by allowing laid-off teachers first chance to interview for other teaching vacancies but not guaranteeing them a
teaching post. Those who couldn't find a teaching position
would be given a job somewhere else in the system. Though
this might mean simply paper pushing at the board of education's Pershing Road headquarters, it usually worked out in
practice that the surplus teachers were kept on as tutors in special programs at their old schools or else found full-time teaching positions at other schools. In any case, the number of such
supernumeraries was not large and the whole issue had taken
on more symbolic importance than it deserved. Finally, the bill
contained a small concession to the principals, extending the
length of their performance contracts from three years to
four.[28]

The legislators filed back to Springfield in late November
for the veto session that would write the final chapter in the

year-long school reform battle. The agreement almost came unravelled several times. Black legislators remained angry about the oversight powers of the school finance authority and suspicious of the school reformers' motives. Jesse Jackson held a press conference on November 26 denouncing the bill as a "forced trusteeship" and demanding that the legislators defer it until another session. Bipartisan comity was also strained by end-of-session horsetrading between Republicans and Democrats. When the roll was finally called in the senate, however, SB 1840 passed nearly unanimously. Only one Republican, Aldo DeAngelis voted, against it. The law passed the house on a vote of 98 yeas, 8 nays, and 10 present. Only two members of the disgruntled black caucus, Monique Davis and Arthur Turner, voted against it. The Chicago school reform law was engraved on the statute books as PA 85-1418.[29]

A Year-Long Battle

The battle for school reform in 1988 proved more protracted and complex than anyone had foreseen. Representative Ellis Levin commented afterwards, "I don't think there's any bill that has had more hours of deliberation both by members of this body and parents and civic leaders and business leaders."[30]

The legislative process, however, represented partisan politics at its best. With a firm majority in one house and a slender one in the other, the Democratic leaders took charge of the bill in its final stages, ensured that all interested parties had a full opportunity to press their cases, then enacted the law not once but twice. Republicans may call this boss rule, but Democrats deem it a fine example of New Deal-style, broker politics. Mary Dempsey, who wrote more lines of the final act than any other individual, has concluded categorically, "Without Mike Madigan, without Art Berman, and without John Cullerton, school reform never would have passed."[31]

Many reformers didn't trust Speaker Madigan at the time, and some still cannot fathom what his motives were, even in retrospect. Yet Roberto Rivera, who sat in Madigan's office during the bargaining sessions as a delegate of Senator Miguel del Valle, has summed up Madigan's role very well. According to Rivera, Madigan knew that some variety of school reform was inevitable, the outrage growing out of the school strike demanded a response, so he probably decided, "Why not be a hero?" As a master of conflict management (which is another definition of the word *politics*) Madigan knew when to become a "champion rather than a target."[32] A brilliant tactician, Madigan proved once again that he runs one of the tightest legislative ships in the country, on a par with Speaker Willie Brown's California House of Representatives.

In the best of all possible worlds, a bipartisan approach might have been preferable. Renee Montoya has astutely pointed out that Republican cooperation would enable the reformers to return to the legislature year after year for fine-tuning, without fear of reopening old wounds and risking attacks on the basic features of the law. No one believed the law was perfect; indeed, almost everyone admitted it would need some refinement in the future. Bipartisan harmony would ease the process of continual change.[33]

Yet such cooperation between Republicans and Democrats simply wasn't realistic in 1988. Madigan and the Democrats harbored too much anger at Governor Thompson's manipulation of the income tax increase: against it when running for office, championing it once safely ensconced in the governor's mansion. The Republicans, for their part, were sick of the Chicago schools coming hat-in-hand to the legislature. Though ready for drastic action, such as fragmenting the Chicago district into pieces, they didn't feel cooperative. Given the circumstances, a partisan strategy and Speaker Madigan's revenue-neutral decree were the necessary prices to pay for school reform.

Madigan admitted that he could probably accept the governor's amendatory veto without changes and muster sufficient bipartisan support for it in the veto session of the legislature. "But there would be no black votes," the Speaker pointed out. "In a system where the majority of children are black, I am not comfortable with the message that would be sent with that type of vote."[34] In the racially charged politics of Chicago in the eighties, keeping the black and white factions of the Democratic party together was more important than building bridges between Democrats and Republicans.

The black caucus had been cruelly whipsawed by a conflict of loyalties throughout the school reform debates. The Chicago Board of Education, under minority control since Harold Washington's election, provided a sure source of jobs and contracts for the black middle class; yet the system was not providing the quality education that black and Latino children needed to prepare for good jobs. The dilemma that this presented to black legislators can be illustrated by the example of Carol Moseley Braun. She represented a heavily middle-class district that encompassed Hyde Park, South Shore, and Kenwood, where many teachers, principals, and school administrators lived, and she had long worked as legislative spokesperson for both the city of Chicago and the Chicago Board of Education. One of the extra lobbyists that the board employed to fight the school reform bill was a close personal friend of Braun's, Billie Paige. Yet, Al Raby, a strong advocate for C.U.R.E., was also a friend and neighbor and had promised to act as campaign manager when she ran for citywide office at the end of 1988. Braun sponsored the original C.U.R.E. bill and chaired the house task force that wrote a later version of the bill; yet she continued to harbor many reservations about the wisdom of the legislation.[35] Speaker Madigan wisely placed a high priority on resolving the dilemma of Representative Braun, and others like her, and thus retaining biracial support for school reform.

Tom Coffey, the overall strategist for C.U.R.E., believes the reformers tried too hard to earn Republican support in the early stages. "We should have kept our eye on the ball," he concludes. "Democrats controlled the legislature and we should have concentrated all our efforts on them."[36]

Michael Madigan, John Cullerton, and Arthur Berman were the principal legislators responsible for the passage of school reform; yet they would have had no bill to pass if the reformers had not mounted such a broad and deep campaign. Cullerton admitted candidly, "We always said, the legislature didn't draft the bill, the parents' groups did."[37] C.U.R.E., the education summit, and the ABCs coalition all represented broad multiracial, multiethnic constituencies. The often tense, always fragile, but ultimately creative cooperation between groups that are usually at each other's throats was the single most decisive factor in the passage of school reform.

Yet the reform coalition also enjoyed unusual depth of research and intellectual resources. Nearly all the reformers agree that Don Moore of Designs for Change was the intellectual father of the movement. Even Moore's archrival, Fred Hess, acknowledges as much. Yet Moore did not stand alone. Chicago was unusually well endowed with educational advocacy and research groups. The long, abrasive battle over desegregation and the sharp financial crisis of 1979 spawned groups such as Designs for Change and the Chicago Panel on Public School Policy and Finance. The discovery of the Latino dropout problem led Aspira to sponsor important research as well, and Michael Bakalis had conducted two full studies of Chicago schools even before he founded C.U.R.E.

The unusually large number of private foundations in Chicago, established by the heirs to the city's mercantile and industrial fortunes, provided crucial financial support for these educational research efforts. In the mid-1980s, the Donors Forum of Chicago, the foundations' local trade association, conducted an internal examination of their philanthropic efforts and determined to increase funding for public school reform. Both the Community Trust and the MacArthur Foundation helped underwrite expenses of the education summit, and the president of MacArthur, John Corbally, headed up the executive committee of the summit.[38]

A wealth of ideas and cash, therefore, fueled Chicago's year-long battle for school reform, from the teachers' strike and the convocation of the education summit in October 1987 to the veto session on December 1, 1988. Tom Coffey believes that the successful reform drive provides a textbook model of how community organizations can change society. Building on the research and experience already amassed during previous years, C.U.R.E. fashioned a bill and a strategy early in the game. Coffey emphasizes that you cannot develop a winning strategy on the run, you cannot merely react to others. Yet C.U.R.E. remained flexible and willing to compromise, and at crucial intervals, they made new allies, such as the business executives of Chicago United and the Latino community organizations federated in UNO. Lacking the financial expertise to write the spending cap provisions, they cooperated with Fred Hess and Diana Lauber of CHIPS who drafted the appropriate language.

The coalition just kept getting larger. By the time ABCs organized the September rally to overcome Governor Thompson's veto, they listed 44 school reform, business and civic, or community and neighborhood organizations on their roster. This broad-based alliance finally secured the most radical school reform law of the 1980s.

Notes

1. *Chicago Tribune*, 29 May 1988, sec. 2, p. 1; 3 June 1988, 1; 10 June 1988, 1.

2. See Michael D. Klemens, "Mike Madigan and the 'Party of Economic Opportunity'," *Illinois Issues* 14 (August-September 1988): 18-21, for Madigan's opposition to the tax increase.

3. Arthur Berman, interview by authors, 30 September 1991.

4. "Comparative Analysis: Key Chicago School Reform Proposals," C.U.R.E.-Haymarket papers; *Journal of the Senate*, 85th General Assembly, 1988 sess., 1: 1572-73; *Chicago Sun-Times*, 3 June 1988, 20.

5. Berman interview.

6. *Chicago Tribune*, 8 June 1988, 1; Carol Moseley Braun, interview by authors, 5 February 1991.

7. *Chicago Sun-Times*, 16 June 1988, 4; *Chicago Tribune*, 16 June 1988, sec. 3, p. 3.

8. *Chicago Sun-Times*, 19 June 1988, 3; 21 June 1988, 9; *Chicago Tribune*, 17 June 1988, sec. 2, p. 7; 20 June 1988, 12.

9. John J. Cullerton, interview by authors, 4 October 1991.

10. Philip Rock, interview by authors, 27 August 1991.

11. We have based this account on interviews with Tom Coffey (23 October 1990), Mary Dempsey (5 October 1990), Diana Lauber (15 October 1990), Coretta McFerren (11 September 1990), Danny Solis (17 October 1990), Pat Keleher (22 October 1990), David Paulus (16 November 1990), Roberto Rivera (20 September 1990), David Peterson (2 October 1991), Arthur Berman (30 September 1991), and John Cullerton (4 October 1991), all of whom participated in the marathon sessions at Michael Madigan's office. Newspaper accounts were sketchy: see *Chicago Tribune*, 24 June 1988, 1; *Chicago Sun-Times*, 24 June 1988, 3.

12. Cullerton interview.

13. Dempsey, Berman interviews.

14. Cullerton interview.

15. Solis, Keleher, Paulus, Peterson interviews; see also *Chicago Sun-Times*, 28 June 1988, 8; *Chicago Tribune*, 28 June 1988, 1.

16. Peterson, Cullerton interviews.

17. *Chicago Tribune*, 30 June 1988, sec. 2, p. 3.

18. The best account of these climactic hours in the legislature is "Chicago Schools: Reform to Come but No Money," *Illinois Issues* 14 (August-September 1988): 43-44; the vote on SB 1839 is detailed in *Journal of the Senate*, 85th General Assembly, 1988 sess., 3: 4084-85. See also *Chicago Tribune*, 1 July 1988, 8; *Chicago Sun-Times*, 1 July 1988, 7.

19. Most observers, however, believe that the White Sox stadium bill (SB 2022), passed the house with only a simple majority a few minutes after midnight. Speaker Madigan declared that his watch read 11:59 P.M. and his decision stood. *Chicago Tribune*, 1 July 1988, 1; *Chicago Sun-Times*, 1 July 1988, 1.

20. The votes are in *Journal of the Senate*, 85th General Assembly, 1988 sess., 3: 5226; *Journal of the House*, 85th General Assembly, 1988 sess., 4: 7469; and in *Chicago Sun-Times*, 3 July 1988, 8.

21. Thompson's vetoes usually began with the following boilerplate language, outlining his legal authority: "Pursuant to the authority vested in the Governor by Article IV, Section 9(e) of the Illinois Constitution of 1970, and re-affirmed by the People of the State of Illinois by popular referendum in 1974, and conforming to the standard articulated by the Illinois Supreme Court in *People ex Rel. Klinger v. Howlett*, 50 Ill. 2d 242 (1972), *Continental Illinois National Bank and Trust Co. v. Zagel*, 78 Ill. 2d 387 (1979), *People ex Rel. City of Canton v. Crouch*, 79 Ill. 2d 356 (1980), and *County of Kane v. Carlson*, 116 Ill. 2d 186 (1987)..."

22. *Chicago Tribune*, 16 July 1988, 5; *Chicago Sun-Times*, 16 July 1988, 12; Manford Byrd, Jr., "Analysis of Senate Bill 1839 Reforming the Chicago Public Schools," C.U.R.E.-Haymarket papers; Keleher interview.

23. *Chicago Tribune*, 20 August 1988, 5; 22 August 1988, sec. 2, p. 1; Mary Dempsey to John Cullerton, 19 August 1988, and "Governor Thompson: Sign Up for School Reform," (printed flyer), C.U.R.E.-Haymarket papers.

24. Keleher, Paulus interviews; Joyce Mika and Catherine Greenwood to Governor James R. Thompson, 8 August 1988, C.U.R.E.-SON/SOC papers.

25. Michael D. Klemens, "Governor Steps into Chicago School Reform," *Illinois Issues* 14 (November 1988): 25; *Chicago Tribune*, 1 September 1988, 1; 27 September 1988, 1; *Chicago Sun-Times*, 1 September 1988, 1; 27 September 1988, 7.

26. The full veto message is in *Journal of the Senate*, 85th General Assembly, 1988 sess., 3: 5309-22. See *Chicago Tribune*, 27 August 1988, 1, for the other Thompson quote.

27. *Chicago Tribune*, 15 October 1988, 5; 18 October 1988, sec. 2, p. 1; 11 November 1988, sec. 2, p. 1; 12 November 1988, 1; 18 November 1988, 1.

28. Michael D. Klemens, "Chicago School Reform Signed into Law, *Illinois Issues* 15 (January 1989): 28; *Chicago Tribune*, 2 December 1988, 1; 4 December 1988, 1; *Chicago Sun-Times*, 1 December 1988, 1; 2 December 1988, 1.

29. *Journal of the Senate*, 85th General Assembly, 1988 sess., 3: 6200-6201; *Journal of the House*, 85th General Assembly, 1988 sess., 4: 8651.

30. Klemens, "School Reform Signed," 28.

31. Dempsey interview.

32. Rivera interview.

33. Renee Montoya, taped memoir, November 1990.

34. *Chicago Tribune*, 11 November 1988, sec. 2, p. 1.

35. Braun interview.

36. Coffey interview.

37. Cullerton interview.

38. Anne Hallett, director of the Wieboldt Foundation, interview by authors, 17 October 1990.

The Transition

In the year and a half after the Chicago school reform act took effect, nearly all the pieces of the reform plan fell into place. An interim school board, which included three members of the ABCs coalition, dismissed Manford Byrd and hired a new schools superintendent. The interim board made a start at reordering the budget and slashing the bureaucracy, then offered the teachers a historic three-year contract to break the biennial cycle of strikes.

Meanwhile, parents and taxpayers turned out in greater numbers than expected for the first local school council elections. Despite some controversy and confusion, the LSCs completed the first round of contract negotiations with the school principals and started fashioning school improvement plans. The business leaders who lobbied for the reform act's passage provided crucial financial support and management advice to the fledgling councils.

As the interim board prepared to step down and make way for a newly appointed permanent school board, Joan Jeter Slay, a member of both C.U.R.E. and the interim board, concluded, "Reform is alive and well and will continue to be alive and well. The critical pieces in the reform are the local school council members".[1]

Changing Political Winds

Before parents and educators could begin implementing the reform law, however, Chicago's unsettled politics took another unexpected turn. After two decades of boring predictability under Boss Richard J. Daley, the city had been buffeted by eight election campaigns for the mayoralty (counting both primaries and general elections) since Daley's death in 1976. Six of these eight had been turbulent, closely contested affairs. Now in the spring of 1989, Richard M. Daley, Son of Boss, defeated two black Democrats: Acting Mayor Eugene Sawyer, in the Democratic primary on February 28, and Alderman Timothy Evans, running as an independent under the banner of the Harold Washington party in the April 4 general election. For the first time since America's big cities began electing black mayors, a white rival had turfed out a black incumbent.[2]

There was no chance that the election of Richard the Second would usher in a period of renewed machine dominance. Legal attacks on patronage politics and the divisiveness of racial campaigns had decisively shattered the "last of the big city machines" after the death of Richard the First in 1976. Instead of a simple polarization between machine and reformers, the Chicago electorate now broke down into at least four factions, based on race and class. Both the black and the white ethnic voting blocs enjoyed roughly equal strength in the city, whereas much smaller Latino and lakefront liberal groups held the balance of power. Since the death of Harold Washington, a sharp split between "movement" blacks and more traditional black politicians further complicated the picture.

Harold Washington had firmly united all black factions behind him in his two elections, then added the swing votes of the Latinos and the lakefront residents to tip the balance his way. In 1989, Richie Daley reversed the process, holding his white ethnic strongholds and racking up solid majorities in both the Latino and lakefront wards. Thus he defeated the leader of each black faction in turn. Disunity and feuding in the black community greatly reduced the turnout that had buoyed Washington's campaigns, thus easing Daley's electoral victory.[3]

Mindful of both the elder and the younger Daley's penchant for verbal bloopers, campaign advisor David Axelrod and other political strategists kept Richie on a tight leash during the campaigns. Daley did participate in one televised debate, but he otherwise avoided uncontrolled questions from the media, earning himself a reputation as the "stealth candidate."

Nonetheless, candidate and mayor-elect Daley handled the education issue flawlessly. In January, he told a group of businessmen from the City Club that the improvement of Chicago's schools was his "No. 1 priority," and he promised to appoint a deputy mayor for education to coordinate the implementation of reform. After his election, Daley mounted a carefully choreographed issue-a-day transition, showcasing one major program at a time. The day before his inauguration on April 24, he met with the various school reform organizations and repeated his promise to appoint a deputy mayor for education.[4]

The state legislature enabled Dalcy to get a fast start on school reform. On May 1 the governor signed a bill making the school reform act effective immediately instead of on July 1.[5] Daley, therefore, appointed the seven-member interim school board and his promised deputy mayor on May 25.

The new board included three members of the business-parent advocacy coalition that had lobbied so effectively for the law: Joseph Reed, a former AT&T executive, Joan Jeter Slay from Designs for Change and C.U.R.E., and Adela Coronado-Greeley, a magnet school teacher and member of an influential parents' advocacy group. The mayor tapped James Compton, the president of the Urban League, as head of the interim board, and also appointed west side minister Janis Sharpe, who was likely the candidate of influential black leader Nancy Jefferson. Daley reappointed one member of the outgoing board, sociology professor William Liu, to give the Asian-American community some representation. Lourdes Monteagudo, an outspoken magnet school principal, filled the newly created post of deputy mayor for education.[6]

Perhaps the most interesting education appointment was the vice-president of the interim board, William Singer. A former political reformer, who had unsuccessfully challenged Richard

J. Daley in the mayoral primary of 1975, Singer became a partner at the prestigious law firm of Kirkland & Ellis and moved
closer to the regular Democrats during the Council Wars
period. Commentators found delicious irony in the old reformer's service to Richard the Second, and many were surprised at
the high profile he assumed, functioning as a virtual cochair
along with Compton. Singer became the interim board's
spokesman on financial matters, having acquired his expertise
a decade earlier on a state task force inquiring into the board
of education's financial state. Joan Slay recalls that Singer
patiently tutored her and the other members of the board in the
byzantine nuances of the budget, and that he dedicated nearly
a full year of his time to the details of the new teachers'
contract. Singer himself later told a reporter that when he was
young, the public school was the center of the neighborhood,
the center of the local community, and an avenue to rise in the
world. When he ran for mayor in 1975, he discovered this was
no longer the case. Ever since then, he had believed the system
needed radical reconstruction.[7]

All in all, many school reformers did not completely trust
Daley, Singer, and his other appointees. Black political opponents railed against the mayor and his new deputy mayor,
Lourdes Monteagudo, for sending their own children to private
schools.[8] And Hal Baron, the manager of Harold Washington's
education summit, commented tartly on Daley's decision to
spend the week before the closing of local school council
nominations visiting his relatives in Ireland:

> If Harold Washington were still with us as Mayor, he surely
> would not be in Ireland, or West Africa. He would be right
> here, stirring up interest neighborhood by neighborhood, to
> make sure that school reform received the most enthusiastic
> and propitious launching possible.[9]

Yet, Daley did nothing to thwart or slow the progress of
school reform. This attests to the momentum that reform had
gathered. No matter how controversial it had been before the

law was passed, school reform now took on the status of a motherhood issue. No politician wanted to be seen standing in its way. Kids First was no longer a strategy but a doctrine of political faith.

In this new atmosphere of consensus on the need for education reform, House Speaker Michael Madigan finally dropped his long opposition to an increase in the state income tax. On May 17 Madigan announced his own tax plan, a temporary 20 percent surcharge on the income tax whose proceeds would be divided nearly equally between local governments and the public schools. As was usual with partisan proposals in the legislature, the Democrats' tax surcharge passed the house of representatives handily (72 to 45) and the senate by a very close vote (30 to 27).

The two-year tax surcharge, passed on June 30, 1989, raised the individual income tax rate from 2.5 percent to 3 percent and the corporate rate from 4 percent to 4.8 percent. This was expected to produce an additional $363 million annually for education in the state, $334 million for local governments, and about $86 million for local property tax relief. Armed with these new funds, the interim board struck a quick one-year agreement with the teachers' union for the upcoming school year and began negotiating a long-term contract for subsequent years.[10]

Madigan's tax plan solidified his reputation as the shrewdest politician in the state. By funnelling new dollars to schools and local governments he gave both the incoming Chicago mayor and the school reform law valuable breathing room. He also upstaged Governor Thompson by imposing his own temporary tax surcharge rather than the permanent increase the governor had been championing for years. Setting the expiry date for June 30, 1991, was a political masterstroke. This postponed controversy about the tax surcharge's renewal beyond Daley's reelection campaign in the spring of 1991, but ensured that both the mayor and the governor (whoever they might be at that time) would have to court the Speaker if they wanted the tax surcharge extended or made permanent. In any case, Mayor Daley and the interim board enjoyed a temporarily more favorable financial climate than the school boards of the preceding decade, thanks to Speaker Madigan.

Corporate Support

As the political atmosphere changed, corporate commitment to education reform remained constant. CEOs of major Chicago companies had devoted unusual amounts of their own time to the reform cause during 1988, and while they didn't wish to sustain this high level of personal involvement, they expected a return on their investment. Therefore, in February 1989, Chicago United and the Civic Committee of the Commercial Club incorporated a new vehicle for business support of the public schools, Leadership for Quality Education (LQE). The two sponsoring federations of business corporations furnished LQE with an annual budget of about five hundred thousand dollars, and Joseph Reed, the vice-president for external affairs of AT&T, took early retirement to serve as the president of the organization. Reed had helped AT&T adjust to the radical re-structuring of the Bell System under federal court order, so he had some experience with the downsizing and decentralizing of fossilized bureaucracies. The business community also present-ed Reed as their candidate for the interim school board, and Mayor Daley obliged by appointing him to the board in May.[11]

LQE worked in partnership with philanthropic foundations and the school advocacy organizations to get the local school councils up and running. The interim board was positively swamped with work during its short tenure and the permanent bureaucracy at Pershing Road provided precious little informa-tion to prospective LSC members, so the burden of training and support fell to the private sector. Many observers, even sym-pathetic ones, expected school reform to fail. It was hard to believe enough parents would be interested in running for positions on the 540 local councils and capable of performing effectively once elected. Without the support of the business community, the cynics may have been proven right.

Designs for Change, the Chicago Panel on Public School Policy and Finance, and the other reform groups fashioned concise training programs for prospective LSC candidates, and businesses and foundations contributed the funds to make these training sessions widely available. By July, LQE had raised about $600,000 as a local school council election war chest. A five-member panel of foundation executives screened applications from over a hundred groups and awarded $25,000 to each of 22 grassroots organizations to organize parents and taxpayers in their neighborhoods and boost participation in the LSC elections scheduled for October.[12]

Meanwhile, individual corporations encouraged their own employees to run for local school council positions. CNA Financial, for example, Chicago's eighth-largest public corporation with over 15,000 employees, inaugurated Project Participate. Volunteers from the company's corporate training department held seminars and workshops, on company time, to familiarize interested employees with the school reform law and coach them on campaign techniques for the LSC elections. Seventy-six of CNA's Project Participate trainees ran for council positions and 23 of them won. Since their election, the corporation has continued to support them with training seminars and half days off to attend LSC meetings.[13]

Illinois Bell, the local phone company, trained 250 employees to run for LSC positions and 36 of them won election, the most from any corporation in the city. Two of them, Maria Vargas and Grady Bailey, were later appointed by Mayor Daley to the permanent school board that succeeded the interim board.[14]

At First National Bank, CEO Barry Sullivan and Vice-President David Paulus also actively encouraged employee participation. Instead of sending out a memo, Paulus used the bank's telemarketing team to telephone every one of the four thousand employees who lived within the city and urge them to get involved with their local school, either as a candidate or a voter. Designs for Change conducted training seminars at First National, and over one thousand individuals took advantage of this training. About 95 actually ran for office and 23 won posts on the LSCs. After the elections, First National granted one thousand dollars to each of the LSCs where one of their employees served.[15]

First National Bank went even further. Like most large corporations, the bank conducted an extensive program of corporate philanthropy. In 1989, however, instead of doling out money in small amounts to worthy charities, CEO Barry Sullivan decided to target the bank's philanthropic funds on two minority communities, one black and one Latino. Bank executives would forge a partnership with indigenous businesses and organizations, such as churches, neighborhood chambers of commerce, social service agencies, and community organizations, to improve the neighborhoods. They focused initially on the upcoming LSC elections as the first test for these partnerships.

Originally, the First National team had singled out the Grand Boulevard community on the south side, where Sokoni Karanja's Centers for New Horizons formed a strong organizing base, and the Puerto Rican community on the near northwest side, where the march on Clemente had kicked off the school reform movement years before. However, Danny Solis from UNO convinced Dave Paulus that his Mexican community on the southwest side was better organized than the Puerto Ricans and would make a stronger base for the partnership. Since the bank executives desired the greatest possible return for their investment, they bowed to this argument and designated Solis's Little Village neighborhood along with Grand Boulevard as First National's partners. First National Bank funnelled $150,000 into each of the target neighborhoods for the LSC elections.[16]

Tomas Sanabria, the executive director of Network for Youth Services on the northwest side, viewed Solis's maneuver as a direct challenge. He hustled up a much smaller grant from other corporate sources and set out to match UNO's organizing effort. This competition between UNO and NYS in the Latino community had a healthy effect; it led to an unexpectedly large turnout of Mexicans and Puerto Ricans at the LSC elections. UNO used about half its grant from First National to mount a major information campaign on Spanish language radio and television. Since these stations broadcast citywide, they helped increase turnout not only in UNO territory but in Sanabria's neighborhood as well.[17]

The LSC Elections

If businesses and community organizations had not been fully engaged, the first LSC elections in October 1989 might have flopped. Skeptics predicted that parental apathy would doom school reform before it even started. At the end of August, the naysayers looked clairvoyant. About six weeks before the elections and less than a month before nominations were scheduled to close, only eight hundred candidates had stepped forward to run for more than four thousand parent and community positions on the 540 LSCs.[18]

So Dave Paulus and Ron Gidwitz, cochairs of the election committee for LQE, unleashed the telemarketers again. Gidwitz, a Republican ward committeeman as well as a business executive, hired a New York telemarketing firm he had used in election campaigns. They logged over 50,000 phone calls per day, reaching nearly every parent of a public school student in the city. LQE then hired five hundred part-time workers to follow up the phone leads with LSC nomination forms.[19]

As the late September deadline approached, the newspapers reported many LSC positions were still going begging. But when nominations closed, only 18 of Chicago's 540 schools did not have full slates of candidates. Ninety-three percent of the high schools recruited enough candidates to contest elections for all 10 elected seats on the councils; 97 percent of the elementary schools presented full slates. Nearly 17,000 candidates (about 9,500 parents, 4,500 community residents, and 2,500 teachers) stepped forward to run.[20]

When three hundred thousand parents, teachers, and community residents voted for LSC representatives on October 11 and 12, no one felt quite sure whether this marked a good or a bad turnout. There were no other elections exactly like these anywhere else in the country. The vote totals equalled about 15 percent of registered voters, a much lower percentage than in general elections. School officials, however, pointed out that suburban school board elections regularly draw only about 10 to 12 percent of the electorate. And the school reformers noted with satisfaction that the most recent election in New York City's decentralized school districts attracted only 7.2 percent of the voters.[21]

Virtually 100 percent of the teaching staff voted for their two allotted teacher representatives on the LSCs and parents of school children, who had the greatest stake in the elections and a majority of seats up for grabs, produced a turnout of about 35 percent in the elementary schools, lower in the high schools. The expected low interest among community residents without children in the public schools, many of whom did not even know where their local school was located, depressed the final turnout totals. All in all, Chicago's first experiment in local school democracy proved satisfactory, but not overwhelming.[22]

The highest parent turnout came in some surprising places. The organizing rivalry between Solis's UNO and Sanabria's NYS brought out 13,576 parents (37.5 percent of those eligible) in the northwest side Puerto Rican district 3 and 12,257 (34.8 percent) in the Mexican district 5 on the southwest side. With only a fraction of the money and organizers that UNO enjoyed, Sanabria turned out the largest number of parents of any school district in the city. On a percentage basis, however, district 9, which included both the middle-class black neighborhood of South Shore and the South Chicago Mexican community organized by UNO, produced the greatest parent-voter participation (44 percent). Clearly, minority parents cared enough about their local schools to show up in respectable numbers and vote for representatives on the new local school councils.[23]

The First Big Test

Several days after the LSC elections, the interim board announced their selection of a new general superintendent, Ted Kimbrough, a Chicago native currently serving as superintendent in Compton, California. The outgoing board had granted Manford Byrd a one-year extension to his contract in March 1989, but the interim board released Byrd from his duties and allowed him to fulfill his contract as a consultant. They appointed one of Byrd's deputies, Charles Almo, as acting superintendent for the beginning of the 1989-90 school year and mounted a nationwide search for Byrd's permanent successor. Kimbrough was scheduled to take office in January 1990.[24]

School reformers greeted the new superintendent with caution and mixed emotions. No one doubted Kimbrough's toughness, intelligence, or competence. James Compton and Bill Singer from the interim board had sought him out specifically for these traits. Yet Compton, California, a tough, largely black suburb of Los Angeles, contained only a small fraction of Chicago's massive student body. More important, Kimbrough's background suggested a business-as-usual superintendent rather than an audacious reformer. In retrospect, Don Moore has suggested that the school reform law should have eased the requirement for the superintendent to be a professional educator. Since political constraints required the hiring of a black superintendent, the pool of black educators with the necessary qualifications for a big-city superintendency is quite small, no more than about 20 people. It might have been better to hire a black business executive, a turnaround specialist who had successfully salvaged a failing corporation.[25]

A superintendent can hasten or hinder the progress of reform, yet ultimately the Chicago school reform act will rise or fall with the fate of the local school councils. Skeptics predicted parent apathy, but the first round of LSC elections proved them wrong. They then forecast confusion on the newly elected councils, and events conspired to partially validate this prediction.

The bureaucrats at Pershing Road did not supply information to the fledgling councils in a timely fashion. It may have
been simply inertia and unfamiliarity with a totally new system,
but the massive lack of support suggested a more systematic
campaign of sabotage. In any case, the members of the LSCs
floundered for the first few months after the elections. They
even had to hustle around looking for meeting places. It cost
about three hundred dollars to keep a school building open at
night, since union rules demanded the presence of a building
engineer paid at overtime rates. The board of education said
they could afford only two such meetings per year for each
LSC; other meetings would have to be held in park field
houses, church basements, or some other makeshift venue.
Eventually, the unions and board compromised and made the
school buildings available more frequently, but this abrasive
issue simply added one more uncertainty to the start-up process.
When ABCs commissioned a poll of LSC members in January
1990, the majority of council members rated the administration
very low for its support of reform.[26]

In the long run, these early vicissitudes experienced by the
LSCs produced healthy side effects. Some council members
grew discouraged and resigned, but the large majority who
stuck it out developed a sense of ownership in their jobs. After
making dozens of phone calls to Pershing Road to elicit the
smallest crumbs of information and then calling reform and
advocacy organizations all over town for further details, LSC
members felt pride in their own tenacity and resourcefulness.
They vowed that no politician or bureaucrat would take away
their hard-earned authority. Joan Jeter Slay has nicely summed
up this ironic outcome, "We have reaped the benefit of our own
disasters....The council members took the initiative and no one
is going to take this away from them."[27]

It is fortunate that the LSC members developed some
toughness, for they faced their first big test early in 1990, the
first round of principal selections. The law required that half
the 540 schools in the city choose their principals in 1990 and

the other half in 1991, with a lottery deciding which schools would go first. The central administration at Pershing Road decreed that LSCs should decide whether or not to retain their present principal by February 28 and then, if they dismissed the principal, to choose a new one by April 15. Many council members believed these deadlines were unrealistic and simply added to the pressure and confusion of the start-up period. Nevertheless, they threw themselves into the lengthy and tedious task of evaluating the sitting principal and interviewing new candidates for the job.

The principal retention process exploded in controversy at a half-dozen or so schools, and the media pounced on the stories. Journalists find most school reform business tedious and unglamorous, but the firing of principals was full of drama and human interest. At Robert Burns Elementary School in the Latino neighborhood of Little Village, the LSC dismissed a 10-year veteran principal of Slavic ancestry. A large number of students walked out of class voicing noisy protest. Similar demonstrations greeted the dismissal of a 12-year veteran at Spry Elementary in the same neighborhood. The press, particularly the *Tribune*, fingered Danny Solis's UNO as the culprit in both these cases, suggesting that UNO was manipulating the LSCs to hire Latino principals. Solis readily admitted that UNO had assisted many candidates in their council campaigns, had encouraged them to form slates, and had provided leadership training after election, but he denied dictating decisions to the LSC members.[28]

Probably the most bizarre controversy broke out at Wells Community Academy, the neighboring high school to Roberto Clemente on the near northwest side. Principal David Peterson, who had run the school for 13 years, was popular with many of the students and had developed a well-respected honors program that sent many graduates on to college. Yet the dropout rate at the school hovered around 60 percent and critics accused Peterson of "creaming," that is, concentrating his attention on the cream of the crop and ignoring the great mass of students at Wells. The newly elected LSC originally voted not to renew Peterson's contract, but at a subsequent council meeting in March, Peterson successfully challenged the validity of one teacher-member's election and secured the appointment of another teacher who was favorable to him. The LSC then proceeded to vote him a contract renewal.[29]

The media controversy over a few contentious cases nearly obscured the most salient feature of the principal selection process in 1990: 82 percent of the 276 incumbent principals retained their positions. And ironically, after all the accusations of race politics aimed at UNO, the final figures showed that Latino principals suffered the lowest retention rate (50 percent) in the system. Since most of the incumbent Latino principals had been appointed recently and enjoyed only interim status, they had not been able to build an impressive track record and gain retention.[30]

In fact, the local school councils acted rather conservatively in their first big test. The reform act provided a once-in-a-life-time opportunity to clean house in the public schools, but most of the LSCs chose not to seize this opportunity in 1990. Even though the second round of principal retentions was much less controversial, the LSCs did not become more adventurous. They retained about 75 percent of the principals eligible for contracts in 1991.

Mary Gonzales of UNO has aptly summed up the reasons for such timidity on the part of the LSC members:

> If you say, "We should have a Hispanic role model as principal," that is discrimination; if you say, "This guy's been here a long time and we need new blood," that is discrimination; if you say, "This guy is up in age and he doesn't have the energy," that too is discrimination.[31]

Faced with such supersensitive questions as race, sex, and age discrimination, most LSCs gave their principals a pass. This speaks well for the stability of the system. Those who feared wholesale, politically motivated firings were proven wrong. Still the high retention rates are a bit misleading. Many principals voluntarily retired or transferred rather than risk the scrutiny of LSCs. So the overall principal turnover is higher than these figures suggest.

The Pieces Fall Into Place

Throughout the rest of 1990, additional pieces of school reform fell into place. In March, the school board nominating commission, composed of one member from each of the 11 subdistricts in the city plus five mayoral appointees, submitted 45 candidates for the 15-member school board to Mayor Daley. Three names were grouped together on slates for each position and the mayor was required to pick one name from each slate or else reject individual slates and ask for more names. Daley found that many of the nominees were political enemies and thus he stalled for time. The law ambiguously called for the interim board's authority to "expire on May 15, 1990, or upon the appointment of the new board, whichever is later." Daley's critics considered the May 15 date an absolute deadline, whereas the mayor deemed it merely a target.[32]

On May 11, Daley named only seven of the required 15 members for the new board and asked the nominating commission to produce additional slates of names for the remaining vacancies.[33] Since the new board could not take office until all members had been appointed and confirmed by the city council, Daley's ploy extended the tenure of the interim board indefinitely. Though the mayor found many of the initial nominees politically unsuitable, he had a deeper reason for stalling. He wanted to give the interim board sufficient time to negotiate a landmark three-year contract with the teachers' union. Though his foot-dragging caused a sharp controversy and drew protests from black political leaders, the interim board and most school reformers welcomed the extra time. If a completely new board had taken office in May 1990, they would have had to start from scratch on the contract negotiations and this might have caused another disastrous strike if the contract wasn't ready by September.

Bill Singer from the interim board wrapped up his negotiations with the Chicago Teachers Union at the end of July. The three-year pact was the longest ever in the school system's history, and it provided for raises of 7 percent in each of the three years. The agreement also raised the starting salary for new teachers and provided a one thousand dollar bonus payment for outstanding teachers. The teachers hailed this contract as a belated recognition of their professional status, and political leaders welcomed its promise of labor peace for three years. No one wanted to reenact the drama of the 1987 teachers' strike.[34]

Unfortunately, the three-year contract did not turn out to be quite the achievement it seemed at the time. The contract contained an escape clause allowing the board to cancel the annual 7 percent raises should sufficient funds not be available. In 1991, the second year of the contract, the board of education offered no raise whatsoever, and the teachers responded by threatening a strike. The teachers, however, showed much more reluctance to walk out than they had in the past. They continued to bargain for the first two months of the 1991 school year and ultimately settled for a 3 percent raise that year and a guarantee of the full 7 percent in the third year of the contract. The lessons of the 1987 strike prevented the teachers' union from taking hasty actions in this case, but the promise of the three-year contract to provide labor peace and stability bumped against hard fiscal realities.[35]

With the interim board's work at last completed, Mayor Daley appointed the final eight school board members, and the full roster was sworn in on October 3. The board was cleverly constructed to represent a wide range of groups and interests without allowing any single group to dominate. The seven African-American appointees fell just short of a clear majority. Three Latinos, three whites, an Asian-American, and an Arab-American rounded out the slate. Several members, such as LSC member Stephen Ballis from the north lakefront and Saundra Bishop, a former city staffer with the parent/community council, had extensive experience in the school reform movement. Bertha

Magaña, a Mexican-American attorney and mother, was a staff member of UNO, which had been at the center of the storm throughout 1989 and 1990. At its first meeting, the new board elected black university professor, Clinton Bristow, as board president.[36]

The three-year teachers' contract cleared the way for appointment of the permanent school board, but the contract was built on financial quicksand from the very beginning. The legislation implementing this contract tapped unused portions of the teachers' pension fund and the school building fund to provide $66 million for teachers' salaries. Though questioning the wisdom of such financial gimmickry, Governor Thompson approved the measure, but he exercised his amendatory veto to change some other provisions of the bill. The legislature finally repassed the funding measure during the veto session on November 29.[37]

The final piece had fallen into place. Jackie Vaughn, the teachers' union president, remarked brightly, "The three-year contract can be implemented, the education programs and the local school councils that are developing can be funded, and we can look forward to three years of peace and stability in our system." The *Chicago Tribune* editorialized, "School reform: All in place at last." *Crain's Chicago Business* concurred, "After slow start, school reform is beginning to make the grade."[38]

A year and a half into Chicago's experiment with radical school decentralization, everything seemed to be going well. Too well, as it turned out.

Notes

1. Joan Jeter Slay, interview by authors, 2 August 1990.
2. *Chicago Tribune*, 2 January 1989, 1; 1 March 1989, 1; 5 April 1989, 1; *Chicago Sun-Times*, 1 March 1989, 1; 5 April 1989, 1; Paul M. Green and Melvin G. Holli, eds., *Restoration 1989: Chicago Elects a New Daley* (Chicago: Lyceum Books, 1991).

3. The Republican party has rarely mounted a credible campaign in mayoral elections since the 1930s, except for the racially charged candidacy of Bernard Epton in 1983. In 1989, Edward Vrdolyak, Harold Washington's old nemesis, ran as the Republican candidate but won only 3 percent of the votes.

4. *Chicago Tribune*, 10 January 1989, sec. 2, p. 1; 24 April 1989, sec. 2, p. 3.

5. This fast-track legislation indicates that a firm consensus had formed behind school reform. Senators Arthur Berman and Robert Kustra introduced SB 651 the day after Daley's election. It passed unanimously in the house on April 11 and with only one dissenting vote in the senate on April 26. When the governor signed the bill, it became the first law passed by the 86th General Assembly, PA 86-0001. See *Chicago Tribune*, 2 May 1989, 1; *Chicago Sun-Times*, 2 May 1989, 1.

6. *Chicago Tribune*, 26 May 1989, sec. 2, p. 1; *Chicago Sun-Times*, 26 May 1989, 1.

7. Slay interview; "Chicago Voices—William Singer," *Chicago Sunday Tribune Magazine*, 9 December 1990, 9-10; *Chicago Sun-Times*, 26 May 1989, 4.

8. Monteagudo became the center of a political storm on 27 March 1990 with an impolitic statement that no Chicago public school was good enough for her daughter. Though the mayor was greatly embarrassed, he defended his appointee and refused to ask for her resignation despite sharp protests by black activists. See *Chicago Sun-Times*, 27 March 1990, 3; 28 March 1990, 3; *Chicago Tribune*, 28 March 1990, sec. 2, p. 8; 29 March 1990, sec. 2, p. 1; 30 March 1990, sec. 2, p. 2; 5 April 1990, sec. 2, p. 1.

9. Harold Baron, "What Would Harold Be Doing About School Reform?" Unpublished manuscript.

10. *Chicago Sun-Times*, 17 May 1989, 1; 18 May 1989, 1; 1 July 1989, 1; *Chicago Tribune*, 18 May 1989, 1; 1 July 1989, 1; 2 July 1989, 1, 14, 15.

11. *Chicago Tribune*, 2 February 1989, sec. 2, p. 10; "Leadership for Quality Education," privately published brochure, 1990.

12. *Chicago Tribune*, 25 July 1989, sec. 2, p. 3; 7 August 1989, sec. 4, p. 1.

13. *Chicago Tribune*, 24 August 1989, 1; "Helping Chicago's Schools Make the Grade," *Inside CNA* (May-June 1990).

14. Alex Poinsett, "Corporate Chicago Weighs In With Clout, Money, Time," *Catalyst* 2 (March 1991), 3.

15. David Paulus, interview by authors, 16 November 1990.

16. Paulus interview; Danny Solis, interview by authors, 17 October 1990.

17. Solis interview; Tomas Sanabria, interview by authors, 5 October 1990.

18. Nominations for the 469 elementary schools were due by 27 September, for the 71 high schools by 28 September. Elementary school council elections were held on 11 October, high school elections 12 October. See *Chicago Sun-Times*, 24 August 1989, 15, and 5 September 1989, 4, for details.

19. Paulus interview.

20. *Chicago Sun-Times*, 26 September 1989, 17; 29 September 1989, 16.

21. *Chicago Sun-Times*, 12 October 1989, 1; 13 October 1989, 7, 38; *Chicago Tribune*, 12 October 1989, 1.

22. Not surprisingly, the second round of LSC elections, in October 1991, produced a much smaller response. About half as many candidates ran for election and about half as many voters turned out to vote. Though this was considered a negative development at the time, it's possible that this lower turnout simply indicated general contentment with incumbent LSC members and a desire for stability on the councils. See *Catalyst* 3 (December 1991), 18.

23. These figures are based on the official voter participation counts supplied by the board of education. Charles L. Kyle has analyzed them in, "Hispanic Voter Participation in Local School Council Elections in Chicago in 1989," Paper presented to the Midwest Sociological Convention, 14 April 1990.

24. *Chicago Tribune*, 9 March 1989, sec. 2, p. 1; 5 August 1989, 5; 17 October 1989, sec. 2, p. 3; *Chicago Sun-Times*, 19 August 1989, 1; 20 August 1989, 3; 17 October 1989, 3.

25. The following individuals offered cautious opinions about Kimbrough: Don Moore (1 August 1990), Joan Jeter Slay (2 August 1990), Kelvin Strong (12 September 1990), Sokoni Karanja (16 October 1990), Pat Keleher (22 October 1990), and Dave Paulus (16 November 1990). *Crain's Chicago Business* published a thoughtful editorial (22 January 1990, 12) urging Kimbrough to listen to the school reformers not the entrenched bureaucrats.

26. *Chicago Sun-Times*, 24 October 1989, 11; 8 November 1989, 7; 25 January 1990, 76; *Chicago Tribune*, 25 January 1990, sec. 2, p. 1.

27. Slay interview.

28. *Chicago Tribune*, 27 February 1990, sec. 2, p. 1; 28 February 1990, 1; 1 March 1990, sec. 2, p. 1; 11 March 1990, 1; *Chicago Sun-Times*, 1 March 1990, 1; Solis interview.

29. *Chicago Sun-Times*, 7 March 1990, 1; *Chicago Tribune*, 8 March 1990, sec. 2, p. 6; 4 April 1990, sec. 2, p. 10.

30. *Chicago Tribune*, 28 March 1990, sec. 2, p. 1; *Chicago Sun-Times*, 28 March 1990, 7.

31. Mary Gonzales, interview by authors, 12 October 1990. The guidelines for selection of principals issued by the board of education on 1 February 1990 were very explicit on this point: "<u>No applicant or candidate may be selected or rejected on the basis of race, sex, creed, color or disability unrelated to ability to perform,</u>" (underlining in the original)'

32. *Chicago Tribune*, 3 May 1990, 26; 6 May 1990, 1; 8 May 1990, sec. 2, p. 6.

33. *Chicago Tribune*, 12 May 1990, 1; *Chicago Sun-Times*, 12 May 1990, 1.

34. *Chicago Tribune*, 31 July 1990, 1; *Chicago Sun-Times*, 31 July 1990, 1.

35. *Chicago Sun-Times*, 18 November 1991, 1, 19; *Chicago Tribune*, 18 November 1991, 1; 19 November 1991, 1, 18; 24 November 1991, sec. 2, p. 1.

36. *Chicago Tribune*, 3 October 1990, 1; 25 October 1990, sec. 2, p. 3; *Chicago Sun-Times*, 25 October 1990, 48. School board members are profiled in the *Tribune*, 4 October 1990, sec. 3, p. 16.

37. *Chicago Sun-Times*, 17 August 1990, 1; *Chicago Tribune*, 17 August 1990, 1; 30 November 1990, sec. 2, p. 1. The authorization for the use of pension funds was contained in SB 1591.

38. *Chicago Tribune*, 17 August 1990, 1; 30 October 1990, 14; *Crain's Chicago Business*, 5 November 1990, 6.

16

The Bombshell

Just one day after the Illinois legislature cleared the way for a three-year teachers' contract to buy labor peace and give school reform time to work, the Illinois Supreme Court declared the 1988 school reform law unconstitutional. The *Chicago Tribune* called the high court's decision, issued on Friday, November 30, 1990, a "judicial megabomb...dropped on the Chicago public schools."[1]

Many public school principals had never reconciled themselves to the loss of tenure decreed by the reform act, so the principals' professional association filed suit to invalidate the law on grounds that it violated a contractual agreement with the tenured principals and deprived them of valuable property rights (a lifetime job) without due process of law. In order to widen the scope of their suit, the Chicago Principals' Association also lined up several registered voters and taxpayers who challenged the voting procedure for the local school councils. By taking a shotgun approach in its lawsuit, the association hoped that at least some of the legal buckshot would hit the mark.[2]

The plaintiffs filed their complaint on April 17, 1989. The lawyers for the city of Chicago and the board of education confidently petitioned the circuit court for a summary judgment and a prompt decision. The court agreed, issuing a summary judgment that dismissed the suit on August 29, 1989. The principals' association appealed, however, and over a year later, after the first LSC elections and the first round of principal selections had been completed under the reform act, the Illinois Supreme Court issued its bombshell overruling the trial court and declaring the law unconstitutional.

The Supreme Court Decision

Ironically, the supreme court denied the principals' main charge, that the loss of tenure violated contractual rights and due process. The justices, however, ruled that the voting procedure for electing local school councils violated the one person-one vote doctrine that the U.S. Supreme Court had enshrined into law with its landmark decision of *Reynolds v. Sims* in 1964.[3] The school reform act mandated that only parents vote for the six parent representatives on the LSCs, only teachers vote for the two teacher reps, and only community members who were not teachers and did not have children in the public schools vote for the two community members. This meant that parents cast a weighted vote, a violation of the one person-one vote doctrine; thus the entire law was unconstitutional. This judicial decision threatened to topple the entire structure laboriously erected by the school reform movement during the decade of the 1980s.

The decision referred to as *Fumarolo* was an unusually clear and carefully reasoned judgment.[4] Chief Justice Daniel Ward, a Chicago Democrat who had previously served as state's attorney in Cook County, wrote the majority opinion. Ward stated at the outset that his court was sailing on uncharted waters, "We are not aware of any legislation similarly structuring a public school system." Therefore, the court had no exact precedents to follow.[5]

The key question before the court in applying the one person-one vote doctrine to the local school council elections was whether these councils possessed "general governmental powers." If they did, then the court was obligated to follow a "standard of strict scrutiny"; that is, they must find some compelling reason for departing from the one person-one vote formula. If the councils did not enjoy general governmental powers, however, the court could apply the "rational basis test." Under this more relaxed standard, it would be permissible to depart from the one person-one vote formula if the legislature made any reasonable case for doing so.[6]

Though no exact precedent existed to guide the court's deliberations, there were other cases in which federal courts had allowed exceptions to the voting equality rule. For example, in two cases in the western United States, the U.S. Supreme Court had permitted an irrigation district and an agricultural improvement district to limit voting privileges only to landowners in the district.[7] School reform lawyers argued that the local school councils were similar to these agricultural improvement districts; that is, they were special purpose bodies, with important but limited powers, that primarily affected just one class of people, the parents of schoolchildren, not the general citizenry. Therefore, the LSCs should be deemed not to possess general governmental powers.

The Illinois Supreme Court disagreed:

> Considering the whole Act, and the local school councils in particular, we hold that the local school councils are essential units of educational governance, empowered to make important budgetary, educational and administrative decisions....The Reform Act creates a unique system in which local school councils play an important role in one of the most critical of governmental functions, the providing of public education.... The administration of education through the operation of our schools is a fundamental governmental activity in which all members of society have an interest....We hold, therefore, that the local school councils exercise general governmental functions....[8]

Two facets of the school reform act appeared to weigh heavily upon the justices' decision: the budgetary powers of the LSCs and their role in nominating members of the Chicago Board of Education.

The LSCs did not possess the power to levy taxes or issue bonds (these were retained by the central school board), but their approval was required for the local school's budget and expenditure plan. They enjoyed wide discretion in disbursing the Chapter I funds made available to low-income schools. This fiscal authority prompted the court to conclude that "the powers exercised by the local school councils are broad."

Furthermore, each LSC appoints one of its members to sit on the subdistrict council, and each subdistrict council then elects one member to serve on the school board nominating commission. That commission presents slates of candidates to the mayor and he appoints the board of education from these slates. The court ruled that "the nominating commission is simply too closely connected to the unconstitutionally selected local school councils to conclude that it has been properly selected or that it can properly select candidates for the board of education."[9]

Ironically, the school reformers had done their job too well. The reform act clearly granted the local school councils substantive powers, not merely advisory status. The Illinois Supreme Court appeared very impressed with this fact. "The legislature has made the local school councils the indispensable foundation of the school system," the majority opinion stated. The school reform movement had successfully distinguished the LSCs from PTA committees or other parent advisory councils, and the court therefore ruled that they were endowed with general governmental powers and must be elected on the one person-one vote principle.[10]

The supreme court justices specifically rejected the argument that parents enjoy a substantially greater interest in the schools than other citizens do:

> The administration of education through the operation of our schools is a fundamental governmental activity in which all members of society have an interest. Furthermore, educational activities are financed by and affect virtually every resident....A school is not an island within the community; the school system is an integral part of the whole city.[11]

This is precisely what the leaders of the SON/SOC coalition had been arguing for years. Taxpayers who do not have children in the public schools still have a vital interest in the health of the public schools and should possess an equal voice in their maintenance. The supreme court vindicated this judgment.

Having struck down the school reform law as unconstitutional, due to its faulty voting procedure, the justices were not legally bound to consider any other aspects of the principals' lawsuit, but they decided to consider the main complaint, denial of tenure, since "these issues may arise again should the legislature choose to reenact the legislation." The court gave short shrift to the principals' argument that their previously granted tenure created a contractual obligation the legislature could not alter: "A party who asserts that a state law creates contractual rights has the burden of overcoming the presumption that a contract does not arise out of a legislative enactment." In other words, the burden of proof is on the principals. The justices then continued, "The legislature must be free to exercise its constitutional authority without concern that each time a public policy is expressed contractual rights may thereby be created." In short, the legislature giveth and the legislature taketh away. In this case, the lawmakers took away principal tenure and replaced it with four-year performance contracts. The supreme court ruled that "the plaintiffs . . . did not have a contractual right to continued employment."[12]

In retrospect, the *Fumarolo* judgment on the voting rights matter clearly could have gone either way. The justices readily admitted they had no clear precedents to guide them. Reasonable people could argue that the LSCs, though they enjoyed important powers, were not really general governmental bodies. Parents of schoolchildren probably do have a much greater interest in their decisions and are much more greatly affected by them.

These are not just theoretical musings. One supreme court justice actually argued along these lines in dissenting from the majority opinion. Justice William G. Clark, a Chicago Democrat who had served as Illinois Attorney General before his appointment to the bench, filed a minority opinion. Clark noted that "the local school councils cannot levy taxes, issue bonds, enter into employment contracts, purchase, lease or acquire by condemnation buildings or real estate" and therefore concluded that they are limited purpose units of government, much like the water irrigation districts ruled on in previous cases.[13]

The decision, therefore, could have been different. Critics who argue that the school reformers were legally sloppy and should have foreseen the constitutional objection have the benefit of hindsight, which is always 20/20.

The Try for a Quick Fix

The court's decision caught the school reform forces off guard. Leaders of the advocacy organizations had been puzzled and irritated by the intransigence of Bruce Berndt, president of the principals' association, during the drafting of the reform act, but they considered his association's lawsuit merely a nuisance. Important state legislators such as Senator Berman and House Speaker Madigan had invested considerable time and personal influence in the passage of the act and they did not want to see it all swept away. As for Mayor Daley, he had been pursuing a "stealth strategy" leading up to his reelection campaign in the spring of 1991, carefully deferring consideration of all contentious issues until after the elections. The last thing he wanted was for school reform to leap back onto the front pages. Most disconcerted of all, however, were the 6,500 local school council members whose positions as the keystones of reform were put in jeopardy. One LSC member remarked to a reporter, "We've been working like dogs for a year and a half, with no pay, and now this thing is a real kick in the teeth for us."[14]

Immediately after the court's decision was announced, therefore, reformers and politicians scrambled to their posts in a damage control exercise. The *Sun-Times*, which had covered the long saga of school reform more closely and sympathetically than its rival the *Tribune*, crossed over the line of objective journalism and used its front-page story of December 1, 1990, to reassure the public rather than inform it. Both in that article and in a longer follow-up the next day, the paper printed a soothing litany:

· "Nothing changes; local school councils are not disbanded,"
Mary Dempsey, attorney, Sidley & Austin.
· "There should not be any implication here of a panic, that the
whole school system is thrown out the window," Senator
Arthur Berman.
· "Nothing has really changed. We will go through a process,
and that process will be one to make reform even better,"
School Superintendent Ted Kimbrough.
· "I don't view this as a major setback. I view it more of a
technical problem that has to get worked out," Governor-
elect James Edgar.
· "I think it is more of a legal glitch than anything else," James
Compton, president, interim school board.[15]

These statements were disingenuous and not strictly
accurate. The supreme court had explicitly pointed out that "the
decision today that there is a denial of equal protection under
the Act is not simply a decision that there is a type of technical
omission or defect in the statute." Mary Dempsey, the principal
drafter of the reform act, had prudently included a severability
clause in the law, so that if one section were declared unconstitutional the rest of the act could stand without it. The justices,
however, overruled this clause, declaring, "After the portion of
this statute which has been declared unconstitutional because it
denies equal protection is stricken, the remainder of the statute
cannot stand independently."[16]

The violation of the one person-one vote principle in the
school reform act was not, therefore, merely a technical glitch.
It struck at the very heart of the act. The reformers knew this.
Control of the LSCs by a parent majority was the distinguish-
ing feature that set off the Chicago reform from other school
systems. In New York's decentralized school districts, for example, parents enjoyed very little influence. The court did not
say that a parent majority on the councils was impermissible,
but it did disallow the unusual voting mechanism whereby only
parents voted for parents, only teachers voted for teachers, and
only community members voted for community representatives.

It would be possible to fix this problem by letting all
interested parties (parents, teachers, and community members)

cast 10 votes, one for each elected member of the LSC, but this would destroy the unique feature of parent predominance in the voting procedure and open the door to political slate making by politicians or community groups. If every member of the local school district had 10 votes, whether he or she had children in the school or not, a vigorous turn-out-the-vote effort for a political slate of candidates could easily swamp the parents of schoolchildren and skew the process. This is one of the major reasons the reformers adopted the like-votes-for-like procedure that the court ultimately disallowed. Finding a new procedure that would satisfy the court and meet the purposes of school reform would not be easy.

Furthermore, the reformers feared that reopening the school reform question would allow all sorts of amendments and political deals to gut the law. No one believed the 1988 act was perfect. Indeed, each of the reformers had a list of small changes they would like to see enacted. One technical change with universal support was a provision to remove LSC members who did not show up for two or three successive meetings.[17] Despite the desire for improvements, however, reformers feared a wholesale reconsideration of the act. The upcoming legislative session in 1991 looked especially crowded and controversial. The lawmakers would have to consider political redistricting after the recent census, the expansion of the McCormick Place convention center and the possible building of a domed football stadium, and the renewal of Mike Madigan's income tax surcharge. School reform would likely be pushed down into a lower priority and would be used for bargaining and deal making on these higher-profile issues. No one could predict just what might happen to the law under these circumstances.

Therefore, the reform coalition decided to push for a quick fix of the law to minimize confusion and disruption. A *Chicago Tribune* editorial demanded that outgoing Governor Jim Thompson call a special session of the legislature right away to fix the school reform law. The governor declined to do so. The next window of opportunity, then, was the one-day, end-of-session meeting of the legislature in early January. Every two years, after legislative elections, the outgoing General Assembly meets for largely ceremonial purposes; the following day the newly elected senators and representatives take over, choosing a house Speaker and senate president. If the reform forces could reach consensus on what was needed to fix the school act, they might be able to sneak it through the legislature during its one-day, closing session.[18]

Accordingly, the ABCs coalition of businessmen, school reform organizations, and community groups, now reinforced by the local school council members, sprang back into action. Sidley & Austin, a leading law firm, provided a team of 6 to 10 lawyers working *pro bono*. They ultimately performed about two hundred thousand dollars worth of free legal work. The first order of business, agreed upon by everyone except the principals, was for the legislature to retroactively validate all the actions that the board of education and the local school councils had taken since the reform act went into effect in 1989. In particular, the LSCs had completed the first round of principal selections early in 1990 and it was vital that their choices be ratified. A second priority was that the legislature somehow confirm the LSC members in office until their terms ran out in October 1991. The easiest way to do this would be to make the offices, technically speaking, appointive, permitting the mayor to reappoint all the sitting LSC members for the rest of their terms.

The reform coalition swiftly reached agreement on these first two points, then labored over a new voting mechanism to fix the fundamental defect in the law. The team of lawyers from Sidley & Austin drafted a voting procedure granting 10 votes to all interested parties in a school district (parents, teachers, and community members). The ABCs coalition then held a news conference on December 13 to publicize the plan.[19]

Opposition to the quick-fix approach surfaced quickly. The principals, of course, wanted to gut the law and reduce the

LSCs to merely advisory status. Professionals in the school board administration, who had much to lose from thoroughgoing reform, also wanted to slow down the process. They found a sympathetic audience in Superintendent Ted Kimbrough and Board President Clinton Bristow, who convened a series of caucuses to discuss a fuller range of amendments to the school reform law than the minimum three that the ABCs coalition was pushing. Even those who wanted to rush through a change in the law found themselves stumped by the problem of magnet schools that drew students from all over the city. Should anyone in the city be allowed to vote for the two community representatives at these schools?

The most significant opposition to the quick fix, however, came from the established black community organizations, such as Operation PUSH and the Urban League, which had not exercised much influence on the shaping of the 1988 law. Black leaders complained that they had been shut out of the bill-drafting process in Springfield in 1988. This wasn't literally true. Many of the school reformers were black and the bargaining process in Mike Madigan's office was open to any interested party. Yet, there was one sense in which the black community groups did have a grievance. Reform organizations with paid staff or large grants could afford to keep a delegate continuously in Springfield, whereas others could not. More fundamentally, however, the black organizations were distracted and exhausted by mayoral politics after the death of Harold Washington and therefore did not devote sufficient attention to the bargaining process in Springfield the first time around. They didn't intend to make the same mistake twice, and thus they opposed the rush for a quick fix.

Accordingly, a new group, the African-American Education Reform Institute, composed largely of black educators and community groups, began discussing the issues. Inevitably, the debate became entangled in the mayoral election campaign. Black candidate Danny Davis, running against Mayor Daley in the primary, stated, "We reject the approach of working behind closed doors, of having a team of lawyers at Sidley & Austin put a legal Band-Aid on the part of the law found unconstitutional." Though Speaker Madigan convened public hearings in the first week of January to give everyone a chance to air their views on school reform, these sessions failed to reach a consensus on how to fix the law.[20]

When the 86th General Assembly convened for its final day on Tuesday, January 8, 1991, it adopted only two of the three proposals in the ABCs coalition's quick fix. HB 3302, titled the School Reform Protection Act, validated all past actions of the Chicago Board of Education and the local school councils and authorized Mayor Daley to appoint all current members of the board and the LSCs for the remainder of their terms. These two actions removed any doubt about the legality of principal selections and budgetary actions taken since the passage of school reform. The legislature declined, however, to settle the voting procedure for future LSC elections, postponing action until the full session of the next General Assembly. Lacking consensus among the school reform groups, Speaker Madigan and Senate President Rock did not want to split their Democratic caucuses and jeopardize their own reelections as leaders of the legislature. Black legislators had made it clear they were not ready to settle the voting procedure and enact a quick fix. They preferred a full airing of their own amendments to the reform act in the next legislative session, and Madigan and Rock deferred to them.[21]

The Marathon Session

Richard M. Daley was easily reelected mayor of Chicago in April 1991, defeating two black candidates, Danny Davis in the Democratic primary and Eugene Pincham running on the Harold Washington party ticket in the April 2 general election.[22] Despite his renewed mandate, however, he showed no inclination to take the lead in fixing the school reform law. Indeed, a month after his reelection, his controversial deputy mayor for education, Lourdes Monteagudo, resigned and Daley waited a full four months before naming her replacement. When he finally chose Leonard Dominguez, a former school principal, for the deputy mayor's post, however, Daley confirmed the prominent role that Latinos had played throughout the school reform debate.[23]

With the approval of both Democratic leaders in the legislature, Senator Arthur Berman, chairman of the education committee, assumed the role of political point man for school reform. He introduced two shell bills, SB 10 and SB 11, at the very beginning of the new legislative session, one to carry the revised voting procedure for LSCs and the other for any other amendments the reformers devised. Berman made it clear that the reform organizations would have to reach consensus before he would act. "If the reform groups are agreed on an approach, it will pass," Berman stated.[24]

Some of the black politicians wished they could eliminate the school reform act altogether or at least weaken the power of the local school councils. They viewed the LSCs as potential breeding grounds for political rivals. Furthermore, some of their most vocal constituents, black professionals employed at Pershing Road, feared for their jobs under a thoroughgoing reform regime. One black legislator, Representative Monique Davis, was herself an employee of the Chicago Board of Education. Davis was one of only two black Democrats to vote against the final reform act in 1988 and she became an outspoken opponent of the law, but most members of the black legislative caucus did not dare voice their strongest negative opinions publicly. Black parents of public school children, and particularly their elected representatives on the LSCs, supported reform and would not brook any direct attack on the reform law.[25]

The African-American Education Reform Institute, a coalition of about 20 groups headed by the Urban League, became the main spokesman for the black position on school reform. They unveiled a plan in March 1991 that would grant each voter in LSC elections only three votes for the 10 elective positions. This would give each voter's ballot equal weight, as the supreme court required, but would insure that no one group (parents, teachers, or community members) could dominate the voting procedure. In addition to the voting change, the institute also proposed that principals be given complete control over their schools, with authority over building engineers and food service workers.

Finally, the African-American groups insisted that the section of the reform law phasing in an open enrollment plan for public school students be scrapped. Black teachers and administrators greatly feared any freedom-of-choice plan as a direct threat to the viability of the public schools. Though open enrollment would only apply within the public school system, many feared it as a first step towards tuition vouchers and open enrollment in both public and private schools. James Deanes, the president of the parent/community council and a member of the institute, repeatedly stated that school reform should be given a chance to "make every school a school of choice."[26]

After the African-American Institute staked out its position in March, the debate began to focus on the main problem, fixing the voting procedure for the LSCs. The ABCs coalition stuck with its proposal to grant each voter 10 votes, which they would divide among the six parent representatives, two teachers, and two community representatives (the principal would, of course, continue to serve ex officio and the LSC membership would continue to total 11). The African-American Institute, however, feared that this would lead to slate making, which might be dominated by the teachers' union, as in New York, or by white community residents surrounding a school with a black minority. Particularly in schools where black students were bused in, the surrounding white neighborhood residents could use their 10 votes to out-poll the parents of the bused students. The institute, therefore, stood firm for their three-vote plan.

The teachers' union complicated the picture by objecting to the general community voting for teachers' representatives. They wanted to retain a special status for teacher members by making them appointive positions. The board of education could appoint the teacher reps on the LSCs after the teachers in each school held a nonbinding straw vote. Continuing his long-standing alliance with the teachers' union, Danny Solis of UNO endorsed the proposal for appointive teachers' positions and advanced a plan for voters to cast eight votes for the remaining parent and community reps. Solis argued that parents would likely turn out in much larger numbers than general community members, so the arguments of the African-American Institute were groundless. Of course, very few Latino children were bused into white neighborhoods so he didn't share the blacks' fears of a surrounding white community dominating elections. Furthermore, Solis's UNO enjoyed a strong organizing position in several Latino neighborhoods. If any group engaged in slate making and tried to dominate LSC elections, it would probably be UNO.[27]

Senator Berman and Speaker Madigan finally gathered all the reform groups and other interested parties for a two-day summit in Springfield on June 18 and 19. The procedure employed three years previously, when the original reform bill was hammered out in Madigan's office, paid dividends once again. Senator Berman, however, noted that the process proved more acrimonious this time. In 1988 the bargaining sessions in Madigan's office were so novel that the participants felt happy just to be listened to. Three years later, however, everyone's expectations were higher and the search for compromise much harder.[28]

Finally, after much wrangling, the reform summit deferred to the teachers' union and agreed that the board of education should appoint the two teacher reps on each LSC after the teachers had made their wishes known in a straw vote. Senator Rock and Speaker Madigan then proposed a simple numerical compromise on the voting procedure, granting each of the voters in LSC elections five votes for the remaining eight positions (six parents and two community reps). Under this proposal, if any slate making took place, no slate could elect more than five members, less than a majority of the LSC membership. This compromise won grudging agreement. The summit members also agreed to postpone the open enrollment plan until the 1994 school year. They tried to convince the food service and janitorial unions to cede control to the principals at each local school, but failed to get more than token concessions.[29]

Before the legislature could act on these agreements, however, school reform got swept aside temporarily as the Democratic majority in the legislature battled the new governor, Jim Edgar, over budgetary matters. Edgar had proposed deep cuts in welfare spending to balance the state's recession-reduced budget and had promised suburban homeowners property tax relief in the form of a tax cap limiting property tax increases to 5 percent or the rate of inflation, whichever was less. Democrats, on the other hand, opposed the tax cap and called for less severe spending cuts. The governor had campaigned on a pledge to make the state income tax surcharge permanent, but then to resist any further tax increases. Speaker Madigan insisted instead that the surcharge be renewed for only two more years, so that the governor would have to return to the legislature yet again if he wanted more money. Various attempts to compromise these positions failed and the legislature went into overtime in July.[30]

Jim Edgar, a strait-laced downstater who had spent a lifetime in state government, chose not to deal or compromise with Speaker Madigan and Senate President Rock but insisted on making at least part of the income tax surcharge permanent and effecting some property tax relief for the suburbs. The legislative process, therefore, stalled, and the marathon overtime session of the legislature extended nearly three weeks into July.

Pressure built up on the lawmakers when the state's employees went without paychecks the week of July 15. Finally, the governor and the Democratic leaders reached an agreement that the house approved on July 17 and the senate on July 18. The governor won a 5 percent property tax cap for the suburban collar counties surrounding Chicago, and the Democrats succeeded in reinstating some of the proposed welfare cuts. Both sides compromised on the surcharge extension. The portion of the income tax surcharge designated for education became permanent. This was characterized by the press as a victory for Edgar, for he had promised this in his gubernatorial campaign, but Madigan and the Democrats found it congenial as well since they had invested so much personal prestige in school reform. The remaining portion of the surcharge, designated for municipalities and for paying overdue state bills, was renewed for only two years, as Madigan insisted.[31]

After the budget logjam was broken, the exhausted legislators swiftly cleared their calendars in just one day and adjourned shortly after midnight, in the early morning of Friday, July 19. Before adjournment, however, they approved the plan to expand McCormick Place, financing the construction mainly with taxes on the tourist industry in Chicago. They also passed the two school reform bills, revising the voting procedure for LSCs and adding some subsidiary amendments to the reform act.

SB 10 enacted the compromise voting procedure that had been agreed to by the school reformers in June. The principal continues to sit ex officio on the local school council, two teacher representatives are appointed by the board of education after an advisory vote of the school's teachers, and then every resident of the school's attendance district is eligible to cast five votes for the six parent representative positions and the two community rep posts. In addition, on high school councils, the one student representative, who had been a nonvoting observer under the original act, is granted the right to vote on all matters except personnel decisions. This student delegate is appointed like the teachers, after a nonbinding vote of his or her peers. Finally, the bill authorizes the board of education to draw voting boundaries for the magnet schools so that community representatives will not be drawn from all over the city but only from areas where most of the students live.

SB 11 failed to solve the thorny question of how much authority a principal should exercise over nonteaching school staff. Principals were given the right to evaluate the performance of building engineers and food service workers semiannually, but many reformers remained unhappy that the unions retained considerable power over the final shape of this bill.

The legislation delayed the start of open enrollment until the 1994 school year and provided that LSC members could be removed after absences from three consecutive meetings or five meetings within one year. The power of the LSCs over school principals was also clarified and enhanced. If the principal repeatedly failed to implement the school improvement plan approved by the council, the LSC could remove him or her before the principal's contract expired. Finally, Senator Miguel del Valle managed to add a provision encouraging the use of translators at the LSC meetings of bilingual schools and establishing the preexisting bilingual advisory committees as standing committees of the LSCs.[32]

Despite the longest and most contentious session of the legislature in recent Illinois history, the lawmakers retooled the school reform act and overcame the edict of the Illinois Supreme Court that had declared it unconstitutional. The unusual cooperation between businessmen, community organizations, and politicians held up through yet another round of close bargaining and compromise. The local school councils could now direct their attention to improving their schools and preparing for new elections to the councils in October.

Still a Rocky Road

Overcoming the constitutional obstacle by no means assured the success of school reform, as formidable challenges still faced the Chicago public schools. Even as the reform organizations were negotiating the details of a new voting procedure for LSCs, another financial crisis was unfolding at the board of education's central offices on Pershing Road.

Shortly after Mayor Daley's reelection in April, Superintendent Ted Kimbrough revealed that the school board was facing a huge deficit of over three hundred million dollars in the

upcoming fiscal year. Much of this projected deficit resulted
directly from school reform. The 1988 act had mandated a
gradual shift of all Chapter I compensatory education funding
to the disadvantaged schools it was intended for. Previously the
central board had used this money to balance its budget, and it
was now finding the loss of that extra revenue difficult. More
important, the three-year teachers' contract that the interim
board had negotiated was built on financial quicksand. The
first-year raise of 7 percent was paid for with funds borrowed
from the teachers' pension funds, but no explicit source of
funding was provided for the second- and third-year raises.[33]

Howls of derision greeted Kimbrough's Cassandra-like
warnings. The school board had outlined horrendous deficits
nearly every spring in living memory, and somehow they rarely
turned out to be as bad as predicted. Mayor Daley, attending a
mayors' conference in Washington when Kimbrough's budget
numbers were released, remarked offhandedly, "I don't believe
them. They have had a long history...." In his May 6 inaugural
address, Daley made his skepticism more explicit. Holding up
the school board as an example of bureaucracy run amuck, he
stated, "The school bureaucracy still stands in the way of
change, rather than leading it." Daley then added a warning,
"And if we can't break the stranglehold of bureaucracy and
school board politics in Chicago, we may have to take that next
step." The next step was tuition vouchers allowing public
school students to attend private schools.[34]

More dispassionate observers agreed that Kimbrough's
budget plight was real, but exaggerated. Fred Hess, whose
Chicago Panel on Public School Policy and Finance had
established a solid track record for credible analysis of school
finances, estimated that the real deficit probably stood at about
$200 million, rather than the $315 million that Kimbrough
officially projected for the Chicago School Finance Authority.
Hess told a public television audience that the superintendent
could easily cut eight hundred jobs from his administration for
a saving of $40 million and then save another $60 million by

closing and consolidating underused schools. The rest of the deficit, however, would have to be erased with new money from the legislature (unlikely) or a renegotiation of the teachers' contract (difficult, but possible).[35]

Kimbrough proposed various doomsday budget alternatives, such as a hit list of school closings; then as the legislature approached its scheduled wind-up in June, his political allies in the black caucus attempted to secure at least part of the money he needed. An amendment to SB 158, sponsored by Senator Emil Jones in the senate and Representative Ron LeFlore in the house, would delay the redistribution of Chapter I funds to individual schools for one year, thus making about $78 million available to Kimbrough to help balance his budget. The surprise amendment passed the house on June 21, without any consultation with reform organizations that were down in Springfield at the time, but the advocacy groups rallied over the weekend and prevented its passage in the upper house. Despite the looming financial crisis, school reformers remained adamant that compensatory funds for disadvantaged children not be sacrificed once again.[36]

As the legislators staggered home in July, after their marathon session wrestling with the state's financial problems, the Chicago Board of Education's fiscal difficulties remained unresolved. The board reneged on the 7 percent raise stipulated in the second year of the teachers' contract, and though the Chicago Teachers Union seemed reluctant to push for a strike, their membership eventually authorized a walkout for November 18. Negotiations went right down to the wire, with the school board unwilling to offer even a token raise for the teachers. Finally, three days before the strike deadline, Mayor Daley stepped in, as his father had so often, and brokered a settlement that kept the schools open. The board made additional staff cuts and the mayor refinanced some bonds to free up funds for a three percent raise. No one had any idea, however, where the money would come from for teacher raises in the final year of the contract.[37]

A repetition of the autumnal cliffhanger, therefore, seemed likely for 1992. Though school reform had marked some notable achievements in the 1980s, it continued to be threatened by inadequate finances and the weight of a costly bureaucracy as the decade of the nineties began.

While all this was going on, one final piece of school reform legislation unexpectedly fell into place in 1991. The nationwide movement for school reform in the 1980s began with "A Nation at Risk"'s call for greater accountability from educators. In Illinois, the first wave of reform legislation, in 1985, mandated standardized tests in 3rd, 6th, 8th, and 11th grades (the Illinois Goal Assessment Program), and required the publication of a school report card detailing how each school and school district measured up on these tests and other performance measures. The shockingly low scores of Chicago schools provided a powerful impetus to the second wave of school reform. These school report cards, however, provided no sanctions, other than public ignominy, for low-performing schools. So in 1991, a commission of businessmen and educators secured the passage of an academic bankruptcy act to put teeth into the report card process.

The 29-member regulatory process committee, funded by the Illinois Manufacturers' Association (IMA) and headed by a vice-president of Northern Illinois Gas, recommended that the Illinois State Board of Education adopt a tough accountability plan pioneered by the state of South Carolina in 1984. In return, IMA and the Illinois Chamber of Commerce agreed not to oppose extension of the income tax surcharge for education. The old theme sounded once again: no money without accountability.[38]

Representative Terry Steczo introduced HB 885, and the legislature passed it overwhelmingly on June 27, 1991. The law requires the state board to monitor the performance of all schools across the state. If any school or district's performance measures decline markedly or stagnate at very low levels, the board is empowered to put that school or district on an "academic watch list" and appoint a committee to fashion an improvement plan. If the school or district does not improve after four years, the state board can invoke severe penalties, including the removal of the local school board, the appointment of an "independent authority" to run the school, or as a last resort, the closing of the school. This law, therefore, provides for academic receivership and the ultimate sanction of the death penalty for inadequate schools.[39]

Fifteen years ago, Chicago's public schools were virtually unaccountable to anyone, fashioning illusory budgets with smoke and mirrors; publishing bogus statistics that masked an enormous dropout problem; blaming the victims, low-income minority students, for their low performance on standardized tests; and stiff-arming parents who dared to complain. After a decade of school reform, the schools are now supervised by local councils of parents, teachers, and taxpayers; their finances are subject to review and approval by the School Finance Control Authority; they are compelled to publish honest test scores and dropout statistics in a yearly report card; and the state board of education can put them out of business if they don't educate their students. Whether the city's public schools will improve over the next decade remains an open question, but at least they now have a fighting chance.

Notes

1. *Chicago Tribune*, 2 December 1990, sec. 4, p. 2.

2. The case was officially known as *Arthur Fumarolo et al. v. The Chicago Board of Education et al.* The lead plaintiff, Arthur Fumarolo, was the secretary of the Chicago Principals' Association.

3. *Reynolds v. Sims* (1964), 377 U.S. 533, 12 L. Ed. 2d 506, 84 S. Ct. 1362.

4. *Arthur Fumarolo et al. v. The Chicago Board of Education et al.*, Docket No. 69558-Agenda 22-March 1990. See also *New York Times*, 1 December 1990, 10; *Chicago Tribune*, 1 December 1990, 1; *Chicago Sun-Times*, 1 December 1990, 1.

5. *Fumarolo*, 2.

6. Ibid., 10-11.

7. *Salyer Land Co. v. Tulare Lake Basin Water Storage District* (1973), 410 U.S. 719, 35 L. Ed. 2d 659, 93 S. Ct. 1224; *Ball v. James* (1981), 451 U.S. 355, 68 L. Ed. 2d 150, 101 S. Ct. 1811.

8. *Fumarolo*, 16-17, 22.

9. Ibid., 17, 31.

10. Ibid., 19.

11. Ibid., 22, 41.

12. Ibid., 35-36.

13. Ibid., 51-52.

14. *Chicago Tribune*, 2 December 1990, sec. 2, p. 1; 3 December 1990, sec. 2, p. 1.

15. *Chicago Sun-Times*, 1 December 1990, 1; 2 December 1990, 16. The *Chicago Tribune*'s lead story, 1 December 1990, 1, was far more stark and realistic, laying out the serious nature of the court decision with a minimum of "happy talk."

16. *Fumarolo*, 32, 42.

17. In interviewing people for this book, we routinely asked them what changes they would like to see in the law. Nearly everyone mentioned a removal mechanism for non-attending LSC members.

18. *Chicago Tribune*, 2 December 1990, sec. 4, p. 2; *Crain's Chicago Business*, 10 December 1990, 12.

19. *Chicago Sun-Times*, 14 December 1990, 1; the *Tribune* published a picture of the news conference, 14 December 1990, sec. 3, p. 3, but no story.

20. *Chicago Tribune*, 12 December 1990, sec. 2, p. 1; 13 December 1990, sec. 3, p. 10; 3 January 1991, sec. 2, p. 1; 6 January 1991, sec. 4, p. 4; *Chicago Sun-Times*, 3 January 1991, 14; 4 January 1991, 5; 5 January 1991, 5.

21. *Chicago Tribune*, 8 January 1991, sec. 2, p. 1; 9 January 1991, sec. 2, p. 2; *Chicago Sun-Times*, 8 January 1991, 1; 9 January 1991, 3. Joan Jeter Slay, from Designs for Change, wrote a clear synopsis of HB 3302 in a "Voice of the People" column in the *Tribune*, 7 February 1991, 18.

22. Paul M. Green, "Chicago's 1991 Mayoral Elections: Richard M. Daley Wins Second Term," *Illinois Issues* 17 (June 1991): 17-25.

23. *Chicago Tribune*, 17 May 1991, sec. 2, p. 3; 5 September 1991, sec. 2, p. 3; *Chicago Sun-Times*, 17 May 1991, 5.

24. Michael Klonsky and Susan Klonsky, "LSC Election Defect Still a Flashpoint," *Catalyst* 2 (June 1991): 12; Arthur Berman, interview by authors, 30 September 1991.

regularly sends its finest chefs to teach and provides internships for students at its own hotel restaurants in Chicago.

When the local school council at Clemente faced its first big test, the choice of a principal, it surprised many by passing over the Latino candidates, and promoting the long-time assistant principal, Lou Geraldi, of Italian-American ancestry. Antonio Beltran, the LSC president, explained that they chose Geraldi because both the teachers and the council members trusted him and they believed he was best qualified to bring the community and the school together.

In pursuit of such school-community ties, the LSC arranged for 40 teachers to attend in-service sessions at community agencies on their own time during the summer. These sessions familiarized the teachers with ethnic customs of the neighborhood and helped heal a rift between Anglo and Latino teachers.

The LSC also used its Chapter I funds to provide additional summer school classes for 770 students. Since some students failed to graduate because they lacked only a credit or two at the end of senior year, the council urged these students to finish up during summer school then staged an additional graduation ceremony for them in August. The first year this policy was in effect, 55 students graduated at a ceremony attended by over one thousand members of the community. Efforts to overcome the dropout problem continued to motivate both school and community leaders.

Finally, with the assistance of Deputy Mayor Lourdes Montcagudo and with funding from the Joyce and MacArthur foundations, the entire LSC from Clemente flew to New York in 1991 to observe a highly acclaimed high school that has decentralized its operations into a series of schools within the school. The school improvement plan that the Clemente LSC subsequently wrote follows this model. Just as department stores today are retooling as a collection of specialty stores under one roof, Clemente Community Academy will house several specialized schools, each with its own assistant principal.

Though Clemente still has many problems to overcome, its

25. We interviewed Carol Moseley Braun, currently the Cook County Recorder of Deeds, but previously a legislative leader in the state house of representatives, and state Senator Ethel Skyles Alexander, on 5 February 1991. Both stated they would like to see the LSCs become voluntary and advisory rather than elective and authoritative. When we asked point blank whether the 1988 School Reform Act was a mistake, neither was willing to state it quite that baldly, but Braun concluded it was "a defective bill that caused more problems than it solved." Alexander avowed that the legislature should have concentrated on increasing funding for the schools.

26. *Chicago Tribune*, 20 March 1991, sec. 2, p. 3; *Chicago Sun-Times*, 20 March 1991, 5.

27. Klonsky and Klonsky, "LSC Election Defect," is a good account of these conflicting positions. Also, Danny Solis and Rep. Monique Davis debated these two positions on a special edition of John Callaway's "Chicago Tonight" broadcast on WTTW/11, 9 May 1991.

28. Berman interview.

29. *Chicago Tribune*, 19 June 1991, sec. 2, p. 5; 20 June 1991, sec. 2, p. 3; 25 June 1991, 18; *Chicago Sun-Times*, 19 June 1991, 3; 20 June 1991, 22; 25 June 1991, 31; Philip Rock, interview by authors, 27 August 1991.

30. *Chicago Tribune*, 1 July 1991, 1. The lawmakers had previously killed the proposal to fund a domed football stadium in Chicago, but another proposal to build an extension to the lakefront McCormick Place convention center was still very much alive. As with school reform, it was merely waiting for the main event, the budget battle, to be settled.

31. *Chicago Tribune*, 14 July 1991, 1; 18 July 1991, 1, and sec. 2, p. 1; *Chicago Sun-Times*, 18 July 1991, 1.

32. Gabriel Lopez, from the Speaker's office, graciously provided us with legislative summaries and analyses of SB 10 and SB 11. See also *Chicago Tribune*, 12 July 1991, sec. 2, p. 2; 19 July 1991, 1; *Chicago Sun-Times*, 19 July 1991, 4.

33. *Chicago Tribune*, 21 April 1991, 1; 28 April 1991, sec. 2, p. 1; 30 April 1991, sec. 2, p. 3; 2 May 1991, 1; *Chicago Sun-Times*, 25 April 1991, 1, 38, 39; 26 April 1991, 5; 1 May 1991, 1; 2 May 1991, 1.

34. *Chicago Tribune*, 24 April 1991, sec. 2, p. 3; 25 April 1991, sec. 2, p. 1; 26 April 1991, sec. 2, p. 1; 2 May 1991, 1; 7 May 1991, 1; 12 May 1991, 1; *Chicago Sun-Times*, 7 May 1991, 1.

35. John Callaway, "Chicago Tonight," WTTW/11, 9 May 1991; Hess's views were also outlined in *Chicago Tribune*, 5 May 1991, sec. 2, p. 1.

36. *Chicago Tribune*, 21 June 1991, sec. 2, p. 2; 24 June 1991, sec. 2, p. 1; *Chicago Sun-Times*, 22 June 1991, 1; 26 June 1991, 31.

37. *Chicago Tribune*, 24 November 1991, sec. 2, p. 1.

38. Michael D. Klemens, "Stricter Accountability for Schools? Rewards for Success, Consequences for Failure," *Illinois Issues* 17 (June 1991): 8-9; Rock interview.

39. *Chicago Tribune*, 21 February 1991, 1; 28 June 1991, sec. 2, p. 1; 4 July 1991, 12; *Chicago Sun-Times*, 28 June 1991, 26.

17

Lessons from Chicago School Reform

It is far too early to evaluate the success or failure of school reform in Chicago. The reform act set five-year goals and targets for the improvement of education, and the clock began ticking after the election of the first local school councils. The standardized tests that students took during the 1989-90 schoo year will be used as benchmarks to measure progress c decline.

If Chicago's schools do not show substantial improveme by the 1993-94 school year, pressure will build for even mo radical changes. Many feel that if the present school refor fails, the next step will be a choice plan, granting each stud a tuition voucher and authorizing him or her to use it at a private or public school. This could mark the end of the pul school system.[1] Thus the stakes remain very high.

A Case Study

At this time, it does seem appropriate to present s evidence of progress from the high school where the sc reform movement began, Roberto Clemente. Subsequent t Latino community's dramatic march on the school, the l of education designated it a community academy, makin school eligible for over a half million dollars annua supplemental desegregation funding. This new money ha used to add badly needed personnel and increase securit

In 1989, the school formed a partnership with Hyatt to establish an up-to-date culinary arts program. Hyatt in a modern teaching kitchen at the school, and the corp

experience so far illustrates the best aspects of school reform in Chicago: community support, interethnic cooperation, corporate and foundation assistance, and innovative school improvement plans.

It is also possible at this time to reflect on the Chicago school reform movement and consider its wider implications for reform politics in general. Teachers, principals, and parents of schoolchildren may want to read the lessons of school reform, but so too should community organizers, social reformers of all kinds, and political leaders responsible for making social and economic policy in the upcoming decade.

An unusual combination of circumstances fostered change in the Windy City, so it may not be possible to exactly duplicate Chicago's reform model elsewhere. Yet the politics of school reform in the 1980s does hold several lessons of wider applicability.[2]

Farewell to Gradualism

First of all, successful reform of an entrenched bureaucracy is not likely to be a gentle, gradual process. A policy of incrementalism—step-by-step reform, pilot programs, phased-in experiments—is unlikely to work. A meat ax, not a scalpel, will be needed.

This flies in the face of conventional political wisdom. Since the New Deal of the 1930s, liberal reformers have pursued political and economic change through a policy of pragmatic incrementalism, step-by-step changes to existing laws and institutions. John F. Kennedy called this process "the art of the possible," but Franklin D. Roosevelt characterized it best:

> Civilization is a tree, which, as it grows, continually produces rot and deadwood. The radical says: "Cut it down." The conservative says: "Don't touch it." The liberal compromises: "Let's prune it, so that we lose neither the old trunk nor the new branches."[3]

Yet evidence is beginning to accumulate that incremental change may be appropriate for advancing or extending social programs but insufficient when curbing or redirecting them. The Civil Rights Act of 1964, Voting Rights Act of 1965, and Open Housing Act of 1968 completely uprooted a one hundred-year-old system of Jim Crow in the American South. Lyndon Johnson did not ask the southern states for gradual change, he personally implored the Congress to bury Jim Crow, proclaiming "We Shall Overcome." Similarly, Jimmy Carter's deregulation of the airline industry in the 1970s swept away four decades of intricate fare and route arrangements, and Ronald Reagan's tax cuts and tax reforms were breathtaking in their scope. The dismantling of a government program requires more radical action than instituting a new one or enlarging an existing one.

Edward B. Fiske, veteran education writer for the *New York Times*, has applied this insight to school reform. "After nearly a decade of making incremental changes in public education," Fiske wrote in 1990, "a growing number of political and educational leaders have decided that far more basic, thorough-going structural changes are necessary."[4]

The example of Eastern Europe is instructive in this connection. Four decades of incremental change built a barnacle-encrusted bureaucracy that repressed political freedom and throttled economic growth. When the Soviet Union withdrew its heavy hand from the region in 1989, Communist party bosses, such as Erich Honecker in East Germany, attempted to preserve their power by making small reforms and concessions. It didn't work. Popular pressure for democracy and consumer capitalism swept away the Communists in one wave. The old protest song from the 1960s proved literally true: "He who gets hurt will be he who has stalled, for the times they are a'changing."

The lesson for reformers is clear. Be bold. Don't heed those who caution you to proceed more slowly or gradually. None of the school reformers interviewed for this book believe the

Chicago reforms went too far; most wish they had gone even further. Dropping a bomb on Pershing Road is a frequent suggestion. Kelvin Strong presented a solution only slightly less radical: "All Pershing Road should do is cut the checks. Let the local school principal act as CEO of the school. All the central board should do is provide services to the CEO and act as his auditor."[5]

From Political Machine to Community Organization

The history of school reform in Chicago also illustrates a fundamental change in big-city politics. Community organizations have replaced political bosses as the "cogwheels of democracy."[6]

During the mayoralty of Richard J. Daley, Chicago's Democratic party was widely hailed as the "last of the big city machines." Pundits marveled that such an unattractive, old-fashioned politico as Daley and such an archaic institution as the Democratic machine could survive into the modern, media age. After Daley's death, however, the machine swiftly crumbled. Two blows sufficed to send it into oblivion. The Shakman Decree, a judicial consent decree settling a lawsuit filed by a maverick legal reformer, banned the firing of government workers for political reasons and thus dried up the chief source of machine power, patronage jobs. Then, the great snowstorm of 1979, which Jane Byrne rode into the mayoralty, exposed the hollowness of Chicago's slogan, the "city that works." The remnants of Daley's machine couldn't clear away the snow or run the trains on time.

Ten years later, Richard M. Daley won election as mayor, but he has not tried to restore his father's machine, nor could he if he wished. In his surprising victory of 1989 and his easy reelection of 1991, Richard the Second relied on the manipulation of his media image not the manpower of political bosses.

An old-time political machine was not a dictatorship, as many believed. It was, in its own way, a service organization, providing jobs and favors to recent immigrants in exchange for votes, and an expression of small-scale democracy. Ward bosses and precinct captains knew their turf extremely well, and the people identified with them and their party. The bosses found jobs for their constituents, accompanied them to naturalization hearings, distributed food baskets at Christmas and buckets of coal in the winter. They deferred to each ethnic group's customs, faithfully attending wakes and weddings and religious festivals. For all its centralization, the machine represented government with a human face.[7]

It is widely acknowledged that television has hastened the demise of political machines. Voters today identify with politicians who look glamorous and decisive on the tube. They ingest their political information in 30-second sound bites rather than chats with the precinct captain. What is not so widely recognized is that other small-scale institutions have cropped up to replace the personal contact of the old-style machine.

A good place to begin exploring this idea is in suburban town halls. Political scientists have long decried the proliferation of governmental units in metropolitan areas. Hundreds of suburbs around each big city have their own town or village councils. In addition, numerous county boards, park districts, sanitary districts, and other special purpose agencies are superimposed upon the crazy quilt of government. Abstract theorists propose the consolidation of all these superfluous bodies into one large metropolitan government. But in the real world, citizens like their small-scale suburban boards and councils. They fear absorption by the big city and annihilation by large, impersonal bureaucracies. Thus they resist annexation, consolidation, or metropolitan government.[8] They may not vote in impressive numbers for their local municipal officers or school board members, but they like to know they are there if they need to complain.

This addiction to small, local units of government is not restricted to the suburbs. City dwellers who own condominium apartments participate actively in the elected condo boards that set the rules and regulations for their buildings. Young professionals who would never think of engaging in politics or running for city office, battle fiercely for spots on these boards. In many areas of the city, community organizations have experienced a renaissance.[9] The confrontational organizations that follow the Alinsky tradition, such as the Back of the Yards Council or the Woodlawn Organization, garner most of the publicity, but no neighborhood is too small or too middle-class to hatch some sort of community organization. Even public housing residents have their own government-mandated tenants' councils. In Chicago, the president of this council, Artensa Randolph, is a political power in her own right and sits on numerous advisory boards and study commissions. Latino immigrants have used bilingual advisory councils at local schools as important levers of influence.

In short, community organizations and small-scale democratic bodies, such as condo boards or suburban town councils, fulfill some of the functions of the old machine. They give the voters a sense of identification with a larger community, offer them a chance to have their say-so, and humanize the impersonal workings of government bureaucracies.[10]

Viewed in this context, Chicago's local school councils are not so radical and eccentric as their opponents maintained but rather are part of a larger trend in society and government. School reformers recognized this, arguing consistently that a local school council in Chicago would be no smaller than the average school district in the suburbs or downstate.[11] Rather than a radical departure from normal practice, the school reform act brought Chicago's schools more closely into line with the rest of the state.

Even the most dedicated citizen, however, cannot devote full time to making small-scale democracy work. The old-time political machine used to outlast the efforts of volunteer reformers. Tammany Hall boss George Washington Plunkitt phrased this point poetically, reform committees "were mornin' glories—looked lovely in the mornin' and withered up in a short time, while the regular machines went on flourishin' forever, like fine old oaks."[12]

Yet nowadays, community organizations like UNO and advocacy groups such as Designs for Change, funded by foundation and corporate grants, can contribute at least two full-time, paid staff members to a reform cause, the executive director and the issues coordinator. Diana Lauber of the Chicago Panel on Public School Policy and Finance has suggested that the groups with paid staff had an advantage in Springfield during the "Don't Come Home Without It" campaign, for they could sit continuously in Speaker Madigan's office whereas others could not.[13] At least some community organizations now enjoy money and staying power like the ward bosses and precinct captains of old.

Harold Washington based the policies of his entire administration on this insight that local, neighborhood organizations were the logical successors to the political machine. Community organizations in the African-American community provided the impetus for his nomination and election, and Washington listened closely to such community leaders as Leon Finney from TWO and Nancy Jefferson of the Midwest Community Council. In addition, he endeavored to break the grip of downtown business interests on city government and return more services to the neighborhoods. He didn't view the decentralization of the school system in isolation but as part of a long-range plan to revitalize local neighborhoods and govern through local organizations. Convoking a parent/community council to foster the reform movement, then moving towards decentralized control of the schools, came very easily and naturally to Harold.[14]

Community organizations played key roles in the drama of Chicago school reform. Network for Youth Services mounted the march on Clemente in 1984 that first exposed the dropout problem in the public schools. Groups such as the Save Our Neighborhoods/Save Our City coalition and the Near North Development Corporation brought expertise and energy to the deliberations of C.U.R.E., and the leaders of TWO and the Midwest Community Council hastened a settlement of the 1987 teachers' strike. During the 1988 lobbying campaign in Springfield, Danny Solis's United Neighborhood Organization turned out more parents than any other group.

The second lesson of Chicago school reform, therefore, is an old one put forward by Saul Alinsky years ago. Work with the indigenous institutions that already exist in the community. If the Catholic church and the Democratic party are no longer so powerful as they once were, then work with community organizations, block clubs, and issues advocacy groups. Small-scale democracy can be just as powerful today as it was in the New England town meeting or in the precincts of the Daley machine.

Alliance with the Powers That Be

A third lesson from Chicago's school reform campaign contradicts the advice of Saul Alinsky, the legendary community organizer. Alinsky-style organizations generally treat business and political leaders with contempt and try to embarrass them publicly, hoping to shame them into action. Yet, the Chicago school reform movement treated the powers that be (businessmen and politicians) as partners in the reform process, not enemies to be confronted. They followed the advice of Tom Coffey and the Haymarket Group, "There are no enemies here, just allies we haven't convinced yet."

The alliance between business executives and parents, which was forged during the sessions of the education summit, was one of the most remarkable features of the Chicago school reform movement. Harold Washington had consciously attempted to bring such diverse individuals together as allies, rather than let them rail noisily at each other to no purpose. The alliance was often marked by suspicion and tension, but mutual self-interest (business leaders wanted well-educated employees and parents wanted their children to be employable when they left school) ultimately resulted in a cooperative relationship, not a confrontational one. The resources that business brought to the reform movement (mainly money and legal expertise) proved crucial.

The reformers, moreover, treated politicians with respect and finesse, not hoots and catcalls. Protest politics had produced some stunning achievements in the 1960s and 1970s, most notably the federal civil rights acts and the end of the Vietnam War. Yet in these more conservative times, a cooperative approach to politicians seemed better advised. School reformers lobbied and demonstrated in Springfield, but they kept open lines of communication to the Democratic leaders of the legislature, Speaker Michael Madigan and Senate President Phil Rock. Finally, the reform act was hammered out behind closed doors in the office of Speaker Madigan.

Phil Rock, of course, had been involved with the issues of school reform since the march on Clemente in 1984, but few would have considered Madigan a likely ally for any reform cause. Indeed he is a more authentic survivor from the old machine tradition than the present Mayor Daley. Yet he ultimately became a prime mover behind the 1988 school reform act, because the reform coalition insisted on treating him as a potential ally, not an enemy.

It was difficult for groups like UNO and SON/SOC, which grew out of the Alinsky tradition, to adapt to this gentler, more persuasive approach. That is the main reason UNO almost missed the school-reform boat. But Michael Bakalis, who convened C.U.R.E., saw from the start that school reform was so complex it could not be dramatized in one burst of lobbying or protest marches. It required a continuous, involved, informed process of joint legislating alongside the leaders of the General Assembly.

At least one community activist involved in school reform, Miguel del Valle, entered politics himself. While lobbying in Springfield in 1984, del Valle decided he could do more for education in the capitol chambers than out in the streets. He became one of the sponsors of the original C.U.R.E. bill and helped negotiate the final form of the law that overcame the supreme court's decision.

Business executives still command much respect in these Reaganesque times, whereas politicians enjoy very low prestige and voter turnout has fallen to alarming levels. No matter. Both businessmen and elected officials of government control the levers of power. They can be important allies in movements for social change.

Kids First—Primero Los Niños

Finally, the most important aspect of Chicago school reform is that African-American, white, and Latino politicians and organizations worked together in a common cause. More commonly, ethnic and racial divisions fragment the city as each group pursues its own self-interest. Chicago's school reform coalition was always fragile and uneasy, and since the passage of the school reform act in 1988, the African-American community has threatened to break it completely.

C.U.R.E. and the ABCs coalition held together long enough to decentralize Chicago school governance for one reason only: they put kids first. Kelvin Strong summed up the success of C.U.R.E., "We all came out of this with a sense that our kids had won, not that we had won or that any group had won."[15] In Chicago's poisonous racial atmosphere, only the innocence of little children could unite so many different groups and individuals. Politicians and pundits routinely label a noncontroversial program or policy a motherhood issue. School reform was very controversial, but eventually the reform coalition turned it into a motherhood issue by focusing quite literally on children and their parents.

Reformers elsewhere should not fear that Chicago's experience is unique or confined merely to educational matters. There will be many political issues amenable to a Kids First strategy in the coming decade. Due to the Reagan-Bush economic policies, the elderly are no longer the poorest age-segment in American society. Children are. Twenty percent of American children, more than 12 million kids, live below the poverty line, and an even larger percentage are growing up in single-parent families.[16]

American children are nearly twice as likely as the elderly

to live in poverty, yet the federal government spends more than four dollars on the elderly (mostly Social Security and Medicare) for every dollar it spends on youth. Since 1965 the share of social welfare spending aimed at children (this even includes education) at all levels of government has declined from 37 percent to 24 percent. The percentage of such spending targeted for senior citizens has risen from 21 percent to 33 percent. According to the *Washington Post*, "No other country has so large an age bias to its poverty rates nor so wide an age tilt in its allocation of resources."[17]

Important political leaders have begun to recognize this. Governor Mario Cuomo of New York recently proclaimed the 1990s the Decade of the Child. Similarly, L. Douglas Wilder of Virginia, the first African-American governor ever elected in the U.S., declared that the upcoming years will be the Decade of Youth and Families. Governor John D. Rockefeller IV of West Virginia chaired a bipartisan National Commission on Children that recommended a one thousand dollar tax credit for each child in a family. All three Democrats are considered potential presidential candidates, and even if they do not run, their focus on children, families, and health care will help define the political debate in both 1992 and 1996.[18]

The day after the Persian Gulf War ended, a group of business executives calling themselves the Committee for Economic Development released an "unfinished agenda" for domestic policy featuring a "new vision for child development and education." Nationally syndicated columnist David Broder concluded, "The real question the report raises is whether a nation that coordinated brilliantly an international military rescue mission for Kuwait can coordinate a similar mission to rescue its own children."[19]

If political or community leaders wish to attack the problems of poverty, crime, health care, or family breakdown in the coming years, they might do well to heed the final lesson of Chicago's school reform movement. In any language, put Kids First, *Primero Los Niños*.

Notes

1. Patrick Keleher, one of the business leaders of the school reform movement, now heads a pro-choice organization, Teach America, funded by the City Club of Chicago. The November 1990 edition of *Catalyst*, the semi-official voice of Chicago school reform, devoted the whole issue to a discussion of "School Choice: Bane or Benefit?" Mayor Richard M. Daley mentioned the possibility of tuition vouchers in his 1991 inaugural address.

2. We have benefited from reading other studies of the Chicago school reform movement: Donald R. Moore, "Voice and Choice in Chicago" in *Choice and Control in American Education*, eds. William H. Clune and John F. Witte, (New York: The Falmer Press, 1990), Vol. 2, pp. 153-98; Mary O'Connell, "School Reform Chicago Style: How Citizens Organized to Change Public Policy," a special issue of *The Neighborhood Works* (Spring 1991); G. Alfred Hess, Jr., "Chicago School Reform: What It Is and How It Came to Be," (Chicago Panel on Public School Policy and Finance, March 1990); and Hess, *School Restructuring, Chicago Style* (Newbury Park, Calif.: Corwin Press, 1991). The opinions and conclusions in this chapter, however, are our own.

3. Edward R. Kantowicz, "The Limits of Incrementalism," *Journal of Policy Analysis and Management* 4 (1985): 217-18. The Roosevelt quote is from a September 1932 campaign speech, quoted in Walter Johnson, *1600 Pennsylvania Avenue* (Boston: Little, Brown, 1960), 47.

4. Edward B. Fiske, "Starting Over: Piecemeal Change Gives Way to Radical School Reform," *New York Times*, 4 April 1990, sec. 2, p. 6.

5. Kelvin Strong, interview by authors, 12 September 1990.

6. Sonya Forthal coined this phrase as the title of her classic study of the precinct captain (New York: William-Frederick Press, 1946).

7. The best introduction to the lost world of the political machine is the "memoir" of Tammany Hall boss George Washington Plunkitt, *Plunkitt of Tammany Hall*, ed. William L. Riordon, (New York: E. P. Dutton, 1963), and the insightful introduction to that volume by Arthur Mann. See also Edward R. Kantowicz, "Politics," in the *Harvard Encyclopedia of American Ethnic Groups*, ed. Stephan Thernstrom et al., (Cambridge: Harvard University Press, 1980).

8. Robert C. Wood made this point in *Suburbia: Its People and Their Politics* (Boston: Houghton Mifflin Co., 1958).

9. *Illinois Issues* ran a special series of articles on "Community Organizing in Illinois" from January 1988 to July 1989. These have been collected and published in book form as *After Alinsky: Community Organizing in Illinois*, ed. Peg Knoepfle, (Springfield, Ill.: *Illinois Issues*, 1990).

10. Albert Hunter provides a pioneering exploration of the functions of community organizations in chapter five of *Symbolic Communities: The Persistence and Change of Chicago's Local Communities* (Chicago: University of Chicago Press, 1974). Hunter wrote: "They [community organizations] serve as an integrating mechanism between the citizens of the local community and the governmental bureaucratic structures of the city as a whole" (p.172). This is precisely what the political machine used to do.

11. Politicians noticed this also, pointing out that school board elections have often been "breeding grounds for baby politicians." One member of the black caucus opposed the concept of LSCs because he didn't want to do anything to help produce his next election opponent. Carol Moseley Braun related this story in an interview with the authors, 5 February 1991, but she did not identify the politician.

12. Riordon, *Plunkitt of Tammany Hall*, 17.

13. Diana Lauber, interview by authors, 15 October 1990.

14. Both Harold Baron and the Reverend Kenneth Smith made this point eloquently in interviews (4 December 1990 and 29 November 1990, respectively).

15. Strong interview.

16. The interim report of the National Commission on Children reported these figures. See, *New York Times*, 27 April 1991, 22. In 1990 the Center for the Study of Social Policy began publishing an annual directory of social statistics dealing with children, *The Kids Count Data Book*.

17. Paul Taylor, "Like Taking Money from a Baby," *Washington Post National Weekly Edition*, 4 March 1991, 31.

18. National Commission on Children, "Beyond Rhetoric: A New American Agenda for Children and Families" (Washington, D.C., 1991); *New York Times*, 25 June 1991, 18; *Chicago Tribune*, 25 June 1991, 1; Paul Taylor, "Jay Rockefeller and the Fortune of Children," *Washington Post National Weekly Edition*, 1 July 1991, 15.

19. David Broder, "Execs Put Kids Atop 'Unfinished Agenda'," *Chicago Tribune*, 3 March 1991, sec. 4, p. 3.

Appendix 1

The First Round of Illinois School Reform
Key Bills, Illinois General Assembly, 1985 Session

The Omnibus School Reform Bill	SB 730 (PA 84-126, July 2, 1985) · mandatory testing in reading, math, and language at 3rd, 6th, 8th, and 10th grade levels · skill testing for new teachers · annually published school report card · creation of Illinois Mathematics and Science Academy · new programs for the handicapped · transportation reimbursement for private school students · $400 million in new education funding
Dropout Prevention Bills	HB 2158 (PA 84-662, June 24, 1985) defines a dropout and requires annual reports of dropout statistics HB 2165 (PA 84-663, June 30, 1985) reduces the student-counsellor ratio to 250 to 1 HB 2167 (PA 84-664, June 24, 1985) requires non-discriminatory testing of special education students SB 210 (PA 84-682, June 24, 1985) requires phone call to parents to notify them of student absences SB 1212 (PA 84-710, June 29, 1985) creates statewide advisory council on bilingual education SB 1215 (PA 84-711, June 26, 1985) forbids schools to deny a student admission for lack of records SB 1218 (PA 84-712, June 29, 1985) authorizes educational partnerships between universities and high schools
Safe School Zone Bills	SB 206 (PA 84-1074, July 1, 1985) upgrades the charge for selling a firearm to a minor SB 207 (PA 84-1075, July 1, 1985) toughens penalties for gang recruitment, selling firearms, or selling drugs in a school zone SB 202 (PA 84-718, June 27, 1985) creates a Department of Alcohol and Drug Abuse

Appendix 2

The Second Round of Illinois School Reform, 1988
Key Bills, Illinois General Assembly, 1988 Session

	C.U.R.E. Bill HB 3707 SB 2144	Berman Bill SB 1839 Amendment #1	Braun Bill HB 4101 Amendment #6	SB 1839 Passed 7/2/88	SB 1840 Passed 12/1/88 PA 85-1418
Local School Councils	19 members 6 parents 6 comm. reps 6 teachers 1 principal (Directly hire principal by majority vote)	19 members 10 parents 4 comm. reps 4 school staff 1 principal (Indirect power to approve principal appointment)	11 members 6 parents 2 comm. reps 2 school staff 1 principal (Directly hire principal by 3/5 vote)	11 members 6 parents 2 comm. reps 2 teachers 1 principal (Directly hire principal by 7/10 vote)	11 members 6 parents 2 comm. reps 2 teachers 1 principal (Directly hire principal by 7/10 vote)
Principals	· Hired on 3-year contract · No additional qualifications beyond state certification	· Hired on 3-year contract · Additional qualifications permitted	· Hired on 3-year contract · No additional qualifications	· Hired on 3-year contract · No additional qualifications	· Hired on 4-year contract · No additional qualifications

Appendix 2, continued

	C.U.R.E. Bill HB 3707 SB 2144	Eerman Bill SB 1839 Amendment #1	Braun Bill HB 4101 Amendment #6	SB 1839 Passed 7/2/88	SB 1840 Passed 12/1/88 PA 85-1418
Teachers	· Hired on merit, not seniority · 60-day remediation period · No teacher advisory commission · No special provisions for supernumeraries	· Hired on merit, not seniority · 45-day remediation period · 10 member teacher advisory commission · No special provisions for supernumeraries	· Hired on merit, not seniority · 45-day remediation period · 10 member teacher advisory commission · No special provisions for supernumeraries	· Hired on merit, not seniority · 45-day remediation period · teacher advisory commission (undetermined numbers) · Supernumeraries guaranteed a teaching job	· Hired on merit, not seniority · 45-day remediation period · professional personnel advisory commission (Undetermined numbers) · Supernumeraries guaranteed job at central board
Central Board	· Current board replaced as soon as possible · No interim board · New 11-member board · Nominating comm., 20 sub-district reps	· Current board replaced 1/89 · No interim board · New 15-member board · Nominating comm., 20 sub-district reps plus 5 mayoral appointees	· Current board replaced 7/89 · Current board serves as interim · New 15-member board · Nominating comm., 20 sub-districts reps plus 5 mayoral appointees	· Current board replaced, 30 days · 7-member interim board until 5/15/90 · New 15-member board · Nominating comm., 20 subdistrict reps plus 5 mayoral appointees	· Current board replaced, 30 days · 7-member interim board until 5/15/90 · New 15-member board · Nominating comm., 20 subdistrict reps plus 5 mayoral appointees

Appendix 2, continued

	C.U.R.E. Bill HB 3707 SB 2144	Berman Bill SB 1839 Amendment #1	Braun Bill HB 4101 Amendment #6	SB 1839 Passed 7/2/88	SB 1840 Passed 12/1/88 PA 85-1418
Oversight Commission	5 members 1 each appointed by governor, mayor, speaker, senate pres., 1 chosen by other 4	5 members 2 appointed by governor, 2 appointed by mayor, 1 appointed jointly	No oversight commission	7 members 4 appointed by mayor, 3 appointed by governor	Current school finance authority serves as oversight commission
Funding Equity	· All State Chapter I funds go to disadvantaged children · Hold harmless clause · Non supplanting clause	· 4-year phase-in of Chapter I redistribution · No Hold harmless clause · No Non supplanting clause	· No Chapter I redistribution · No Hold Harmless clause · No Non supplanting clause	· 4-year phase-in of Chapter I redistribution · Partial Hold harmless clause · Non supplanting clause	· 4-year phase-in of Chapter I redistribution Hold Harmless clause · Non supplanting clause
Spending Cap	Management study to set a spending cap	No spending cap	Administrative expenses held to statewide average	Administrative expenses held to statewide average	Administrative expenses held to statewide average

Appendix 2, continued

	C.U.R.E. Bill HB 3707 SB 2144	Berman Bill SB 1839 Amendment #1	Braun Bill HB 4101 Amendment #6	SB 1839 Passed 7/2/88	SB 1840 Passed 12/1/88 PA 85-1418
Unique Features	5-year phase-in of school choice plan Removal of LSC members for non-attendance 3-year transition period for training SB 1839 Passed 7/2/88	SB 1840 passed 12/1/88 PA 85-1418	Parental pick-up of report cards required	Study of school choice plan mandated	Limited school choice plan after 3 years

Index